ADVANCE PRAISE FOR *THE NEW SCIENCE OF TEACHING AND LEARNING*

"Tracey Tokuhama-Espinosa's book is not only an excellent guide for teachers and a most needed review of the cutting-edge research on neuroeducation, but also a model of pedagogy. The author has made a generous effort to guide readers step-by-step in the fascinating exploration of the new transdisciplinary field called MBE—Mind, Brain, and Education Science. I recommend this book to every teacher. It will clarify many issues and promote many educational initiatives."

—Antonio M. Battro, M.D., Ph.D., President of IMBES, International Mind, Brain and Education Society

"Tracey Tokuhama-Espinosa has written a highly accessible, extraordinarily well-documented compilation of essential information for all educators. She firmly establishes the links between neuroscience and psychology and provides the background knowledge needed to evaluate research for validity. . . . Teachers who want to provide the best opportunities for their students' success and influence the incorporation of valid mind, brain, education research in their schools and the nation need to be educated, critical consumers. . . . This breakthrough book guides informed decision-making using the best science has to offer to return joy and authentic learning to our classrooms."

—Judy Willis, M.D., M.Ed., neurologist, middle-school teacher, author, and renowned speaker on brain-based education

"What an impressive book. Tokuhama-Espinosa has pulled off quite a feat—not only distilling a huge amount of content on teaching and learning, but also telling the story in a compelling way. This book provides a fascinating review of state-of-the-art research and is very well-organized. It does more than just debunk myths, it also points toward tried-and-true tenets and principles of education. It is written with clarity, freshness, and a sense of urgency that is apt given the subject matter. This is a book that every educator—and everyone who cares about children—should read."

—Craig Pohlman, Ph.D., Director, Mind Matters at Southeast Psych in Charlotte, NC, author of *How Can My Kid Succeed in School?* and *Revealing Minds*, and co-author of *Schools for All Kinds of Minds*

The New Science of Teaching and Learning

Using the Best of Mind, Brain, and Education Science in the Classroom

Tracey Tokuhama-Espinosa

Foreword by Pat Wolfe

TEACHERS COLLEGE PRESS

Teachers College, Columbia University
New York and London

Published by Teachers College Press, 1234 Amsterdam Avenue, New York, NY 10027

Library of Congress Cataloging-in-Publication Data

Tokuhama-Espinosa, Tracey, 1963–
    The new science of teaching and learning : using the best of mind, brain, and education science in the classroom / Tracey Tokuhama-Espinosa ; foreword by Pat Wolfe.
        p. cm.
    Includes bibliographical references and index.
    ISBN 978-0-8077-5033-9 (pbk. : alk. paper)
    ISBN 978-0-8077-5034-6 (hardcover : alk. paper)
        1. Learning, Psychology of. 2. Learning—Physiological aspects. 3. Teaching.
    4. Cognitive science. I. Title.
LB1060.T645 2010
370.15′23—dc22   2009030485

ISBN 978-0-8077-5033-9 (paper)
ISBN 978-0-8077-5034-6 (hardcover)

Printed on acid-free paper

Manufactured in the United States of America

17   16   15   14   13   12   11   10   8   7   6   5   4   3   2   1

*This book is dedicated to
all of my children's teachers—
past, present, and future.*

It is by teaching that we teach ourselves, by relating that
we observe, by affirming that we examine, by showing
that we look, by writing that we think, by pumping that
we draw water into the well.

—Henri-Frédéric Amiel (1821–1881)

Contents

Foreword

Anyone involved in the field of education for any length of time has seen many innovations and programs come and go. The pendulum swings are so frequent in schools that many educators have adopted a "Sit tight, these too will pass" attitude. The newest "breakthrough" in education is neuroscience, or brain research, a field that has garnered many proponents, books, and programs that purport to be brain-based.

However well-meaning this new interest may be, it too will go the way of other innovations if we are not careful. What many new programs lack, and the reason many fail, is a firm foundation based on research and a clear definition of their application to the teaching/learning process. Also sorely needed is a set of standards on which to judge the validity of what is being touted as "research-based" practices for educators.

Tracey Tokuhama-Espinosa does an excellent job of addressing both these needs in this timely, well-researched book. Up to this point, there has been little consensus among researchers and educators as to the potential applications of the brain research to educational policies and practices. Understanding this, Tokuhama-Espinosa used a Delphi technique to poll recognized experts in both education and neuroscience to gain agreement as to what is well-established in this newly emerging field, what is probably true, what is intelligent speculation, and what are "neuromyths."

This seminal book has the potential to change the way we think about teaching and learning.

—Pat Wolfe

Preface

Teachers have the most important job in society. As a teacher, you impact the quality of professionals from every other field as they pass through your classrooms before going out into the community. Good teachers know this, take their responsibilities seriously, and strive to improve their practice through reflective processes. Whether you are a master teacher on the cutting edge of education who trains others or a teacher-to-be going through licensing on a fast track, this book has something for you. Part of the continual improvement of the field of education means that independent of your current level of expertise, you want to sort out the barrage of promises about new teaching methods and to understand the hows and whys of student results when these methods are applied. Great teachers know what works and why.

One of the most popular waves in teaching practice in recent years is *brain-based education*. It has come to light that much of the "brain-based information" does not enjoy full scientific backing and in some cases may even be harmful or simply a waste of money. The intention of this book is twofold: First, address the confusion around the misuse of concepts in brain-based education, and second, identify and apply the well-substantiated findings about the brain to classroom practice and teaching.

I was lucky enough to grow up in Berkeley, California, in the 1960s and attended public schools that were bursting with creative, rebellious minds (teachers and students alike). Granted, I didn't learn how to spell for a long time (we were always encouraged to express ourselves first; spelling would come later—much later), but we did get some solid basics in innovation, linking ideas, and questioning authority. These skills have come in handy as a teacher myself now, bombarded with promises of cure-alls for difficult students and extra stimulation for my bright stars. Unfortunately, some of these promises have been broken. At first blush it seems that brain-based education has a tremendous amount of merit, but what part of it is fad and what part is fact? Or is any of it completely credible? Luckily in Berkeley we also learned some things about babies and bath water.

In 2008 I undertook a large-scale international study to help define standards in brain-based learning as part of my doctoral studies. First, a study was used to determine the parameters of the field based on an analysis of the literature over the past 30 years. This began with a review of over 4,500 books, articles, Internet sites, university programs, and conferences that resulted in a new model of brain-based learning that is found at the intersection of neuroscience, psychology, and education, now called Mind, Brain, and Education: The Science of Teaching and Learning, or MBE Science for short. This model went through many changes in my dissertation research.

To test this model, I went to the experts. The top names in brain-based learning contributed their insights to the views of world-renowned neuroscientists and psychologists. After the initial study, other experts added their voices and opinions. These giants, already known in their own fields, are now also recognized as the seminal leaders of the new discipline of MBE Science. These experts submitted their beliefs about education to the scrutiny of the new field and have found it to reflect the best possible teaching practices known in the world today but humbly open the findings to further review by you.

This book is divided into 10 chapters. Each chapter can be used as a stand-alone text related to a specific aspect of MBE Science. If you are a seasoned teacher, a practitioner in MBE Science, or a teacher trainer, then you will probably want to read the chapters in order. If you are a new teacher and looking for immediate, usable knowledge, then you may want to start with Part II of the book, Applying Mind, Brain, and Education Science in the Classroom, and then go back to Part I, The Scientifically Substantiated Art of Teaching, when you have more time.

Chapter 1 defines the parameters of the new academic discipline of MBE Science. This chapter begins with a basic explanation of how the intersection of neuroscience, education, and psychology is the "new and improved" (read: "scientifically substantiated") version of brain-based education; it is followed by a look at the establishment of a new academic discipline through the events in education around the world that have led to the birth of MBE Science.

Chapter 2 looks at five well-established facts about the brain and the teaching–learning processes that are the backbone of excellent teaching.

Chapter 3 explores information that scientists now believe is probably true about the brain, learning, and teaching but that still needs just a bit more backing to be accepted as a complete "truth." Unlike the "well-established" category, this category of concepts deserves our attention but needs further research.

Chapter 4 considers the other end of the spectrum and looks at what is intelligent speculation, or what we would like to believe is true about the brain and learning processes but just don't have the evidence to support it at this time. These are often concepts that tend to be overestimated in education.

Chapter 5 examines the large number of neuromyths, or false beliefs, about the brain and the teaching-learning processes that exist in education today. These claims are often commercially driven and they range from the laughable to the reproachable. They waste valuable resources and time, as well as mislead teachers with false promises.

Part II, Applying Mind, Brain, and Education Science, explores the classroom implications of this information. Chapter 6 reviews the core tenets—that is, the individual aspects—of how brains differ in the way they take in information. Chapter 7 looks at the fundamental, universal principles about the brain and learning processes found in all humans. Together the tenets and principles presented in Chapters 6 and 7 point to the 10 instructional guidelines that make up the basic teaching elements of MBE Science found in Chapter 8.

Chapter 9 gives teachers concrete tools to judge the quality of information in the popular press, on the Internet, and in their teacher training programs using simple critical thinking skills. This chapter is crucial in helping teachers determine how to filter out the proven information from the unproven.

Finally, Chapter 10 looks at the future of MBE Science and helps individual teachers contribute to the field by recognizing and documenting what they can do to better their own personal practice. Additionally, this chapter suggests how professionals from education, psychology, and neuroscience can inform one another in order to advance their common intersection of MBE Science.

Mind, Brain, and Education Science challenges current teaching practices and calls for a reality check on beliefs about the teaching-learning process, especially as they relate to "brain-based education." Teacher application of scientifically based information about the brain, guided by a common set of standards, can potentially shape a new conceptual framework for educational best practice in the future. The tenets, principles, and instructional guidelines behind Mind, Brain, and Education Science point to one of the most important paradigm shifts in education of this generation.

How do we learn best? What is individual human potential? How do we ensure we reach every learner's highest potential? These questions and others have been posed by philosophers, neurologists, psychologists, and educators for as long as humans have pondered their own existence. Mind, Brain, and Education Science benefits teachers in their efficacy and supports learners in their ultimate success. Is it possible we are on the verge of answering these questions through studies in Mind, Brain, and Education Science? Though the prospect is intellectually enticing, only time will tell.

Acknowledgments

Acknowledgment and gratitude are due to all the members of the Delphi panel and the external experts who were both beacons and benchmarks for quality information in the emerging field of MBE Science. Thank you, Daniel Ansari, Michael Atherton, Virginia Berninger, Jane Bernstein, Sarah Jayne Blakemore, John T. Bruer, Renate Nummela-Caine, Donna Coch, David Daniel, Stanislas Dehaene, Marian Diamond, Kurt Fischer, Howard Gardner, John Geake, Usha Goswami, Christina Hinton, Paul Howard-Jones, Mary Helen Immordino-Yang, Eric Jensen, Jelle Jolles, Hideaki Koizumi, Michael Posner, Marc Schwartz, Rita Smilkstein, David Sousa, and Judy Willis. A special thanks to Robert Sylwester for critiquing the pilot survey for these experts.

Warm thanks go to my doctoral committee, who guided the research for this book. Thanks to Bruce Francis, Patricia Wolfe, Pamela Hanfelt, and Elena Kays for their enthusiasm and encouragement.

My gratitude is due to Carlos Montúfar, president of the Universidad San Francisco de Quito, for his insistence that I research MBE Science, as it promises to be the most exciting paradigm shift in educational history in our lifetime.

Big hugs and love to my mom and one of my best editors, Reba. More big hugs to my father and first teacher, Al.

Thank you to Daniela Bramwell for her fine detailed reading and comments and to Jean Ward and Judy Berman at Teachers College Press for their excellent editorial guidance.

And finally, thanks to Cristian, Natalie, Gabriel, and Mateo, who financed, fantasized, and philosophized this venture with me.

Introduction

Humans are always on the lookout for things that will help them be more successful (though what qualifies as "help" and "successful" is unique to each individual). I joke with my own students that this is the "law of minimal effort"; it's part of human nature to do as little as possible while trying to get as much as possible. But in teaching there are no easy answers, and success usually comes with plain hard work. In fact, when things appear too easy, red flags should go up in our minds. Titles like *Right-Brain Learning in 30 Days* (Halary & Weintrayub, 1991) or *Boost Your Brain Power Week by Week: 52 Techniques to Make You Smarter* (Lucas, 2006) should actually worry us. If something appears too good to be true, it probably is. By being skeptical about this information, we raise the bar of performance in the teaching profession. An ever-increasing number of scholars have criticized the allure of a "quick fix" in education based on "neurocures." However, determining what information is proven and what is unproven is getting harder by the day.

This is worrisome. Much of the information easily available to teachers is riddled with "neuromyths," or overgeneralizations and misinterpretations about the human brain. While eager to improve practice, we educators need to be cautious about instances where cause and effect have not been critiqued thoroughly or where anecdotes overshadow evidence in claims about the brain and teaching techniques. There are a growing number of researchers who maintain enthusiasm for the link between education and neuroscience but do so with caution, preferring to call quality information Mind, Brain, and Education Science, or MBE Science, to distinguish it from the faddish claims in the press of "brain-based education." These thought leaders offer valuable recommendations, such as the warning that so-called brain-based learning can be dangerous if parameters for quality information are not improved. These skeptics' vibrant challenges are healthy, and they point to a major shift in education that will lead to better classroom experiences and learning. This book explains how this is happening. But before reading further, it is important to understand where the new information in this book comes from and why you can trust it.

WHY MIND, BRAIN, AND EDUCATION SCIENCE IS BETTER THAN "BRAIN-BASED LEARNING"

In 2008, 20 experts from six different countries joined intellectual forces to put parameters around a new academic discipline called Mind, Brain, and Education Science. The panel of experts was comprised of neuroscientists, psychologists, educators, and educational neuroscientists—or Mind, Brain, and Education specialists—in a structure known as a Delphi survey. This survey is named after the Oracle of Delphi who, in Greek mythology, led people's quests for knowledge with the mantra *know thyself*. A Delphi survey is a research method in which

> the opinions or judgments of a group of people, often leaders and experts in a given field, are solicited and processed through several rounds. . . . The responses are then compiled and evaluated with the aim of promoting a consensus among respondents. (Putnam, Spiegel, & Bruininks, 1995, p. 533)

The philosophy behind this union is that assessments made by a group of experts are more likely to be right than assessments made by the same individuals working alone. There are wonderful ideas about learning and teaching that come from the fields of psychology, neuroscience, and education. Each of these disciplines approaches the process of learning and teaching in a slightly different way. The moment these three visions are united, however, they produce ideas, insights, and concepts that are superior to any single vision. The united vision reached through the experts' generous collaboration is reported in this book.

The Delphi survey was followed by a review of the findings by six additional experts and commentary from two others. The Delphi panel members came from Australia, Canada, France, the Netherlands, the United Kingdom, and the United States, and additional input came from individuals from Japan, Germany, Argentina, and Belgium. The experts whose input was used to devise this model can be found in Appendix A.

The Delphi Expert Survey

As with any meeting of intellectuals, far more questions were raised than answered, including the fundamentals of just how the brain learns; the true definition of *learning*; whether or not there is a more "natural" way to develop classroom instruction; whether there is such a thing as a "critical period" for learning a first language (and why there is no such thing as a critical period for academic skills); who is responsible for uniting the efforts of neuroscience, psychology and education; and just how some practices can be accepted in education and psychology but produce no evidence in neuroscience.

Despite these differences in opinion, the Delphi panel did achieve its primary goal of identifying basic standards in the emerging field. Most panel members, for example, said the field was an independent academic discipline and should be named *Mind, Brain, and Education: The Science of Teaching and Learning*, not *brain-based learning*, which they felt was a label associated with unscholarly research and commercial claims. Most agreed that the parent fields were neuroscience, psychology, and education and that equal input from each of these disciplines was the hallmark of a new, independent academic discipline. The panel also agreed on the overarching research, practice, and policy goals of the new field, as well as on how standards in the new field should be reached, and on the steps to identify quality information in the emerging field. Perhaps of greatest use to teachers is that the experts categorized concepts in this new field and determined their importance for education. These teaching concepts were organized on a continuum from "what is well-established" to "what is probably so" to "what is intelligent speculation" to "what is a misconception or neuromyth," based on the evidence in MBE Science. These categories point to a clear set of tenets, principles, and instructional guidelines for better teaching and more effective learning. And now that the expert researchers have had their say, you, the expert in the field, are asked to join the discussion.

As suggested by Patricia Wolfe (2006), one of the thought leaders of the emerging field, "no one will consider educators true professionals unless we act like professionals in analyzing and applying the research" (p. 11). So before asking the experts what they did and did not agree upon, a thorough review of the field was needed.

Grounded Theory Meta-Analysis

Before the Delphi survey, I began my look at brain-based education with a meta-analysis of the literature that contributes to MBE Science. This meant reviewing any material available in both scholarly and popular press genres. All books, peer-review journals, articles, Internet sources, and conference summaries that were related to the brain, learning, and teaching triad were analyzed. I started by critiquing over 4,500 documents spanning publications between 1977 and 2008 and relevant, seminal studies from even further back. Each new document added to my own emerging theory about how the brain learns best and what we teachers should do to take advantage of this knowledge to teach better. The review of the literature also helped me identify experts in the field based on the number of publications they contributed to or the number of times other researchers referenced their work. The experts identified in the literature were called upon to develop a consensus around the new model of MBE Science in the Delphi survey mentioned above.

As with any book, the contents are influenced by the way the author interprets the information. Before launching into the content, it is only fair to offer a brief word about my own personal biases. The description below is meant to make the attitude with which I approach the book's content more transparent.

MY ACCOMPANYING BIASES

Education is a pivotal structure in society that should focus on one child at a time and strive to maximize the potential of all learners. Each person is born with a different set of gifts; there are no two brains alike, and there are no two individuals who contribute to the world in the same way. This book is written with the belief that MBE Science is a teaching and learning model through which all these individual gifts can flourish. This scientifically substantiated art of teaching recognizes the worth of objective truth and the use of the scientific method; however, it also embraces the idea that society is made up of individuals with unique traits, which often cannot be measured on an objective scale.

From a global perspective, the World Bank (2008), McKinsey and Company (2007), and UNESCO (2008) all view education as a key element in development. This is a core concern of mine, as I have spent half of my life in the richest and best educational systems in the world (Japan, Switzerland, and the United States) and the other half in developing countries of Latin America. The development cycle I have witnessed in both rich and poor nations is one in which formal education systems are an integral part of a society's growth and prosperity. Good education systems can produce well-prepared social participants who tend to respond to the needs of their communities. My hope is that the information in this book will contribute to better educational systems, in rich and poor countries alike. "Education is a human right with immense power to transform," noted former United Nations Secretary-General Kofi Annan, "both on a national as well as individual level."

WHAT THIS BOOK WILL OFFER

This book responds to the call for better standards in MBE Science and the clamor for more proven teaching methods to better educational practice. It not only documents how the field has emerged but also shows where it is heading. These findings offer proven ways to maximize student learning that are substantiated by science and confirmed by teachers' best practice. While quality information about the brain and learning does exist, teachers have few instruments to help them gauge what is valid and what is not. If MBE Science standards become more widely applied, teachers will improve their practice, students will gain from an important shift in education, and ultimately society will be the greatest beneficiary because each person will maximize his or her own learning potential.

So, are you a producer of MBE Science (do you research the field)? Or are you a deliverer (do you, or will you, teach)? Maybe you are also an end user of MBE Science (a student). Independent of your role, you will find the information in this book transformative. Even the best of teachers reading this book will find new ways to expand and improve their art. This book is the first to put parameters around the new field of MBE Science, which is a work in progress. You are invited to contribute to its further development by reading, applying, and critiquing its contents.

Part I

The Scientifically Substantiated Art of Teaching

CHAPTER I

The Case for Neuroscience in the Art of Teaching

Mind, Brain, and Education (MBE) Science is the new and improved *brain-based learning*. It is the scientifically substantiated art of teaching. It is the intersection of neuroscience, education, and psychology. And it is a paradigm shift in formal education. This chapter explains its basic parameters and history.

Although concepts from MBE Science have been applied indiscreetly and inconsistently to classroom teaching practices for many years, modern technology now allows a glimpse into the functioning human brain and how it learns, which helps us judge the quality of these claims. But with this knowledge comes responsibility. For example, between the 1950s and the 1980s, the idea of "enriched environments" stirred the educational community. If children were given "extra" stimulus as babies, they would grow up to be "Baby Einsteins." These claims were based on discoveries of increased synapses, or connections between brain cells, in young rats living in "enriched" settings (Diamond, Krech, & Rosenzweig, 1964; Rosenzweig, Krech, & Bennett, 1958). The rats were given cages with extra toys and running wheels, then sacrificed; their brains showed increased synapses. Despite being based on nonhuman subjects, this finding led to a proliferation of educational recommendations about improving learning environments for infants and young children. Most of us have seen, read, or experienced the "enriched environment" enthusiasm. In fact, as new parents or good teachers, we would feel remiss if we did not try to create an "enriched environment."

The authors of the original rat studies now believe, however, that the "enriched" laboratory environments were actually more like "normal" rat environments (i.e., sewers), which does not prove enriched environments are better, but rather that poor environments are worse than normal environments. This means bad environments can harm, but it does not necessarily prove that enriched environments help. Despite this new knowledge, there is a million-dollar industry dedicated to training parents and teachers to design enriched environments. To heighten concerns, it is not known whether or not overstimulation within an enriched environment causes harm. Though it seems that enriching an environment should not be a bad thing, there is little science to prove this. What we do know is that investment in the equivalent of extra rat mazes or running tracks for kids may not necessarily be required to enhance learning; simply providing normally stimulating environments (e.g., helping children learn to ride a bike or skateboard; talking to them over dinner; engaging them in board or ball games; playing circus, house, or school) is probably just as effective.

Substantiating the art of teaching in science represents a paradigm shift in teaching practices. More and more educators base their practice on proven methods grounded in empirical evidence rather than gut feelings. This in no way limits a teacher's creativity in the classroom, but rather stimulates new ways of thinking about activity design, classroom planning, and course structures. This is not only logical; it is also the law.

In the United States, the move toward scientific grounding for education was legalized in 2001 with the No Child Left Behind legislation in which scientifically based research in education was noted as a priority (Einsenhart & DeHaan, 2005). This points to a shift in education that includes a new academic discipline that is nurtured equally by mind (psychology), brain (neuroscience), and education (pedagogy). Education can no longer go it alone; the task is too great. But how do we know what information is proven in the new field? To answer this, we first need to understand the equation making up the new academic discipline.

WHY PSYCHOLOGY + NEUROSCIENCE + EDUCATION = MBE SCIENCE

When the 20 international experts were asked from where MBE Science principles were derived, this is how they responded:

> The emerging field of Mind, Brain, and Education brings together natural, life, neural and social sciences from which the major guiding principles are derived. The most prominent among these disciplines are education, neuroscience, and psychology. Sub-fields of education (i.e., pedagogy, special education, gifted students), neuroscience (i.e., cognitive neuroscience, neuroethics, neuroscience, neuropsychiatry, developmental neuroscience and pediatrics) and psychology (i.e., developmental psychology, and neuropsychology) comprise the major foundations of Mind, Brain, and Education. (Tokuhama-Espinosa, 2008b, p. 215)

The intersection of neuroscience, education, and psychology has been referred to in many ways over the past three decades. The most popular terms are *brain-based teaching, brain-based education, educational neuroscience, educational psychology, cognitive neuropsychology, cognitive neuroscience,* and *educational neuropsychology*. To be sure that MBE Science was distinct from all the others mentioned above, the experts specifically considered whether the emerging discipline was simply a subdiscipline of one of the parent fields of education, neuroscience, or psychology, or whether it was, indeed, a new, independent academic field. After 3 months of discussion, the majority of the experts concurred that MBE Science is an independent academic discipline, though it probably grew out of the same cognitive neuroscience from which many wonderful educational contributions have emerged.

Readers of this book—educators, psychologists, neuroscientists—are potential MBE scientists. Despite different initial disciplinary roots, these professionals can now share a new trajectory of development at the graduate level, where programs began to increase greatly starting around 2003. This new field is nourished by the different approaches that professionals from different disciplines bring. A neuroscientist might work in a lab tracking neural changes in the brain due to different types of learning experiences, for example, while a teacher in a classroom documents her MBE practice for review by peers, and a psychologist uses therapy to stimulate certain behavioral changes in a student. All three professionals are potentially MBE scientists.

So how does MBE Science differ from the existing and already recognized fields of neuroscience, psychology, and education? MBE Science is distinct in its emphasis on teaching versus the more narrow focus of just how people *learn*.

IT IS NOT ENOUGH TO KNOW HOW WE LEARN, WE MUST KNOW HOW TO TEACH

Neuroscientists, psychologists, and educators have studied learning for centuries. It is apparent, however, that while the science of learning is well established, the science of *teaching* is not as advanced. This means that while neuroscience and psychology have been very helpful in establishing theories of learning, education has been more or less left on its own to develop teaching. Usha Goswami, who is a member of the University of Cambridge's distinguished faculty of Psychology and Neuroscience in Education, confesses that "neuroscience does not as yet study teaching." This is ironic, she notes, as "successful teaching is the natural counterpart of successful learning" (Goswami, 2008a, p. 34). Goswami goes on to acknowledge that "[t]he identification and analysis of successful pedagogy is central to research in education, but it is currently a foreign field to cognitive neuroscience" (2008, p. 35).

The recognition of this missing link between learning and teaching is becoming more and more apparent through MBE Science. Thousands of studies establish how and even why different species learn different types of information, but only a handful of scientific studies establish how to teach human students to maximize learning. MBE Science is quickly making up ground.

ESTABLISHING MBE SCIENCE

It is now apparent that most of the literature leading up to the establishment of this new academic field of MBE Science has been limited in its scope. Beginning in the late 1970s and early 1980s, a handful of important works began hinting at the new field, which was followed by an explosion of writing during the Decade of the Brain (1990–1999) as well as technological breakthroughs that provided continually improved means of observing the functioning, healthy human brain. By 2008, publications directly related to MBE Science—rather than derived from the parent fields of neuroscience, psychology, or pedagogy—were numerous and of very high quality. This indicates growing interest in, research on, and application of concepts in MBE Science.

Teaching Popularized the Field

Documents dating from 1977–2008 make it clear that the field had its origins in psychology, yet some of its strongest evidence came from neuroscience, while educators were responsible for popularizing MBE among teachers. This translation from neuroscience labs to classrooms met with different degrees of success depending on the information and the communicators. This has slowly changed, and high-quality information is increasingly more common.

To counter misinformation being published in the field, a small but significant group of MBE scientists began to formalize their union as well as publish more evidenced-based information. This led to the emergence of a new genre of writing at the end of the 1990s specifically aimed at balancing neuroscience, psychology, and education. Several books published by 2009 demonstrated that this new genre of writing will continue to be a powerful force in the field in the coming years. A list of some of the most exemplary works in the field can be found in Appendix B.

Age Focus in MBE Science Work

Not all learners are represented equally in the MBE Science literature. By far the most studied age group so far has been infants through 5-year-olds. This is followed by primary school children, middle school children, high school students, and, last of all, college students and adults. What we now know about the brain and the science of mind makes it clear that learning is a lifelong process. This means it is likely that more and more books will look at the learner as a work in progress, who grows throughout the life cycle.

Professional Focus

The focus in the new field has been on policy issues rather than on how the information translates into classroom practice. This is both logical and problematic. The rules of the field (i.e., policy) are important, but the utilitarian nature of the information (i.e., classroom practice) is also vital to MBE Science.

The lack of emphasis on curriculum design makes it clear that MBE Science principles have been driven by an understanding of how the brain learns from a laboratory perspective, rather than by practitioners and what they know actually works with students. A greater balance should emerge in the near future as more research begins to take place in classroom settings, rather than being initiated primarily by the field of neuroscience.

Some researchers and writers have managed to merge the disciplines successfully. For example, Berninger and Corina's (1998) "Making Cognitive Neuroscience Educationally Relevant: Creating Bidirectional Collaborations Between Educational Psychology and Cognitive Neuroscience" points to the bridge on which the fields meet. This article seeks to mediate the demands of the three parent fields. Two other examples include Goswami's (2006) "Neuroscience and Education: From Research to Practice" and Hall's (2005) "Neuroscience and Education." All three of these works offer specific recommendations about why and how findings in neuroscience can and should be used in education. Something very interesting and at once attractive is that there is a high degree of intellectual humility within this group of authors, who tend to embrace the bridge-building mentality and often speak about the need for more collaboration among neuroscientists, psychologists, and educators.

WHY TEACHING AND LEARNING HAVE CHANGED AND WHAT TEACHERS NEED TO KNOW

High-Stakes Testing

Though many elements of teaching and learning appear eternal, there are at least two things that have changed drastically in recent years. First, the stakes are higher. High-stakes testing has replaced learning goals with test score benchmarks in many school districts. This sadly means that teaching priorities have often shifted toward marking the right answers on a state test rather than instilling enduring understanding about core concepts. While in some exceptional cases these state exams are well designed, in the vast majority these evaluation methods have resulted in reducing class hours in the arts, physical education, and foreign language, as well as sacrificing significant learning experiences for mere regurgitation of enough correct answers to ensure funding for the next schoolyear. This means we risk rewarding mediocrity exemplified through the rote memorization of facts and formulas on standardized tests, rather than stimulating creative and critical thinking. Large-scale studies around the globe have pointed to a consensus that the way we are currently educating our students is not producing the citizens we need for society (PISA, 2009). This is not sustainable. No community can be satisfied and no society made competitive by the current structure. Every teacher has within his or her own means a way to change this by applying MBE Science.

Technology

Technology has improved research about our learning, our practice of teaching, and our means of evaluating. Technology has also given us a look into healthy human brains and how they approach different types of problems that can point to better ways of maximizing individual learner potential. Unfortunately, technology is also frequently in competition for our children's attention in terms of media, computers, and electronic games. How does technology really impact the potential to learn? The role of technology is often splashed across the headlines, but a real understanding of its role in pedagogy or education is just now becoming core knowledge of teaching professionals.

When we speak about brain-based teaching and learning, we often envision such knowledge as splitting at the seams with high-tech input. This technology, however, is not the same as a crystal ball into the brain, and there is still a ways to go before findings in the lab can easily be replicated in the classroom. So how, exactly, can technology help us teach better? We will explore these questions in the coming chapters as we explain the intricacies of MBE Science.

High-stakes testing, new technologies, and the need to balance our knowledge of learning with an improved practice of teaching all seem convincing reasons to support MBE Science. However, there are some people who do not think MBE studies can or should be linked. These voices are important to listen to—not because they are necessarily right, but because they help us improve the field and how we teach.

ARGUMENTS FOR AND AGAINST UNITING EDUCATION, PSYCHOLOGY, AND NEUROSCIENCE

Not everybody thinks education, psychology, and neuroscience should be joined together. Many contend that a link between the fields is "a bridge too far," as Bruer (1997) stated in his classic skeptical article. Bruer has been the cornerstone of debate for over a decade because his controversial article all but rejected the possibility of a union among fields. Some of the laboratory academicians who agree with Bruer simply feel that the gulf between neuroscientific findings and the classroom is just too wide. Other teachers do not feel they need a "blessing" from neuroscience to confirm their classroom results.

A formal bridge linking the fields of neuroscience, psychology, and education was missing until Howard Gardner, one of the major educational thought leaders of this generation, and colleagues, "propose[d] the establishment of a class of professionals, 'neuro-educators'" (Sheridan, Zinchenko, & Gardner, 2006, p. 11). Neuroeducators, or MBE scientists, are (1) teachers who know about the brain and how it learns best and (2) neuroscientists and psychologists concerned with teaching practices. "A new kind of disciplinarity can be realized, one that 'keeps a foot' in each of its parent disciplines but 'the head' in the middle connecting the disciplines," according to Kurt Fischer, the founding President of the Mind, Brain, and Education Society (Fischer & Fusaro, 2006, p. 1). Teachers need MBE Science training because "[m]any teachers working in our classrooms were trained at universities when the coursework focused exclusively on how to teach rather than on how students learn," according to educator Erlauer-Myrah, (2006, p. 16). Conversely, neuroscientists and psychologists need MBE Science training because their focus has been exclusively on learning, rather than teaching, mechanisms.

Great teachers have always sensed what methods worked; thanks to brain-imaging technology and better research techniques, it is now possible to substantiate many of these beliefs with empirical scientific research. However, the standards that were recently developed by the experts reported here, and that will be explained in the next chapter, can only be effective if they are widely applied. Each teacher contributes to making these changes on both an individual as well as societal level, to be measured over time. This is where all teachers have a responsibility to the field. MBE instructional guidelines clearly delineate core knowledge that all teachers should possess by reviewing past brain-based learning promises and filtering out the science behind the concepts from the neuromyths. This can be accomplished, in part, by helping teachers confirm (or deny) their theories in the classroom. For example, since 1972 there has been empirical evidence that if teachers give students several seconds to reply to questions posed in class, rather than the normal single second, the probability of a quality reply increases due to the natural attention span of students (Thomas, 1972). Information about response time is shared in some teacher training schools, but not all. Standards in MBE Science would ensure the inclusion of information about the brain's attention span and need for reflection time in teacher training.

THE BASIC PREMISE OF MBE SCIENCE: TEACHING AND DIAGNOSING LEARNING PROBLEMS IS NOT EASY

The basic premise in MBE Science is that fundamental academic skills, such as reading and math, are complex and require a variety of neural pathways and mental systems to work correctly. This complexity means that there are a lot of different ways things can go wrong. Just as more sophisticated methods of transportation changed human mobility for the better (from bikes to jet planes), this change also meant there were more ways for things to go wrong. If your bike gets a flat tire, you change it. However, if part of your plane is broken, you may be stuck for a long time until the replacement part arrives. This means that improved transportation gets us places faster, but when problems occur, they can be more complex. In a similar fashion, the more sophisticated our knowledge of the brain is, the more ways we know of for learning to go wrong. MBE Science helps teachers understand why there are so many ways that things can go awry in the learning process, and this impacts how we should teach.

This means that MBE Science can keep educators from jumping to conclusions too quickly. Good MBE scientists never say, "He has a problem with math"; instead, they cautiously identify the true roots of a child's math difficulties: "He has a problem with number recognition (or quantitative processing, or formula structures, etc.)." As noted in a report from the Organisation for Economic Co-Operation and Development (OECD, 2002), "Such a model suggests that there may be several different reasons (rooted in processing in different brain regions), why difficulties . . . arise" (p. 37). MBE Science standards make teaching methods and diagnoses more precise. Think about diagnosis in medicine. As with health issues, understanding the roots of learning problems goes a long way toward understanding how to treat them. Teachers who can diagnose the causes of a child's delay in math (or reading, social skills, memory) are better equipped to apply more appropriate teaching methods that remedy the child's problem.

THREE THEORETICAL AND CONCEPTUAL VIEWS IN MBE SCIENCE— BRINGING THE PERSPECTIVES TOGETHER

One way to understand the conceptual perspectives in the field is to recognize that neuroscience is focused on the neuron as the primary unit of study, while psychology's unit of study is the mind, and pedagogy is interested society, as it relates to formal educational practice. Each of these three foci is considered below.

Neuroscientists: Many neuroscientists believe that the primary goal of MBE Science is to understand how the brain learns and, more precisely, how neurons are changed in the brain based on experience. Neuroscience has been the primary source of evidence-based research in MBE Science.

Psychologists: Many psychologists believe MBE Science's goal is to explain learning behavior and the processes of the mind. That is, while neuroscientists are occupied with the brain, psychologists are more concerned with the mind. When neuroscience and psychology have similar goals, then their research is complementary. For example, both psychology and neuroscience seek explanations for the role of emotions in decision making, and their findings can be complementary. Another example can be seen in motivation studies: Explanations of human motivation through behavior as well as through neurotransmitter release can be mutually illuminating.

Educators: Many educators feel that the purpose of MBE Science is to improve teaching and classroom practices, with a primary focus on individual students and their learning processes. Educators look to neuroscience and psychology, to quote the title of Armstrong's (1998) work, to "awaken the genius in the classroom" and to identify clear classroom applications for neuroscientific research. Others believe that MBE Science should serve as a wake-up call to a greater paradigm shift in the way we assess student learning in the classroom.

These three perspectives mean that MBE Science joins the knowledge of how neurons change (neuroscience) and how behaviors are modified (psychology) with how students learn (education). Despite different goals, neuroscientists, psychologists, and teachers share a common ground in MBE Science, though achieving common objectives can require compromise among the fields.

An interesting example of how educators, neuroscientists, and psychologists have had to compromise in order to create MBE Science can be seen in the experts' work toward developing a definition of the word *learning*. Their definition, informed by the three parent fields, is the following:

Learning can be said to take place in the mind in a psychological sense, and in the brain, in a neurological sense. Learning is instantiated in the brain and is prompted by internal thought processes, sensory input, motor training, or simulated perceptual input in the mind resulting in a physiological and measurable change in the neural networks, as well as changes in the muscles and other parts of the body. Human learning is complex and is intricately related to emotions, cognition, action, volition, and perception. Learning is always

accompanied by brain changes, which in fact underlie learning itself as well
as changes in behavior including thought and feeling. Human learning can be
achieved through active and constructive processes such as in formal school
contexts. Much learning can be observed neurologically before being expressed
in behavior, as in implicit learning, which results in subtle changes in behavior
and is usually only noticeable when new learning is scaffolded upon it, as is
much of the early childhood learning. (Tokuhama-Espinosa, 2008b, p. 23)

There is no doubt that this definition will need to be improved upon in the
coming years. However, the imperfections count less than the disposition
to seek a definition in the first place. This progress should be applauded as
up until recently communication among the disciplines was not amicable
enough to even start this conversation.

This conflict is clear in a recent article:

The differences in the vocabularies of education and neuroscience might ultimately be too great to allow multidisciplinary theorizing. The vocabulary
of education belongs to the social sciences and includes mental terms such as
understanding and *identity*. . . . By contrast, the vocabulary of neuroscience belongs to the biological sciences. It includes material terms such as *hemodynamic
response* and *white matter tract*. It is tailored for the description of physical phenomena. These differences are problematic. (Varma, McCandliss, & Schwartz,
2008, p. 143)

Constructive dialogue will be hampered without a broader, more balanced
lexicon that equally represent the parent fields of neuroscience, psychology,
and education. A basic glossary of terms is included in the back of this
book to help begin the development of an approved lexicon for MBE
scientists. Professionals who know these terms, and are able to apply them
and evaluate their appropriate use, will be able to read and comprehend
articles and books in which the terms are used, discuss and debate with
appropriate terms, and write and hypothesize about the emerging field
using the correct terminology. Shared vocabulary and definitions will
facilitate future discussion and debate in the field.

MBE Science has a long history, which is rooted in our human desire to
know ourselves better. At some levels this means knowing why we can or
can't learn a school subject as fast or as accurately as the kid sitting next to
us (as in academic knowledge), but on another level we also want to know
how we can improve our memory, pay attention to what is important, and
better manage our interactions with others (as in human survival skills).
On yet another level we want to know why we are here, what our purpose is, and just how we know the world. Based on the story of the Hindu
Parabrahma, the human spark was ignited by an initial desire to know one-

self. *Who am I?* asked the Hindu godhead Parabrahma. Around the same time, the Oracle of Delphi made it clear to the Greeks that the guiding human principle was to *know thyself.* MBE Science is not only a necessary paradigm shift in education; it also satisfies a basic human urge to know ourselves better. To better understand the roots of this new academic field, we turn next to a brief history of the field, which is not only a saga of collective breakthroughs but also a celebration of innovative technological findings allowing glimpses into the functioning human brain and an understanding of their impact on education.

THE MBE SCIENCE SAGA

Successful history teachers present their content as a collection of life stories and, perhaps even more exciting, a parade of human failure and triumph. This kind of record characterizes academic and scientific histories as well. One of the most fascinating tales related to education is in the roots of MBE Science. Where did it come from? What pivotal discoveries or grand ideas triggered its conception? To know where we are heading, we first need to know whence we came. So, before going further, a brief history of the new field is called for.

A Short History

The history of MBE Science reaches back to formal education settings spanning thousands of years of our collective past. In this book we will focus on what has happened in the past decade, developments that would not have evolved as they have without major cross-disciplinary thinkers; the advent of new imaging technologies; and the new links being forged by experts in neuroscience, psychology, and education who have begun to work together for the benefit of students.

The Birth of a New Discipline: 2000 and Beyond

It can be said that the field of MBE Science was "born" in several different places at once, all across the globe. Formal attempts to unify interdisciplinary concepts in learning and teaching were numerous at the turn of our century. In 2000, the Australian National Neuroscience Facility was founded as a consortium between Monash University, the University of Melbourne, the Howard Florey Institute of Experimental Physiology, and the National Stroke Research Institute. In 2000, the Neurosciences India Group was also founded with the mission to "empower through education." Some of the earliest formal organizations promoting the new field around the world included INSERM (French National Institute of Health and Medical Research), the Cognitive Neuroimaging Unit in France (2001), and the Oxford Cognitive Neuroscience Education Forum (2001) in the United Kingdom. The Organisation for Economic Co-Operation and Development (OECD) conducted three international conferences at this time to synthesize opinions and concerns and to design agendas for research in the emerging field. These conferences took place in New York (2000), Granada, Spain (2001), and Tokyo (2001), resulting in international agreement on outlines of the field's scope and content. The 400th anniversary meeting of the Pontifical Academy of Sciences in November 2003 also focused on MBE Science, uniting lay and spiritual leaders in the use of science to enhance educational opportunities.

Several government programs related to the emerging field started at this time. The Japan Research Institute of Science and Technology (2001) and the RIKEN Institute in Japan (2002) emphasized flexible, interdisciplinary research about the brain and learning. At the end of 2002, the Dutch Science Council (NWO), in consultation with the Dutch Ministry of Education, Culture and Science, set up the Brain and Learning Committee. The Dutch Science Council undertook initiatives to stimulate an active exchange among brain scientists, cognitive scientists, and educational scientists on the practice of education. This was followed by a publication of the Dutch Science Council and the Ministry of Education, *Learning to Know the Brain* (Jolles, 2005).

This trend toward the educational applicability of neuroscientific concepts was paralleled by an increasingly receptive society. In 2004, the formation of the International MBE Society was announced at the Conference on Usable Knowledge in MBE at Harvard University. In 2005, the Mexican Society for the Neurosciences was founded. At this time an innovative doctorate program, created in 2005, called the Joint International Cognitive Neuroscience PhD Program, which is currently sponsored by the University of Bologna (Italy), Université Claude Bernard (Lyon, France), University College of London (England), University of Bangor (Wales), and the Wake Forest University School of Medicine (North Carolina, United States), united various world perspectives on MBE Science. All of these academic programs called national attention to the importance of uniting neuroscience, psychology, and education in different parts of the world.

Innovations in the field began to snowball by mid-2005. Between 2000 and 2005, there was a refinement of knowledge about the developmental processes of learning, which led to a proliferation of neuroscientific information written for and by educators such as Levine (2000), Sousa (2000), Weiss (2000a), Westwater and Wolfe (2000), and Wolfe (2001a, b). Many of these books and articles sold into the hundred of thousands, attesting to teachers' hunger for guidance about brain-based learning and their slowly developing sophistication about evidenced-based methodologies.

These various initiatives converged to create the global transdisciplinary field of MBE Science. Between 2004 and 2006, there were many concrete suggestions about improving interdisciplinary communication in the emerging field and testaments to the utility of joining the forces of the parent fields of neuroscience, psychology, and education. Daniel Ansari (2005a) at the University of Western Ontario wrote that it is "time to use neuroscience findings in teacher training" (p. 466). John Geake (2005) of Oxford Brookes University also suggested that there needs to be "a mutual middle way" between educational neuroscience and neuroscientific education (p. 10). Usha Goswami (2005a) suggested that unifying neuroscience and education meant finally putting "the brain in the classroom" (p. 17). Howard-Jones (2005) alluded to Bruer's (1997) article when he made specific suggestions for "an invaluable foundation for better bridges" by including educators in the wave of new discovery brought on by neuroscience in the classroom (p. 470). Varma and colleagues (2008) offered concrete observations on the "scientific and pragmatic challenges for bridging education and neuroscience" and optimistically considered the challenges and potential opportunities for better relations (p. 140). Others simply spoke of "improving learning through understanding of brain research" (Wunderlich, Bell, & Ford, 2005, p. 41). All of these calls in the early 2000s landslided into the inevitable: the formation of a new type of professional who united neuroscience, education, and psychology.

For the first time, professionals formally trained in all three fields of pedagogy, neuroscience, and developmental psychology began to emerge. They began to publish work both acceptable to neuroscientists and useful to educators. Judy Willis, for example, is a neuroscientist who has turned to teaching. *Research-Based Strategies to Ignite Student Learning: Insights From a Neurologist and Classroom Teacher* (Willis, 2006) was an acclaimed work in which Willis identified best practice in teaching and then confirmed these practices through neuroscience. Her *Brain-Friendly Strategies for the Inclusion Classroom* (Willis, 2007) is one of the clearest guides for teachers, grounded in both classroom practice and neurological evidence. Likewise, Usha Goswami's (2007) latest book, *Cognitive Development: The Learning Brain* did much the same to move neuroscience into the classroom.

The number of institutes and organizations devoted exclusively to the goals of the emerging field, such as the Oxford University Institute for the Future of the Mind (started in 2006), continued to grow, indicating a continual formalization of the field. The book *The Brain and Learning* (OECD, 2007) added to the global recognition of the new discipline as a view shared by the 30 OECD member countries. In a landmark event, the new discipline of MBE Science launched the first issue of the *MBE* journal in March 2007, thanks to the efforts of Kurt Fischer and David Daniel. Starting in 2005, there were concerted efforts to further integrate teachers into the research process through conferences and society meetings. Developmental psychology, neuroscience, and learning theory became a more common combination in publications, as in Coch, Fischer, and Dawson's (2007) *Human Behavior, Learning, and the Developing Brain* and *The Jossey-Bass Reader on the Brain and Learning* (2008).

With such dramatic scientific advances came concern that, as the field became more established, the consequences of its work needed to be considered, along with a growing concern about neuroethics. Should brain scans be used in school admissions? Should the use of memory-enhancing drugs be approved? Many authors on neuroethics identified dozens of questions in this vein (e.g., Gazzangia, 2005a), and a handful even tried to make recommendations about how decisions should be made in the field (e.g., Illes, 2006). Linked to ethical concerns were greater and greater numbers of articles that challenged findings of brain-based learning in the 1990s and refuted some "accepted" norms, such as the debate about enriched environments mentioned earlier. New self-criticisms are reflective of the maturation of the field, which is now old enough to look back at its own research. By the start of 2008, the new MBE Science field had a clear set of goals.

As described in the Introduction, the international Delphi panel survey united 20 experts in the emerging field and sought to create a framework for standards in MBE Science. In March 2008, the international workshop Explorations in Learning and the Brain—for experts in cognitive neuroscience, neuropsychology, and educational science—was organized under the auspices of the Dutch Science Council; in April 2008, the 20th biannual conference on Learning and the Brain took place in Cambridge, Massachusetts.

By the end of 2008, it was clear that MBE Science had experienced a pendulum swing. Throughout the Decade of the Brain in the 1990s, there was an insatiable demand to ground teaching in science, or, more specifically, in biological information about the brain. Around the start of the 21st century, however, there was a change. Many scientists and neuroeducators reminded the field that it was "losing its mind in favor of the brain" (Siegel, 1999, p. xii) and that a move toward "biological determinism" (p. xiii), which claimed that everything we are is based on the genes we inherit, was unbalanced at best and dangerous at worst. These observations returned a more human face to the emerging MBE Science field. This pendulum swing brings the balance back to the middle and values both the science and the art of teaching. It also gives us cause to celebrate what is well-established in the field and to use these tools to be more effective teachers.

CHAPTER 2

Using What We Know as Fact

One of the main objectives of MBE Science is to confirm best-practice teaching through scientific evidence of how humans learn and, as a result, improve the ways we teach. This means that as educators we need to review our prior knowledge about what we know works in our classrooms and to take a little time to understand *why* it works or how it could work better. However, some of the best practices in classroom settings have yet to be confirmed by science. Our role, and that of other MBE scientists, is not to reject all practice that can't be shown to work in lab settings, but rather to help establish which practices are really proven, and which are simple myths, and use this knowledge to inform teaching. How? First and foremost, we in education should share medicine's first rule: *Do no harm.*

Before we apply the latest fad in teaching in our classrooms, we should stop and think for a moment. When a doctor consults, she uses past knowledge to guide her patient but also has in mind new information she has been exposed to. This doesn't mean that she necessarily pushes her patient into taking the latest drug on the market; rather, she thinks about all the options before prescribing a solution. In a similar way, we teachers need to use our past knowledge as well as consider new information. We need to scrutinize this new information before using it. Just like the doctor, we teachers need to caution ourselves to *do no harm* before enthusiastically jumping on the bandwagon of quick cures. Is the new medicine as good as or better than the old one (is the new classroom activity as good as or better than our old practices)? How much of our willingness to believe in the new product (practice) comes from successful marketing rather than our own knowledge of the product (practice)?

A secondary objective of MBE Science is to move the science of teaching (pedagogy) from being a "soft" to a "hard" science based not only on anecdotal but also on empirical evidence. This means substantiating the art of teaching through hard science. Why should this be done? One of the best reasons is to enhance professional credibility. In order to be respected on the same level as other professions like medicine and law, teachers need to scrutinize the methods we use in class and choose only the very best tools as we exercise our craft. Through MBE Science, we now have the tools to prove what we have suspected and observed through practice as teachers.

MBE Science helps us distinguish which specific types of teaching activities actually lend themselves to better student learning and which do not. To do this, in this chapter we begin by sorting out the science from the neuromyths. We will then explore how the evidence points to a new (or confirmed) set of instructional guidelines that emerge and show how this may change the way we teach.

TRUTHS AND NEUROMYTHS IN MBE SCIENCE

Truths, in science, are beliefs or concepts that have been validated by hypotheses in testing. Myths are the opposite; they tend to have "an imaginary or unverifiable existence," according to the Merriam-Webster Dictionary; neuromyths are imaginary or unverifiable claims about the brain and are normally born of a partial truth. They are typically overgeneralizations or, in some cases, outright misconceptions about the brain. The Organisation for Economic Co-operation and Development (OECD, 2007) explains that neuromyths are "hypotheses which have been invalidated, [but which] nevertheless leave traces and if these have captured a wider imagination, 'myths' take root" (p. 108). The experts in MBE Science who participated in the Delphi panel survey were asked to identify as many neuromyths as they could and then to categorize a list of concepts often used in brain-based education. Based on the panel responses to these two sets of questions, we were able to place the concepts on a continuum from well-established information with scientific backing to pure neuromyths (see Table 2.1). These categorizations were then compared with evidence in the literature.

The commonly used terms or concepts in brain-based teaching and the neuromyths generated by the experts were placed on a continuum of four categories (OECD, 2002, p. 29; see Figure 2.1). They are:

1. *What is well established:* These are essential concepts that form the basic foundations of best-practice teaching (e.g., *plasticity*, or the malleable nature of the brain and its ability to form new connections throughout the life span, which now has hundreds of credible human studies behind it).

2. *What is probably so:* There are important concepts or practices that we need to keep our eye on, as they may soon become well-established, but still lack unanimous backing from at least one of the three areas of neuroscience, psychology, and education (e.g., *sensitive periods*, which has hundreds of studies behind it, though not all conducted on humans).

Table 2.1. Four categories of information in MBE Science and their criteria

Four Categories of Information in the Emerging Field of Educational Neuroscience/ MBE Science (OECD, 2002)	Best Evidence Encyclopedia Criteria	What Works Clearinghouse Criteria
WHAT IS WELL-ESTABLISHED E.g., "Human brains are as unique as faces; while the basic structure is the same, there are no two which are identical. While there are general patterns of organization in how different people learn and which brain areas are involved, each brain is unique and uniquely organized."	*Strong Evidence of Effectiveness* At least one large randomized or randomized quasi-experimental study, or multiple smaller studies, with a median effect size of at least +0.20. A large study is defined as one in which at least 10 classes or schools, or 250 students, were assigned to treatments. Smaller studies are counted as equivalent to a large study if their collective sample sizes are at least 250 students. If randomized studies have a median effect of at least +0.20, the total set of studies need not have a median effect size.	*Positive Effects* Strong evidence of a positive effect with no overriding contrary evidence. Two or more studies showing statistically significant positive effects, at least one of which met WWC evidence standards for a strong design. No studies showing statistically significant or substantively important negative effects.
WHAT IS PROBABLY SO E.g., "Human brains seek and often quickly detect novelty (which is individually defined)."	*Moderate Evidence of Effectiveness* One large matched study or multiple smaller studies with a collective sample size of 250 students, with a median effect size of at least +.0.20	*Potential Positive Effects* Evidence of a positive effect with no overriding contrary evidence. At least one study showing a statistically significant or substantively important positive effect. No studies showing statistically significant or substantively important negative effects and few or the same number of studies showing indeterminate effects than showing statistically significant or substantively important positive effects.
WHAT IS INTELLIGENT SPECULATION E.g., "Learning is enhanced by challenge and is typically inhibited by threat (in which threat is individually defined)."	*Limited Evidence of Effectiveness* At least one qualifying study with a significant positive effect and/or median effect size of +0.10 or more.	*Mixed Effects* Evidence of inconsistent effects as demonstrated through either of the following: at least one study showing a statistically or substantively important positive effect and at least one study showing a statistically significant or substantively important negative effect, but no more such studies than the number showing a statistically significant or substantively important positive effect, or at least one study showing a statistically significant or substantively important effect than showing a statistically significant or substantively important effect.
WHAT IS POPULAR MISCONCEPTION OR A NEUROMYTH E.g., "Humans use about 10% of their brains."	*Insufficient Evidence* Studies show no significant differences. No Qualifying Studies.	*No Discernible Effects* No affirmative evidence of effects. None of the studies show a statistically significant or substantively important effect, either positive or negative. No Qualifying Studies. Potentially Negative Effects. Negative Effects.

Figure 2.1. The MBE continuum.

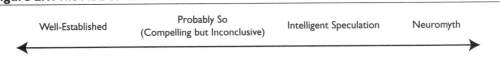

| Well-Established | Probably So (Compelling but Inconclusive) | Intelligent Speculation | Neuromyth |

3. *What is intelligent speculation:* These tend to be concepts that we want to believe are true but that just don't have the science behind them to support the weight of claims attached to them. Some of these concepts may eventually become well-established after more research is conducted or terms are better defined, or they may simply fall into the category of a neuromyth (e.g., *gender differences*, which has thousands of studies behind it, albeit of mixed quality and sometimes with contradictory findings).

4. *What is popular misconception or a neuromyth:* These tend to be "sexy," attractive, and highly marketable concepts about the brain and learning that have little or no evidence behind them. They either reflect their promoters' unintended ignorance about the brain, or they are knowingly promoted misinterpretations sold to the public by unscrupulous consultants (e.g., *right-brain/ left-brain theory,* which has been the subject of thousands of books and articles, some of which promote the claim but most of which criticize its lack of factual accuracy.

To support these four categories of information, in addition to the Delphi panel opinions, each group was compared with the "Best Evidence Encyclopedia Criteria" and "What Works Clearinghouse Criteria." Derek Briggs suggests the use of the Best Evidence Encyclopedia and What Works Clearinghouse to improve the quality of educational research because they are stringent measures in educational research that ensure quality information (Briggs, 2008). For example, in order for a concept or belief to be considered here as well-established, it had to pass the scrutiny of the expert panel and then the criteria suggested by an ingenious category structure. Briggs's article indicates that information can be considered well-established if one of two things occurs. Either, according to the Best Evidence Encyclopedia, there is "[a]t least one large randomized or randomized quasi-experimental study, or multiple smaller studies, with a median effect size of at least +0.20." Or, according to the What Works Clearinghouse, there is "[s]trong evidence of a positive effect with no overriding contrary evidence." This creates stringent criteria against which each educational concept can be judged.

Teachers can use this continuum to distinguish proven from unproven information in brain-based learning literature. It is important to remember, however, that the beliefs and neuromyths are open to continued scrutiny, and it should not be surprising to find that some concepts having little supporting evidence today may be added to a different category when new studies emerge. This is a dynamic field and changes should not be shunned, but rather embraced, if and when new empirical evidence can be found to support the move from one category to another.

Of the many brain-based teaching concepts currently in circulation and with varied levels of application in schools, the expert panel identified 5 beliefs it considered to be well-established in MBE Science, 19 concepts that are probably so, 24 concepts that are intelligent speculation, and 29 concepts that are neuromyths.

WHAT IS WELL-ESTABLISHED

It is very hard to be categorized as well-established, as it should be. Just five educational concepts met these strict criteria (see Figure 2.2). Each of the concepts is explained below, based on the expert commentary and the review of the literature.

Human Brains Are as Unique as Faces

Human brains are as unique as faces; while the basic structure is the same, there are no two that are identical. While there are general patterns of organization in how different people learn and which brain areas are involved, each brain is unique and uniquely organized. (Tokuhama-Espinosa, 2008b, p. 356)

Figure 2.2. What Is Well-Established in MBE Science

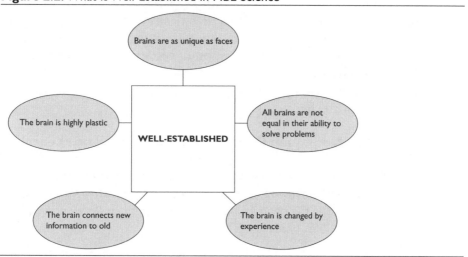

Source: Bramwell, 2009.

The uniqueness of the human brain is perhaps the most fundamental belief in MBE Science. Even identical twins leave the womb with physically distinct brains due to the slightly different experiences they had—one with his ear pressed closer to the uterus wall and bombarded with sounds and light, for example, and the other snuggled down deep in the dark. There are clear patterns of brain development shared by all people, but the uniqueness of each brain explains why students learn in slightly different ways. This well-established belief also explains why different teaching techniques resonate in distinct ways for diverse pupils.

Most experienced teachers can offer countless examples of just how their students differ. Sometimes these differences can be explained by the student's home environment, family values and dynamics, culture, economics, or past schooling experience. For example, it is clear that socioeconomic factors impact learning. However, in other instances learning differences are explained by the raw material the student was born with. There is an ongoing debate as to what percentage of intelligence is genetically based and what percentage is due to the person's teaching and upbringing. Is genius in your genes, or does your environment play a larger role in shaping your potential for school success? Much of the current thinking on this question follows Matt Ridley's belief that it is impossible to separate nature and nurture because all the ingredients of nurture are in genes (nature). Ridley (2003) argues that each human's uniqueness is due to his or her genetic structure. Others argue that environment can advance or suppress development of neural structures. What we know for sure is that no two humans are alike, and this includes their brains.

Having said this, it is clear that humans share the basic parts of both faces and brains. The unique aspect of the brain is not in its overall formation but rather in the subtle ways experiences change the brain. What does this tell us about teaching? It cautions us not to expect the same thing from different students. It reminds us that all students come into our classrooms with different experiences that have changed their brains. It cautions us about overgeneralizing the location of certain skills in the brain or simplifying learning problems ("he has a reading problem"); rather, it forces us to be more precise in our diagnosis and to be more individualized in our treatment of students.

All Brains Are Not Equal: Context and Ability Influence Learning

> All brains are not equal in their ability to solve all problems. Context as well as ability influence learning. Context includes the learning environment, motivation for the topic of new learning, and prior knowledge. (Tokuhama-Espinosa, 2008b, p. 356)

Different people are born with different abilities, which they can improve upon or lose depending on the stimuli, or lack thereof, that they experience. The stimulus one receives is impacted by what one brings to the learning context, including past experience and prior knowledge. This means that children do not enter the classroom on an even playing field. Some are simply more prepared for the world from birth. Both genes and previous experiences contribute to children's success in class. This reminds us to think about the environment we are providing our children.

Children's prior experiences provide their contexts for learning, influencing not only how they learn but also what they enjoy learning and why. For example, some children have parents who have provided them with a variety of experiences, including exposure to a wide variety of stimuli, which increases their chances for success in school—not due to "enrichment" but rather due to broad access to links with prior learning. On the opposite end of the spectrum, other children may have been nurtured by the "one-eyed babysitter" (the television), which offers little chance for interaction or self-reflection about complex themes. Still others find their ability to learn crippled by poor school environments and their enthusiasm for the subject matter dampened by activities that do not motivate them.

Understanding that all brains are not equal in their ability to solve all problems is a key belief in MBE Science that reminds us that differences in student abilities to learn lie not only in the realm of intelligence but also in life and learning experiences. This means that teachers are likely to find students in their classes who appear to "connect" to new information rapidly (due to past experiences), while others are much slower to do so (due to a lack of similar experiences). What can a teacher do to remedy this inequality? Teachers need to know their students better in order to connect to prior experience and identify areas where they need to build new background knowledge for learning. As L. Dee Fink (2003) writes, there is no academic growth without personal growth. Academic learning and individual growth can occur simultaneously and sustain each other. When a teacher knows his students well enough to teach toward personal needs, then the student learns faster. Additionally, when the teacher helps a student gain academically, that student also increases in self-confidence and efficacy, both of which contribute to motivation and learning.

The Brain Is Changed by Experience

> The brain is a complex, dynamic, and integrated system that is constantly changed by experience, though most of this change is only evident at a microscopic level. (Tokuhama-Espinosa, 2008b, p. 356)

You will go to bed tonight with a different brain from the one you had when you awoke. Each smell, sight, taste, and touch you experience and each feeling or thought you have alters the physical form of your brain. While these brain changes are often imperceptible unless viewed under a powerful microscope, they constantly change the physical makeup of the brain. With rehearsal, these changes become permanent. This works in both positive and negative ways. Areas of the brain that are used together tend to be strengthened, while areas that are not stimulated atrophy, as first demonstrated by the Hebbian hypothesis in 1949. This is a physical manifestation of how life experiences change the brain. This means that both use and disuse change the physical structure of the brain. Teachers must remember that the class experiences they design for their students will be recorded, for good or for bad, in their brains. The complexity and dynamic nature of the brain remind teachers that even when they feel they are not reaching students, they may very well be changing them, bit by bit. Research by Peter Giordano (2004) documented numerous cases of what he calls the role of "critical moments" in student development. Giordano's cases show that exchanges, which might seem like inconsequential moments to teachers, may impact students for the rest of their lives.

The concept that our brains are constantly changed by life experiences should caution teachers to be measured in their exchanges with students and to consider the long-term impact that both positive and negative comments can have. Just as a constant drop of water on a rock can eventually wear it down, so can regular comments or actions by a teacher shape a student's belief in himself.

Most of the changes that occur in the brain are apparent only on a microscopic level. Some, but not all, of these physical changes result in behavioral changes that can actually be seen. For example, it is possible that as a child learns to ride a bike, hold a pencil, speak a new language, or play an instrument for the first time, a great many physical changes occur in the brain before the child actually rides the bike, holds the pencil, speaks the new language, or plays the instrument correctly. Some of the things we learn are actions and others are attitudes. The changes in brain mechanisms are similar, however. The brain changes as it learns a new way to approach a problem (or view life, or accept defeat, or face challenges) in a similar way as it changes as it learns a new active skill. This information begs patience from teachers. Learning often occurs in stages that may initially be unseen.

The Brain Is Highly Plastic

> Human brains have a high degree of plasticity and develop throughout the lifespan, though there are major limits on this plasticity, and these limits increase with age. (Tokuhama-Espinosa, 2008b, p. 357)

People can, and do, learn throughout their lives. One of the most influential findings of the 20th century was the discovery of the brain's plasticity. This discovery challenged the earlier belief in localizationism, which had lasted for hundreds of years. Localizationism is the belief that X skill is located in Y part of the brain, as in language is a function of the left hemisphere. Localizationism implies that if, for some reason, Y is damaged, then X is lost forever. We now know that this is not necessarily true, due to testimonies of people who have lost areas of their brain due to stroke. One such case is that of Jill Taylor (2008), who suffered both skill loss (walking, talking, writing) and a change in personality due to her stroke. Given the areas of her brain damage, her story is initially a convincing one in favor of localizationism. What Taylor's story also shows us is the amazing flexibility of the brain not only to recoup lost skills (she now walks, talks, and writes again) but also to tap into lesser-used areas of the brain and, in doing so, expand our repertoire of skills. While different parts of the brain tend to play key roles in certain skills (as in the left hemisphere and language, for example), it has now been documented that neuroplasticity can explain why some people are able to recoup skills thought to be lost due to brain damage. In extreme cases, there are people born with only one hemisphere of their brains who manage to live a completely normal life. Antonio Battro's work "Half a Brain Is Enough" and Mary Helen Immordino-Yang (2007a), one of the brightest new MBE scientists today, offer the detailed story of two such cases in "A Tale of Two Cases: Lessons for Education from the Study of Two Boys Living with Half Their Brains." Immordino-Yang documents how the entire brain works as a single large system—when parts are missing, as in the case of these two children, then other parts of the brain "take over" and learn functions they are not necessarily associated with.

To take plasticity to an extreme, researchers such as Paul Bach-y-Rita make it clear that "we see with our brains, not with our eyes" (Doidge, 2007, p. 14). That is, the brain as a whole, not necessarily a single part of the brain, is responsible for sensory perception. Bach-y-Rita explains this in a simple way: Let's presume you are driving from point A to point B. You normally take the most efficient route, but if a bridge is down or the road is blocked, you take a secondary road. This secondary road might not be as fast as the "natural" route, but it gets you to point B all the same, and it may even become the preferred route if it is reinforced enough.

Perhaps the author who has done the most to explain neuroplasticity to the public is physician Norman Doidge (2007), who has documented studies that "showed that children are not always stuck with the mental abilities they are born with; that the damaged brain can often reorganize itself so that when one part fails, another can often substitute; that is, brain cells die, they can at times be replaced; that many 'circuits' and even basic reflexes that we think are hardwired are not" (p. xv). Neuroplasticity has implications not only for brains that have been damaged but also for basic learning in classroom experiences and how we think about education. Although it was popular in the 1990s to think of the "critical" early years, it is now acknowledged that learning takes place throughout the life span. Does this speak against early-childhood educational practices? Not at all; it simply means that under the right conditions, normal stages of skill development should be seen as benchmarks, not roadblocks, as humans can learn throughout the life span.

Doidge (2007) also writes about "the plastic paradox," describing the "good" and "bad" ways that plasticity affects the brain (p. vxi). He suggests that obsessive-compulsive behavior and racism, for example, are attributed to the brain's plasticity. "It is by understanding both the positive and negative effects of plasticity that we can truly understand the extent of human possibilities" in their entirety (p. vxi). Knowing that the brain is plastic gives hope to teachers in that all students have the potential to learn. The correct choice and application of effective methodologies and differentiated instruction can take advantage of the brain's ability to adapt to change behavior, including learning.

The Brain Connects New Information to Old

> Connecting new information to prior knowledge facilitates learning.
> (Tokuhama-Espinosa, 2008b, p. 357).

We learn better and faster when we relate new information to things we already know. This statement may sound like it needs no evidence—we live this every day. For example, let's say you are going somewhere you have never been before. When someone gives you directions, it is very helpful if she offers you a point of reference that is familiar to you ("you'll see the store you bought the plant at; from there, turn right at the next corner"). Unfortunately, this guidance does not always happen in our classrooms.

It is unfortunate that new concepts are sometimes taught in a conceptual vacuum without anchoring the information to what students already know. This explains why students who have poor foundations in a particular subject will continue to fail. How can a child who does not understand addition move on to understand subtraction? To use a house-building metaphor, if we have a weak foundation, then it is irrelevant how sturdy the walls are or how well built the roof is; the structure cannot be supported. This is an argument for high-quality early instruction. Without a firm foundation in basic mathematical conceptualization (or language, values, artistic, kinesthetic, or social conceptualization), then a student will have a lot of trouble moving on to build more complex conceptual understandings.

The importance of connection to past knowledge is not limited to sequential foundational knowledge, as in mathematics, however. All new learning needs to connect to something already present in the brain, some knowledge or experience to which new learning can attach. This relates to what David Sousa calls "sense and meaning" in class planning (2000). Good teachers take time to carefully plan their classes (they make sense), but they should also take time to link new concepts with prior knowledge (they have meaning to the students). Teachers need to keep in mind that students' past experiences will always impact new learning, for good or ill.

It is impossible for teachers to know everything that their students know, but they should be aware that whatever it is that children bring to the class with them in terms of past experiences will influence learning. Students' past knowledge can serve as a resource, but teachers have to be willing to take the time to dig and understand just what knowledge exists. This well-established belief about teaching and learning confirms that a teacher's first step in teaching is to discover what students already know.

These five well-established facts in MBE Science are the keys to great teaching and are the cornerstones of best-practice classroom design. We now turn to information that includes concepts or practices that we need to keep our eye on because they may soon become well-established but they still lack unanimous backing from neuroscience, psychology, and education.

CHAPTER 3

Considering What to Do with What Is Probably True

Information that is "probably so," or likely to be true, is important for teachers to consider, but we should also watch carefully as new studies emerge. For evidence to be considered probably so, according to the Best Evidence Encyclopedia, there is "[o]ne large matched study or multiple smaller studies with a collective sample size of 250 students, with a median effect size of at least +.0.20"or "[a]t least one study showing a statistically significant or substantively important positive effect," according to the What Works Clearinghouse. In other words, it means that there is, indeed, evidence for the concept but that this comes from few studies. In other cases, it means that while there is support for a concept in this category, it may not enjoy overwhelming support by evidence from all three of the parent fields (neuroscience, psychology, and education).

In this developing field, there is much that is probably so. For purposes of discussion, this information is chunked into four areas in which much MBE research is concentrated (see Figure 3.1):

1. Emotions and their impact on teaching and learning
2. The learning organism
3. Species-related processes
4. Education and teaching processes

EMOTIONS AND THEIR IMPACT ON TEACHING AND LEARNING

Emotions have a special impact on learning processes that have only recently become clear thanks to neuroscientific findings. Emotions are triggered by different types of sensory perceptions and by different memories for different people. The following concepts relate to how emotions influence the way we learn and, therefore, the way we should teach.

Figure 3.1. Beliefs that are "Probably So" in MBE Science

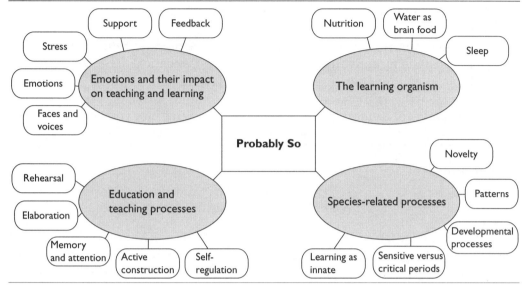

Source: Bramwell, 2009.

Faces and Voices

> The human brain judges others' faces and tones of voices for threat levels in a rapid and often unconscious way, influencing the way information from these sources is perceived (i.e., valid, invalid, trustworthy, untrustworthy, etc.). (Tokuhama-Espinosa, 2008b, p. 360)

As a species, humans are primed to perceive and react to other people's voices and facial expressions and, in doing so, to gauge an individual's threat level or amicability. Without being consciously aware, we make snap judgments from the moment we lay eyes on each other or hear each other's voices. An understanding of this quick judgment is important for teachers. Some teachers manage their classes with an air of confidence and assurance that inspires their pupils to confide in them and to trust their guidance. Students determine the level of teacher self-efficacy in part through their teachers' facial expressions and voices. When a teacher's face shows insecurity, students perceive this; some may act with empathy, others with scorn. According to researchers, when a student feels that her teacher doesn't believe in her abilities to learn—because the teacher "looked at her funny" or his voice seemed condescending—then her actual performance is impaired. Even if students misinterpret facial expressions, what students *think* their teachers think about them influences their performance. This means that teachers should be conscious of the messages they send, intentional or not.

Teacher self-efficacy relates to how teachers appear to feel about their own teaching performance. Student attention is influenced by how interested the teacher appears to be in his own topic. A teacher's level of enthusiasm for his own teaching, as seen on his face or in his tone of voice, influences student motivation: The more enthusiasm a teacher displays for his topic, the more enthusiasm his students have. Teachers need to acknowledge that this enthusiasm is palpable to students. While proven in psychology and evolutionary neuroscience, this concept is not yet well established because documentation in school contexts is sparse.

Emotions

Emotions are critical to decision making. (Tokuhama-Espinosa, 2008b, p. 357)

No decision, no matter how minor, is undertaken without some level of emotion, though recognition of these feelings may not be apparent to the learner. It may seem surprising, but deciding to drop a nuclear bomb, which tie to wear to work, whether to skip a class or not, who to ask out this weekend, or which news station to watch are all emotional decisions. Immordino-Yang and Damazio (2008) have done extensive work in the field of emotions and learning and have documented not only the definition of emotions but also their roles in defining who we are. Their work reminds us as teachers that learning is nurtured by reasoning but also guided by feelings.

Humans make decisions based on past experiences and related to the emotions they experienced at the time. Some educators have proposed that negative emotions can block new learning. As Sousa (2000) expalins, when a concept fights with an emotion, the emotion will almost always win. That is, students may reason to themselves, "I understand the *concept* that attending algebra class is important to passing, but I just feel so *humiliated* by the teacher that I *hate* going." Decisions are influenced by emotions. How we feel influences how we will act.

Teachers who realize the importance of emotions understand how vital they are to the success of their course. Some students do learn through negative motivation prompted by criticism; most people, however, enjoy learning based on positive motivation promoted by encouragement and praise, when merited. Independent of the intelligence and ability levels of their students, teachers can design learning environments that are emotionally supportive. This does not mean that teachers have to like every student they come into contact with, but they do have to respect them to the extent that they protect them from emotional harm. This is not yet well established because documentation in classroom contexts is sparse.

Stress

> Stress impacts learning: "Good" stress (eustress) heightens attention
> and helps learning, while "bad" stress detracts from learning potential.
> (Tokuhama-Espinosa, 2008b, p. 364)

Stress is a part of modern life. When students experience "bad" or negative stress, neurotransmitters in their brains actually block the uptake of new information and new learning. However, a certain level of stress is needed to help students focus and pay attention. "Good," or positive, stress (also known as *eustress*) can be helpful in class. To use a racing metaphor, this is equivalent to the sprinter at the starting line who needs a certain level of stress (adrenaline) to start on time; however, too much stress will either make him jump the gun or waste his energy.

Teachers can use an understanding of the role of stress in learning to enhance classroom experiences. Teaching techniques that manage stress in the right way can help students stay alert and focused. This eustress involves keeping students "on their toes" without creating panic. For example, teachers can make students aware that they can be called on at any time but also give them warning about when this will happen (by a previously agreed-on nod or light tap on the shoulder, or the simple habit of calling on students with equal frequency). By creating this high-alert setting, students maintain focus but do not experience negative stress. A key element in good classroom learning environments is the level and type of stress(es) the learners experience.

Teachers and classroom experiences can be the source of student stress. However, trouble in the home or in the neighborhood can cause students to bring stress to school with them, too. In some children's lives, schools become a sanctuary from their daily life stress. Teachers have little control over any source of stress outside of school, but they should be aware that it could impact student learning. Teachers must also be attuned to physical or emotional bullying inside or outside the classroom; such bullying is not only morally wrong but also adversely stresses learning. Unfortunately, documentation of these experiences in school settings is weak. For that reason, this concept is not yet considered well established, despite neuroscientific and psychological studies that support it, and teachers' daily experience of it in educational settings.

Support from Others

> Support (academic, moral, or otherwise) from others (often teachers,
> peers, or parents) is critical for learning and optimal academic performance.
> (Tokuhama-Espinosa, 2008b, p. 168)

Student learning is enhanced by external support mechanisms. Extra academic support, such as outside tutoring or homework help, has been shown to give students an edge. Likewise, social support networks, such as friends and family, have also been shown to aid learning. It is said that humans are social creatures. When academic goals or achievements are shared with others, they are elevated in importance to the learner.

From a physiological perspective, this can be explained by how the brain interprets this support. The increased self-esteem and enhanced self-efficacy that come from support by authority figures not only release endorphins in the learner's brain but also suppress stress hormones that can impede learning. Teachers who understand this are able to help students identify their own social networks and/or to create them in class. Group work is an example of "artificially constructed" social networks. When teachers structure small-group or pair activities in a conscientious way, they are in effect helping students design a support mechanism. Small-group work only works well, however, when group members have been chosen for their complementary qualities and the groups are supervised sufficiently to ensure equal input from everyone.

Teachers can also use information about the importance of social networks to establish and encourage helpful parental support. This means explaining to parents that when they show interest in what their children are doing in school, they give students another reason to believe it is worth their time and effort. Some schools go so far as to formalize these support mechanisms and offer after-school homework classes or clubs, which provide a forum for student exchange about class materials. Support systems provided by parents, teachers, and schools all encourage better student learning. While proven in education and psychology, this concept is not yet well established because documentation from neuroscience is sparse.

Feedback

> Feedback and meaningful assessment is important to human learning, though the importance and role of feedback vary greatly across domains and processes. (Tokuhama-Espinosa, 2008b, p. 169).

Information about how well or poorly one does on a task is useful if given in a formative (process), rather than summative (end), manner and with enough detail that the learner can use this information to improve upon his work. It should be remembered that different people react to feedback in different ways and that this can vary across topics. However, numerous educational studies show honest, frequent, and balanced feedback aids student learning.

Honest feedback means a teacher should never tell a student she is "doing great" when she is barely passing. Rather, teachers who let students know they "are improving" give a great boost to otherwise wounded egos when poor grades are given. In this sense, teachers give equal weight to assessing students not only on the final *product* (the results on a test, for example) but also on the *process* and *progress* individual students make in their subjects. Even when students are given "bad" news, the feedback shows the teacher cares enough about their progress to take the time to comment on their work and show them specific steps to improve. This type of caring means a great deal to students.

Feedback can be given verbally and spontaneously as well as in writing. This is distinct from grading. When students take an exam, they receive a letter or number grade. This grade does not help them know what they need to do better, only what they did wrong. However, when students receive more explicit feedback about what they did wrong, they are given tools to improve their performance the next time. Teachers across disciplines have found that students who are given clear feedback do better on subsequent evaluations of a similar nature.

Feedback should be multidirectional. Students should receive constant feedback from their teachers as well as provide constant feedback to their teachers in a subtle but consistent way. For example, students can be asked to keep an index card on the table, one side colored green and the other red. If everything is clear, a student shows the green side; if there is doubt or confusion, the student shows the red side. This type of embedded assessment gives teachers immediate feedback about the clarity of their explanation of concepts and the students' level of knowledge without waiting for a test. While proven in education and psychology, this concept is not yet well established because documentation from neuroscience is sparse.

THE LEARNING ORGANISM

Humans are learning organisms that rely on interaction between the body and mind. The following concepts relate to the ways in which the body impacts the mind and decisions in the mind impact the body.

Nutrition

Nutrition impacts learning (good eating habits contribute to learning and poor eating habits detract from the brain's ability to maximize its learning potential). (Tokuhama-Espinosa, 2008b, p. 172)

The state of the body influences the ability of the mind to learn. Just like the body, the brain needs energy to work properly, which it gets primarily from food. The quality of nutrition impacts the physical structure of the brain. A student's diet contributes to both poor attention and its opposite, improved concentration. What our students eat influences how well they do in our classrooms. Though dietary choices are often beyond teacher influence, teachers need to be aware of the role that nutrition plays in learning. Policy makers and administrators should take this a step further and to recommend that parents adopt healthy eating habits at home, and cafeterias should be required to serve nutritious foods and get rid of vending machines for junk food and drinks.

Poor eating habits stem from both economics (junk food tends to cost less than many nutritious options) and a lack of knowledge about the right foods to eat. Poor nutrition can impact the brain through the balance of chemicals, sugars, fats, and other ingredients found in the foods children eat, and it can also explain the highs and lows of attention many students experience in class. Sometimes a concentration problem can be remedied through the lunchbox, not necessarily through medications. Teachers can use this information in their diagnosis of student learning problems. It should be noted that this concept is not yet well established because comparative school-context studies are missing.

Water

Water is "brain food." (Tokuhama-Espinosa, 2008b, p. 277)

This belief is based on the fact that 75% of the body and 77–78% of the brain are comprised of water. Some researchers suggest that allowing students to drink water in class helps restore the body to its natural state. This presumes that the body is "out of balance" due to a lack of water, which in some cases may be true. Some teachers encourage their students to drink water in class. It has been argued, however, that students seem more alert after having a drink of water not because they needed to rehydrate but because the water break gave them a chance to refocus. This belief was categorized as probably so by the experts because it appears logical, though the claim that drinking water in class makes students learn better has yet to be proven beyond a doubt. (Some teachers have argued against water breaks because they lead to bathroom breaks and missed class time!) While proven physiologically, the benefits of rehydrating are not yet well established because documentation in classroom contexts using neuroscientific criteria is missing.

Sleep

Sleep is important for declarative memory consolidation or the explicit learning that takes place in school (though other types of memories, such as emotional memories, can be achieved without sleep). Sleep deprivation also has a negative impact on memory. (Tokuhama-Espinosa, 2008b, p. 360)

Without a good night's sleep, memory is compromised and learning suffers. This explains why students are able to cram for an exam, pass it, but remember almost nothing shortly after the test is over: The information they studied never got into long-term memory. Memory consolidation is dependent on sleep—specifically, REM (rapid eye movement) sleep, in which certain neurotransmitters are present that help preserve memory (Hobson, 2004). Stickgold, one of the leading researchers in this field, writes of "a memory boost while you sleep" (2006, p. 559), which is probably due to a certain combination of neurotransmitters that are only released in the brain during REM sleep.

Additionally, it has been found that lack of sleep compromises one's abilities to be attentive and to organize mental activity efficiently and effectively. To read, to write, to listen, and to tell, one needs a good night's sleep. This means that students who have not slept well will do poorly in our classrooms. While this is something that few teachers have control over, knowledge of the role of sleep in learning might help convince some students to change their sleep habits. This concept is not yet well established because there are only a few studies available on school-age populations.

SPECIES-RELATED PROCESSES

While there are some things that all animals do, there are others that only humans do. The following group of concepts that are "probably so" are specifically related to how humans have survived as a species.

Novelty

> Human brains seek and often quickly detect novelty, which is individually defined (that is, what is novel for one person is not necessarily novel for another). (Tokuhama-Espinosa, 2008b, p. 165)

We are quick to notice things that are out of place or different, and we actually unconsciously look for things that don't belong. This has been a part of human survival since the human race began. Human evolution has counted on the brain being able to detect novelty and determine when things appear different from what we expected. This includes an unexpected movement out of the corner of the eye, abrupt sounds, and other sensory input that is out of the ordinary. This type of sensory detection allowed the human species to avoid danger. Novelty detection protected our ancestors from harm; in modern times, it can be expanded to the classroom setting as well.

Teachers can take advantage of the brain's natural tendency to look for things out of the ordinary to develop categorization schemes and eventually patterns upon which to create expectations. Sesame Street has a popular game—"One of These Things Is Not Like the Other"—in which children are prompted to figure out which "one of these things just doesn't belong" and then point it out "before I end my song!" This wonderful game encourages the natural process of categorizing and eventually identifying something that doesn't fit. The ability to sort information by characteristics is key to conceptual development and the eventual construction of a mental schema upon which we create our vision of the world. Unfortunately, this natural categorization process is also responsible for the brain's lapses of identifying what is different as also being dangerous, which is not always the case. Distrust of those who are "not like us" comes from this human instinct, which sadly explains racism. Things that are different stand out and call attention to themselves. The attraction to novelty may point to an explanation of some teenage behavior. Humans sometimes like to "be different," as it affords them special attention from others.

Though the search for novelty is a general human characteristic, it is also influenced by individual experiences. Because we are exposed to different things in our lives, we find different things to be "novel." The ability to see things that are different gives individuals the option of using new information in a useful way later on. Students can and do learn in a similar way. A student's ability to see what is similar in and what is different between "2 + 3 = 5" and "5 − 3 = 2" helps him extrapolate from his understanding of addition to learn subtraction. This concept is not yet well established because the individual nature of "novelty" makes it hard to study. However, teachers apply this instinctively when they devise novel ways to engage students. The ability to quickly notice when things are different is closely linked to the ability to develop patterns out of the information we come across.

Patterns

> Human brains seek patterns upon which they predict outcomes, and neural systems form responses to repeated patterns of activation (patterns being individually defined). (Tokuhama-Espinosa, 2008b, p. 162)

We categorize our world in ways that help us understand information. Part of how we do this relates to designing patterns to classify the things we come across. These patterns are like a road map that tells us where to go next. This road map is the neural system or pathway taken in the brain for that group of similar experiences. Students spend a great deal of time developing patterns, and our school systems tend to test student knowledge based on their abilities to recognize patterns. Mathematical skills and formulas are highly pattern-bound, as is the proper structure of a sentence, a paragraph, and an essay. In a similar way, students observe social behavior and generally imitate what they have perceived to be normal patterns of interaction among friends, families, teachers, and students.

Students begin identifying patterns in the earliest years using categories or schemas they build through experiences. For example, 3-year-olds often learn nursery rhythms through sound patterns: "Humpty Dumpty sat on a *wall*; Humpty Dumpty had a great *fall* . . ." In a similar way, teachers develop phonic patterning by helping students understand how *cat, bat, rat,* and *hat* share the last two letters and the sound "-at" although they have different beginning letters. This detection of auditory patterns carries over into visual pattern recognition and eventually into conceptual pattern recognition. In general, formal school systems teach students the basic patterns and then hope they can transfer them to the real world.

The main reason patterning is so helpful to learners is because people make projections about outcomes based on past knowledge of those patterns. We predict what will happen next based on past pattern recognition. This can be helpful to teachers, and it can also be problematic. Teachers, like all humans, can be guilty of overgeneralization. For example, let's say a teacher begins the schoolyear with a certain class "chemistry" she thinks she has seen before and thinks to herself "This group is trouble." She might begin to treat the group as if it were filled with troublemakers even before the new class has done anything to merit the label. I have heard teachers make comments like, "So you are Johnny's sister, eh?"—and then proceed to expect the same behavior from Johnny's sister that they observed in Johnny. At the end of the year, it is not uncommon to hear, "You really surprised me this year! You're so much better than your brother was in my class!" Patterns can be helpful, but they can also lead to both negative and positive expectations that can go unfulfilled.

Teachers need to use the brain's pattern-seeking abilities to take advantage of learning opportunities. Classroom activities that take advantage of students' past knowledge are more efficient than those that teach new knowledge without linking it to known patterns. While this concept is proven in neuroscience and psychology, is not yet well established because of the limited number of classroom studies.

Developmental Processes

> Human learning is achieved through developmental processes, which follow a universal pattern for most skills, including academic skills shared across literate cultures, such as reading, writing, and math. (Tokuhama-Espinosa, 2008b, p. 371)

Despite the unique nature of each of our brains, humans have general sequences for learning specific skills, which occur in typical developmental stages. Just as humans need to crawl before they walk and walk before they run, academic skills are also learned in a predictable order. That is, every-one tends to learn math, reading, writing, and thinking skills in a simi-lar order. There are guidelines for physical development devised by the U.S. National Institute of Child Health and Human Development (www.nichd.nih.gov), as well as emotional, social, and psychological develop-ment stages developed by educational psychologists, for example. These well-respected guidelines are useful in describing the normal patterns of human development, and they are key in noting the order in which certain skills are acquired.

For example, in terms of psychosocial development, Erikson's (1950, 1959) eight stages posit that children must move through a stage of distrust versus trust (stage 1) before they can move on to a stage of autonomy versus shame and doubt (stage 2). This means that a young child begins to trust others before he can experience autonomy. This continues on throughout one's life span. In stage 3, the healthy child moves from the autonomous stage to a stage in which he takes initiative (versus a sense of guilt if he fails in this stage). In stage 4, he can then move on to industry (versus those who fail to do so and develop a sense of inferiority). In stage 5, the young ado-lescent develops a sense of identity (or if he fails at this stage, he remains in confusion). In stage 6, Erikson says adolescents can start to engage in intimacy (versus isolation). In stage 7, humans move on toward generativ-ity (or if they fail to do so, they remain in a stage of stagnation). Finally, in stage 8, Erikson suggests that humans develop a sense of integrity (or if they fail to do so, they move toward a state of despair).

In the cognitive realm, Piaget's (1955) theory of development offers four broad stages. In the sensorimotor period (ages 0–2), the baby's world is dominated by a growing understanding of his senses. In the preopera-tional stage (ages 2–7), children are in a "magical thinking" stage in which they do not yet employ logical thinking and their thinking is rather egotis-tical. In the third stage, the concrete operational stage (ages 7–12), children begin to think logically but rely on practical aids, though they are no longer egocentrically focused. Finally, in the formal operational stage (age 12+), children begin to develop abstract reasoning.

In a similar way, Benjamin Bloom (1956) also recognized the devel-opmental nature of human learning. These begin with gaining (1) basic knowledge, moving on to (2) comprehension, then (3) applying this infor-mation to new situations. Once these basic stages are achieved, a person can move on to higher-order thinking. This involves (4) analyzing informa-tion, then (5) synthesizing findings, and, finally, (6) evaluating and judging information.

The National Institute of Child Health and Human Development fo-cuses on physical development; Erikson, on psychosocial development; Piaget, on cognitive development; and Bloom, on the development of higher-order thinking skills. Yet they are all similar in that they all posit developmental growth processes. Students cannot be expected to "run" with advanced information before they know how to "crawl" using basic information, and good teachers know how to assess this in their students.

The physical manifestation of these developmental processes in the brain was postulated in 1894 by Santiago Ramon y Cajal, who suggested that the ability of neurons to make new connections explained the process of learning in the brain. This, too, is a developmental process. Synapses for certain types of learning are strengthened with rehearsal and build upon one another's structures. The father of American psychology, William James, noted that when two brain processes occur together, after time one will stimulate the other. In terms of classroom practice, this means that students will link concepts that occur simultaneously or in succession.

Teachers need to be aware of the developmental processes involved in all facets of human learning if they are to be effective in the classroom. Despite this evidence, this is not yet well established because the definitions of developmental patterns for some academic skills are disputed, and the work of Erikson, Piaget, and others is theoretical.

Sensitive Versus Critical Periods

There are "sensitive periods" (not critical periods) in human brain development in which certain skills are learned with greater ease than at other times. (Tokuhama-Espinosa, 2008b, p. 177)

There are times in human brain development when life skills and academic skills are more easily learned than at other times. However, these sensitive periods do not imply that such skills must be learned at that time or never learned at all; humans can and do learn throughout the life span. For example, my grandmother decided to learn Spanish when she was 79 because I was marrying an Ecuadorian. She was particularly talented at languages and not shy about practicing; she managed to sail through her basic lessons with ease. As we saw in the examples about neuroplasticity, the brain is amazingly more flexible than was once thought. Although specific age boundaries have not been suggested for most skills sets, it is now believed that the order in which one learns skills is more important than the age at which they are learned. For example, when learning a foreign language, one needs to learn to understand what is spoken before being able to speak; it is impossible to learn to speak if you do not understand what is spoken. This means that if we are accurate in gauging a student's developmental level in a skill area and build upon that knowledge, then the actual age of the learner is of less consequence in determining the final developmental levels.

Sensitive periods are windows of opportunity when skills can be more easily learned due to social as well as cognitive developmental processes. These are not "critical periods," a term once used to imply that you either learned the skill during this time or lost the opportunity to do so forever (as with learning a foreign language). The belief in human critical periods stemmed from studies on rats, monkeys, and cats related to critical visual and motor periods. The only critical period proven in humans to date relates to first-language acquisition, and even this is disputed in some circles because there are so few cases of first-language deprivation. Critical periods in sensory development cannot be generalized to critical periods for learning how to read, write, paint, do math, or other academic skills.

There is, however, a social stigma attached to individuals who fail to learn to read or do basic math by a certain age. Social rejection and grade-level retention can reduce a learner's confidence and thus discourage the learner from even trying. This is seen when students who repeated multiple grades in school eventually drop out because they were not able to grasp the expected skills at the expected ages. Teachers should keep in mind that students can learn if foundational skills can be fixed through remediation. Though this seems logical, it is not yet well established because the definitions of terms and of scope (academic fields versus senses only) need further refinement.

The Innate Nature of Learning

> The search for meaning is innate in human nature. (Tokuhama-Espinosa, 2008b, p. 159)

Humans are naturally curious. Humans do not need to be told to seek meaning; they do so innately. Humans seek out patterns and anomalies in order to create meaning, and they do so based on survival instincts that have now been transferred to the classroom. Evolutionary biologists have made it clear that philosophical ponderings about the meaning of life—and flirtations with questions about why the apple falls down and not up (Newton), why time seems to "fly" sometimes and not others (Einstein), where the earth came from (the Greek thinkers Thales and Anaximander), where "knowledge" is stored in the human body (Aristotle), and what drives human will, motivation, and learning (Hippocrates, Socrates, Aristotle)—are innate in human nature.

Observant parents and teachers recognize the insatiable curiosity of young children. The "why?" years, usually starting around age 3, give weight to the belief that the search for meaning is innate in human nature. What happens to this natural curiosity? Do children grow out of it? While some individuals manage to retain this level of intellectual curiosity throughout their lifetimes, many abandon this questioning nature because they have not been encouraged enough. Teachers can encourage their students to question and, in doing so, to retain their natural curiosity for their world and feed their natural desire to learn about their surroundings.

This cannot be done, however, through worksheets and lectures. Teachers need to employ a certain level of creativity in their class design in order to create significant learning experiences. Wiggins and McTighe (1998) suggest that this can be achieved easily by posing "essential questions." Essential questions have certain characteristics: They get to the heart of the subject, cannot be answered with a simple yes or no, lead to a cross-disciplinary understanding of concepts, and naturally lead to other questions. For example, instead of asking students to think about poverty in Africa—something they probably have no firsthand experience with—Wiggins and McTighe suggest asking them the essential question, "Is there enough?" This question cannot be answered with a simple yes or no; it naturally leads to a myriad of other questions ("Enough of what?" "Enough land? Food? Water? Natural resources? Money? Leadership?"); and it crosses several disciplines, as it could be answered from an educational perspective, an economic perspective, an agricultural perspective, and so on. Best of all, this question naturally leads to others and returns students to their "natural state" of questioning. Exercises such as the essential questions suggested by Wiggins and McTighe help encourage the innate desire of humans to learn. While proven in psychology, this concept is not yet well established because documentation in education using neuroscientific processes is sparse.

EDUCATION AND TEACHING PROCESSES

The final "probably so" category of concepts relates to education and how we teach. Concepts in this category are concerned with the way we currently educate and the reasons that we have variable rates of success in this process.

Self-Regulation for Higher Order Thinking

> Self-regulation (monitoring oneself via executive functions) is an integral part of higher order thinking skills. (Tokuhama-Espinosa, 2008b, p. 321)

According to Facione (2004), higher-order thinking skills depend on an individual's ability to monitor his own actions, including cautious steps that analyze, infer, interpret, understand, apply, decipher, decode, and explore information. Self-regulation is partially related to developmental stages, and one hopes that age brings wisdom—the older the person, the greater the level of self-regulation. However, self-regulation is also managed through emotional intelligence, which depends heavily on early exposure to proper social norms. Knowing when and how to monitor oneself via executive functions has a great deal to do with social integration and influences school success. Students who are not able to "control themselves" in either emotional or intellectual contexts have trouble succeeding in school.

Critical thinking and self-regulation are inextricably linked. A student who is a good critical thinker realizes that he must first unite all the information possible and understand all the concepts he is dealing with. He should then ask where the information comes from in order to gauge biases in the work, after which he should analyze the source of the information for credibility. Independent of how credible he finds the sources, a good critical thinker will still leave himself open to doubt. This allows the critical thinker to become accustomed to uncertainty: Sometimes things don't turn out as expected. Once he has reviewed all the information and checked his sources, he will step back and look at the whole, from which he can generate new or distinct ideas. This is a long process. Students who have intellectual persistence have a high level of self-regulation; they do not stop until this critical thinking process is complete. While this seems like a logical concept, self-regulation is individually defined, and this is hard to measure. Additionally, though accepted in psychology, education, and neuroscience, this concept is not yet well established because documentation in school contexts using neuroscientific criteria is missing.

Active Construction of Meaning

> When a learner actively constructs knowledge, the learner will be motivated and engaged in learning. (Tokuhama-Espinosa, 2008b, p. 159)

The first allusion to active learning in recorded literature is perhaps from an old Chinese proverb attributed to Confucius (551–479 B.C): "I hear and I forget. I listen and I understand. I do and I remember." Active, student-centered learning experiences motivate students and involve them in constructing their own ideas, opinions, and views about new concepts, which help them to create new mental schemas about their world. This results in enhanced and more significant learning experiences. Active learning is essentially based on the concept that "we learn by doing" suggested the Greek dramatist Sophocles (496–406 B.C.). This means that learning is an active, not a passive, process in which the student is the central actor. According to Chickering and Gamson (1987), "Learning is not a spectator sport. Students do not learn much just sitting in class listening to teachings" (p. 3). When a learner actively constructs knowledge, he is involved in more than passive listening. He displays higher-order thinking skills and engages in activities that put less emphasis on the information transmission and greater emphasis on developing skills. Active learning emphasizes student exploration of attitudes and values and creates settings in which students receive immediate feedback from their instructors. To be active, students must have the opportunity to participate. This includes giving all students equal opportunity to ask and respond to questions as well as designing class activities that give the students center stage. When teachers allow students to participate actively in class, student self-confidence can be increased as well.

Large-scale institutional studies also give the benefit of the doubt to active learning techniques. When Tinnesz, Ahuna, and Kiener (2006) pre- and posttested 680 students in a Methods of Inquiry course at a large northeastern university, they found that even students who were unprepared for their coursework could make up lost ground through active learning techniques. In another large-scale study, Hake (1998) queried 6,000 students after an introductory physics course to ask their opinions about active learning techniques compared with traditional teacher-centered instruction. He found overwhelming evidence that students preferred active learning techniques. Not only do students appear to perform better in active learning classes; they also prefer this structure over lecture (McKeachie, Pintrich, Yi-Guang, & Smith, 1986). While proven in education and psychology, this concept is not yet well established in neuroscience.

Elaboration

> The elaboration (overt teaching) of key concepts facilitates new learning. (Tokuhama-Espinosa, 2008b, p. 321)

Overt or explicit teaching of key concepts is important for new learning. Good teachers should understand that they achieve better results if they reiterate explicit instruction of core concepts. This includes priming (preparing the students for a new concept), applying concepts (offering examples of the new concept), assessing concept knowledge (evaluating the new concept understanding), and reteaching concepts when needed.

When priming students on a topic, teachers should clearly explain their goals to the class. For example, teachers can develop grading rubrics for topics with their classes. Before starting oral presentations, a teacher can ask her class, "What makes a great presentation?" With or without prodding, her students will develop the criteria by which they know they will be judged. It is better to share clear expectations and make students work to find the answers rather than to leave them working to guess what will be on the test.

The elaboration of key concepts means making what we, as teachers, see as "obvious" clearer to students. In other words, we need to make the implicit explicit. While we may have taught English literature (pre-algebra, sociology, Spanish, art, or chemistry) a million times, the students entering our classrooms are encountering the subject for the first time. This concept is based on a belief that learners are inherently smart—they seek to understand. Effective teachers know they help by going into depth and/or dividing new concepts into manageable parts. While proven in psychology, this is not yet well established because despite numerous anecdotal references, not enough formal studies are available in classroom contexts.

Rehearsal

> The rehearsal of retrieval cues aids in declarative memory processes. (Tokuhama-Espinosa, 2008b, p. 281)

While memory can be created by emotionally shocking experiences, declarative memory is related with facts (associated with school learning) and can be improved only through rehearsal. Declarative memory is a subtype of long-term memory. Declarative memory is often referred as "fact-based" memory or "textbook" memory because it has to do with things that are explicitly learned (such as facts, dates, names, formulas, etc.). This is in contrast to procedural memory, which is related to different processes (such as walking, riding a bike, playing a musical instrument, etc.). This is why the use of mnemonic cues (including repetition and rehearsal) improves the ability to retrieve information. A clear example of this concept relates to homework. Marzano, Pickering, and Pollock (2004) have done extensive research on what constitutes beneficial homework and what is simply time-consuming busywork. When homework is designed at the appropriate level, relevant to the class topic, supported by parent involvement, monitored in quantity, and accompanied by teacher feedback, it contributes to learning. Rehearsal and retrieval of cues about new concepts help ingrain them as permanent memories and, consequently, as true learning. Their research has shown that the learning curves for new concepts are dependent on repetition. Let's say we are students in a fifth-grade social studies class learning about the names of coastal and mountainous regions. We do a worksheet together in small groups. Research tells us that from this first introduction of regional concepts to the second (the classroom activity), our learning curve peaks—we learn a great deal. However, the third time we revisit the concept, our "new" learning is not so great, though it is measurable. This is true after the fourth, fifth, sixth, seventh, eighth, and ninth time as well. However, when we are given a tenth look at the concept, there is another peak in the learning curve, and we see the concepts in a new light. This means that discussing the concepts in class (third time), calling on classmates to respond to specific questions about the concepts (fourth, fifth, and sixth times), a visual cue such as a Power-Point presentation or handout (seventh time), a summary of the classroom activities of the day (eighth time), and a preview of the homework (ninth time) set us up for improved learning through a well-designed homework project that enhances learning.

This is not yet well established because of lack of consensus on what type of rehearsal aids memory best. Though evidence exists in all three parent fields, there are few, if any, studies that apply neuroscience concepts in classroom contexts.

Memory + Attention = Learning

> Declarative knowledge acquisition depends on both memory and attention. (Tokuhama-Espinosa, 2008b, p. 81)

Attention + Memory = Learning. While this formula is overly simple, it is easily proven that learning cannot exist if either memory (conscious or unconscious) or attention or both are missing. True learning relies on the brain's ability to pay attention and subsequently remember what it has been exposed to. Attention can be either focused or peripheral. Memory can be short-term, long-term, emotional, or sensory-related (visual, motor, olfactory, etc.). In order for something to get into declarative long-term memory, a learner must pay attention to it. When there is both attention and memory, learning can occur.

All of this is important for teachers to consider because it impacts their level of efficiency in the classroom. The first important point to take from this belief is that learning does not occur without declarative memory. Students can feign learning, and even do well on an exam, by cramming and extending their working memory (a subtype of short-term memory). However, when these "A" students are queried about the same test questions a week later, they will have little or no recall of the subject. How is this possible? Because the students managed to keep enough dates, facts, and formulas in their head to pass the test, but as this knowledge never made it to long-term declarative memory, it was never truly learned at all (only memorized in the short term). To avoid such faux results, teachers should devise assessment techniques that allow students to demonstrate their mastery of the knowledge, abilities, and attitudes expected of them over several weeks. One-time multiple-choice exams are not as efficient in measuring students' conceptual understanding and true learning as other tools, such as student presentations or project work.

A second important point is that students can sometimes look like they are paying attention or, conversely, seem not to be paying attention when they actually are. The best way to get students to pay attention is by centering the attention on them. This is an argument in favor of student-centered instruction. It is impossible for students not to pay attention when they are the protagonists of the learning activity. However, it is very easy for students not to pay attention when it is focused on others. Studies originally conducted in the 1960s and replicated by the National Training Laboratories of Alexandria, Virginia, throughout the 1980s and 1990s demonstrated that when students passively listen to lectures, they retain approximately 5% of the lecture content. If the lecture content is supplemented by reading, this goes up to 10%; if audio-visuals are used, retention is elevated to about 20%. If the teacher offers a demonstration of the concepts being taught, then students retain about 30% of the information. However, when the students are encouraged to discuss the content, their retention is raised to 50%. If they are allowed to conduct the demonstration themselves, they retain about 75%. The best way to get information into long-term memory, however, is by asking students to teach others. Then about 90% of the content information is recalled. The movement away from the teacher as "sage on the stage" to "guide on the side" (King, 1993) turns the focus of learning on the student.

This concept is not yet well established because while there are a large number of studies on attention and a large number on memory, there are fewer on memory + attention, and even fewer done in school contexts.

THE BACKBONE OF SCIENTIFICALLY BASED TEACHING

The concepts shared above are intriguing and considered to be "probably so" by the evidence in the literature and by the judgment of the expert panel. Combined with the five well-established concepts in the previous chapter, they provide the backbone for best practice teaching.

We now turn to concepts that are considered to be far from fact and merely "intelligent speculation." There is a great distinction between the quality of information found in the first two categories ("well-established" and "probably so"), as compared with what we find in the second two categories, or "intelligent speculation" and "neuromyths." The information found in the next chapter should be reviewed carefully, and teachers should remain cautious of claims made in these last two categories until better evidence is offered for their support.

CHAPTER 4

Evaluating the Usage of What Is Still Just Intelligent Speculation

Concepts or beliefs that are "intelligent speculation" tend to be concepts that we want to believe are true but that just don't have the science behind them to support the weight of their claims. Much of what appears in this category is supported by psychology and education studies but is not substantiated by neuroscience, so educators will recognize much here as best practice. Educators are encouraged not to universally discard the established practices discussed below but rather to be aware of the level of scientific support or lack thereof. In other cases, the evidence exists in neuroscience and psychology, but there is a lack of documentation in the education field. Sometimes, the individualized nature of certain concepts makes them nebulous. For example, teaching through "differentiated instruction" means treating students as individual learners with varying needs. Studies to measure changes based on differentiation are always individual and therefore are hard to construct. Some of these concepts may eventually become "well established" after more research is conducted, or they may simply fall into the category of a neuromyth.

To be considered intelligent speculation, the Best Evidence Encyclopedia suggests that, "[a]t least one qualifying study with a significant positive effect and/or median effect size of +0.10 or more" is needed. This means that just one study is needed to "prove" a point, though there may also be contradictory findings. The What Works Clearinghouse criteria is slightly less stringent, calling for "at least one study showing a statistically or substantively important positive effect and at least one study showing a statistically significant or substantively important negative effect, but no more such studies than the number showing a statistically significant or substantively important positive effect." This criteria means that information in the intelligent speculation category is often of mixed quality, with some studies "proving" the hypothesis and others negating it.

There are three main reasons that information in this category is complex to judge. First, in many cases the contradictory findings mean that if the hypothesis studied by the Delphi panel was reworded, it could be moved to a different category. For example, the following is intelligent speculation: "Different memory systems (i.e., short term, long term, working, spatial, motor, modality-specific, rote, etc.) receive and process information in different ways and are retrieved through distinct, though sometimes overlapping, neural pathways." However, if the wording was changed and this was made into two separate sentences, then it is possible that at least the first half of the sentence would be accepted as well established: "Different memory systems (i.e., short term, long term, working, spatial, motor, modality-specific, rote, etc.) receive and process information in different ways . . ." However, the second half of the statement enjoys only partial backing: ". . . and are retrieved through distinct, though sometimes overlapping, neural pathways." This means that the information that falls into the intelligent speculation category needs to be continually refined. This information should be reviewed with caution, and the reasons for not being considered well established should always be addressed.

Second, some of these concepts are in the intelligent speculation category because evidence is missing from one of the three parent fields (psychology, education, or neuroscience). A final reason many of these concepts are not well established is that they relate to individual aspects of learning (such as the role of humor in learning), which does not mean that they are not true but rather that designing verifiable studies to measure them are complex. Since these aspects vary for different individuals, designing a study to compare reactions between students is meaningless. For example, if I want to prove that humor enhances learning, I need to have humor in my class. But what some of my students find to be funny may not be funny at all to others.

These concepts have been broken into six common strands of inquiry (see Figure 4.1):

1. Existing mental structures
2. Classroom experiences
3. Modes of learning
4. Activities, environments, and enrichment
5. Physical versus functional workings of the brain
6. Different populations

EXISTING MENTAL STRUCTURES

The first category of concepts in intelligence speculation relates to existing mental structures. Existing mental structures are comprised of the personal relevance that learning concepts have for each individual.

Figure 4.1. Intelligent Speculation in MBE Science

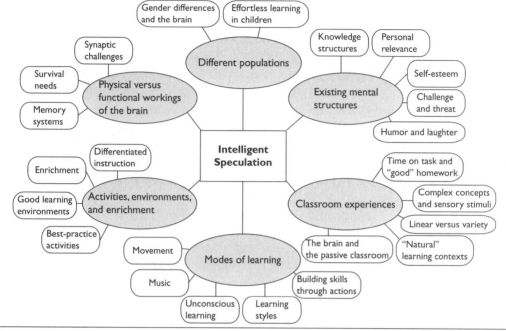

Source: Bramwell, 2009.

Knowledge Structures

> Human learning is a constructive process; humans construct meaning from existing knowledge structures. Such existing knowledge structures are individually defined. (Tokuhama-Espinosa, 2008b, p. 159)

People turn past experiences into conceptual building blocks on which new knowledge is developed. Children begin to build knowledge by categorizing their world; from this understanding of categorization, they then build concepts. Once basic concepts are understood, children build mental schemas, which are basic outlines of understanding. Each child's experiences are unique. The building metaphor is the basis for the constructivist philosophy of education, which is well accepted in education and psychology but not yet in neuroscience. The theoretical and philosophical bases of constructivism are found in the work of John Dewey (1933/1998). Later, Piaget (1972) and Vygotsky (Vianna & Stetsenko, 2006) employed constructivist concepts to develop their models of cognitive psychological development. The core idea is that individuals construct their own knowledge rather than having knowledge spoon-fed to them, or "written" on the blank slates of their minds.

This is "intelligent speculation," and not in the well-established category, in part for two reasons. First, there are still some who believe that students do not construct but rather are taught, making the primary agent in the process the teacher (who does the teaching), not the student (who constructs). This has been a widely contested concept in the past 50 years. Second, even if students do construct their own knowledge, student experiences are so individual that there is no way to measure this construction (and therefore prove this process). In order to move this belief from intelligent speculation into the well-established category, it would be necessary to explain constructivism from a neuroscientific perspective. This may not be as far-fetched as it seems. It is already clear that neurons do build upon one another. Is the day so far off when we will be able to correlate brain constructivism with educational constructivism?

Personal Relevance

> The development of personal relevance to new knowledge makes learning easier. (Tokuhama-Espinosa, 2008b, p. 272)

Things are easier to learn when they are important to the learner. The reason this is intelligent speculation and not yet well established is because "personal relevance" is too broad a concept to define. In order to move this belief to the well established category, a study would have to be conducted in which "personal relevance" is defined for each person in the experiment. The learning processes that participants undergo would then need to be complemented by measured neural growth and by testaments to the ease or difficulty with which the new information was learned. Additionally, it is known that people can and do learn things that they find completely uninteresting or personally irrelevant.

Having said this, each of us has experienced these phenomena in real life and can probably think of classroom settings in which they have occurred. For example, a math teacher can modify a word problem to apply to the students' reality. Instead of saying "Mary went from point A to point B in 10 minutes—how far could she go if she walked twice as fast?" the teacher can replace "Mary" with the name of a student in the class and "point A" and "point B" with real places the students are familiar with. It is possible that better documentation of these experiences from the classroom and from psychological practice will eventually offer enough evidence to merit a move of this belief into the well-established category some day soon. While proven in education and psychology, this concept is not yet well established because documentation in classroom contexts using neuroscientific criteria is sparse. A definition and comparison of "ease" would have to be developed and measured in order to prove this.

Self-Esteem

> Self-esteem impacts learning and academic achievement. (Tokuhama-Espinosa, 2008b, p. 272)

Students who feel good about themselves are more likely to do better in school. While every teacher can attest to this, it remains intelligent speculation, not well-established fact, for at least three reasons. First, the definition of *self-esteem* is still somewhat nebulous in MBE Science. Second, though individual teachers may testify to the importance of self-esteem in learning, studies linking high self-esteem to academic achievement (and low self-esteem to low academic achievement) are few, though they do exist. For example, Gaustad (1992) found that students who liked themselves tended to like school and that liking school was correlated with good grades. Finally, *academic achievement* is a broad term: Does it mean getting into a good college after high school? Overcoming obstacles? Scoring high on standardized tests? It may very well be determined that *academic achievement* is individually defined, making it nearly impossible to design research studies.

To move this belief from intelligent speculation to well established, accepted definitions of *self-esteem* and *academic achievement* are needed. This definition would have to be followed by a longitudinal study of individuals with high and low self-esteem, controlled for all other factors to see if correlation can be established with regard to academic achievement. However, it is important to note that even such elaborate studies would only prove correlation, not causation. An easy alternative would be to simply identify students who are thought to have experienced "academic success" and ask them to rate their level of self-esteem. This type of study would make a strong argument for moving this belief to the well-established category. However, it is important to remember that even if the impact of self-esteem on academic achievement can be proven, enhancing self-esteem may not necessarily be an explicit teaching objective in all classrooms. The real difficulty is that neuroscientific studies related to studies of self-esteem are extremely sparse. A greater collaboration among neuroscientists, educators, and psychologists is needed to research the concept of self-esteem in MBE Science. Though it seems logical that individuals with higher self-esteem would fare better in all aspects of life (academic and otherwise), this has yet to be proven conclusively.

Challenge and Threat

> Learning is enhanced by challenge and is typically inhibited by threat (in which threat and challenge are individually defined). (Tokuhama-Espinosa, 2008b, p. 272)

People do not learn when things are too easy, nor do they learn when they are under too much pressure or feel threatened. While it is well established that stress (but not necessarily threat) impairs learning, it is intelligent speculation that learning is always enhanced by challenge. The lack of evidence in this area is propably due to the individualized nature of "challenge" and "threat." What one person finds challenging, another may find threatening.

To move this into the well-established category, three things need to happen. First, "threat" and "challenge" would have to be defined within an experimental group. Second, these individuals would have to be placed in new learning situations and stimulated by both threatening and challenging elements, according to their self-definitions. Third, the level of correlation between "threat" and low levels of learning and between "challenge" and high levels of learning would have to be measured and evaluated. While this sounds complex, many of us as teachers have already conducted this experiment daily in our own classrooms. Now it is time to document this for others if we believe the concept merits a change of category. Once better documentation of teacher practice can be added to evidence from neuroscience and psychology, then this concept will move closer to being well established.

Humor

> Humor can enhance learning (though it is unclear as to exactly what the mind-body mechanism is that influences this). (Tokuhama-Espinosa, 2008b, p. 281)

Laughter is a sign of enjoyment, and pleasure of this kind is accompanied by the release of endorphins. Endorphins are neurotransmitters that facilitate synapses, or the links between neurons. This, in turn, facilitates the consolidation of information in the brain. This belief is labeled intelligent speculation, however, because while it is well established that *laughter* facilitates learning, it is not clear what types of *humor* prompt laughter. That is, what is humorous is not universally defined. This means that teachers' attempts to inject jokes into their classes may be dangerous unless they share a common sense of humor with the students.

Having said this, many believe the benefits of laughter are worth putting oneself out on a limb for. This sends a mixed message to teachers. Not only should teachers attempt humor in their classes when they feel they share a sense of humor with their students; they should also encourage laughter, perhaps even at their own expense. Sometimes the only point of commonality that students share is their relation to the teacher—meaning that the teacher may end up being the butt of the joke. Teachers who know how to "take it on the chin and keep grinning" and who can laugh at themselves are likely not only to improve the classroom environment but also to increase the chances that the students will learn the topic at hand.

This belief can most certainly be moved from intelligent speculation to well established if we replace *humor* with *laughter*. If, on the other hand, the goal is to prove that humor aids learning, then educators, psychologists, and neuroscientists will need to combine efforts to define the parameters of humor, to determine how it is triggered, and then to measure this in the learning brain. This is not yet well established for the reasons discussed above and because documentation in classroom contexts using neuroscientific criteria is sparse.

CLASSROOM EXPERIENCES

The next category of concepts relates to classroom experiences. Many concepts in this group question whether or not the brain has a "natural" learning system that works differently from the way classroom structures are designed.

The Brain and the Passive Classroom

> The brain is not designed for typical passive classroom instruction; rather it enjoys multimodal, experiential and diverse learning experiences. (Tokuhama-Espinosa, 2008b, p. 193)

Brains hone in on differences and are brought to awareness by changes (in format, activity, form, etc.). This sensitivity means that diverse learning experiences offer the variety that the brain needs to stay alert and attentive to new information. Once again, the reason this belief is in the intelligent speculation, not the well-established, category is related to the terms being used. What is "typical passive classroom instruction" (*is* classroom instruction typically passive?), and what are the definitions of "multimodal, experiential and diverse learning experiences"? It will not take too much to move this belief to a more established category, however. To do this, we first have to determine that a "traditional" classroom (in which students sit silently in rows and the teacher reigns) is what we mean by "typical." Second, we need to define "multimodal" (as in multisensory?) and "experiential" (as in active learning techniques?).

When there is an agreed-upon definition for these three terms, then evidence from neuroscience will have to be established. Then we must ask if it can be proven neurologically that the multimodal delivery of information is more conducive to long-term memory development and subsequent learning. If this can be done, then this belief will most likely be moved to the well-established category.

Natural Learning Contexts

> The human brain learns best when facts and skills are embedded in natural contexts (or concrete examples), in which the learner understands the problems he/she faces, and recognizes how the facts and/or skills might play roles in solving that problem. This is due to the fact that motivation tends to be higher when facts and skills are embedded in natural context. (Tokuhama-Espinosa, 2008b, p. 182)

Context is an important part of facilitating significant learning experiences. When the context is close to the learner's reality, then learning is easier; when it is remote from the learner's experiences, then learning is more difficult. This is why it is not uncommon to hear students grumbling in the hallway as they leave class saying, "When will I ever use *that* in real life?!"

When I was in ninth-grade English class, I remember struggling with the Elizabethan English of Shakespeare's *Romeo and Juliet* to the extent that the beautiful storyline was all but buried under the *thee*s and *thou*s. That is, until Ms. Clayton brought in a video of *West Side Story*. *West Side Story* spoke to us not only because of the vocabulary and dress but also because of the family conflicts and the gang mentality it revealed; this was painfully close to home. We went back to Shakespeare after that viewing, and his brilliance suddenly became clearer to us. In a similar way, teachers who have their students apply the math formulas they learn in the context of architecture, say, or computer programming find their students more engaged than when they simply teach the formula. Likewise, actually planting the potato, deciphering your blood type under a microscope, or writing for the classroom newsletter is more powerful than simply reading about it or being lectured about it.

Framing new information in the context of a student's life is a masterful display of good teaching, but it is hard to measure, which is why it remains intelligent speculation and is not yet well established. Why is it hard to measure? For two reasons. First, an individual student's life context is not obvious and must be uncovered by the teacher, who has to establish a certain level of personal connection with the student before this is possible. Second, it takes far more time to plan contextual activities (building the architectural model, planting the potato, taking the blood sample) than to plan a lecture. Many teachers do not yet see the positive relationship of planning time to learning. Once teachers have learned about students' life contexts and included more contextual activities in their classes, then this belief will become well established. While proven in education, this idea is not yet well established because documentation in classroom contexts using neuroscientific criteria is sparse.

Linear Learning versus Variety

> The brain does not learn in a linear, structured and predictable fashion. This implies the need to use various sensory channels at the same time, including audiovisuals, readings, group work, reflection, and novel activities. (Tokuhama-Espinosa, 2008b, p. 274)

Most epiphanies of learning ("aha!" moments) occur not in an orderly fashion but in unpredictable moments when conceptual links are made in the brain. These links are triggered in different ways for different people; therefore, different sensory channels should be used to connect to different learners. Let's think of a puzzle metaphor. Let's presume that each activity we conduct as teachers can contribute to students' overall conceptual understanding of the new information we are giving them. Let's presume new information is the finished puzzle. We first give students a piece that comes from our lectures. Then we give them a piece that comes from posing discussion questions in small groups. Then we offer a piece through a demonstration. This is followed by another piece when we ask students to do the same demonstration themselves. Then we give them another piece when we ask them to summarize what they think they have just learned, followed by another piece when we ask them to do a modified experiment at home with others. Students will "see" the entire puzzle image based on different combinations of pieces. Each of these activities puts the puzzle pieces in place for the learner and is most effective if these puzzle pieces are designed using a variety of sensory inputs. In these activities, learners are sometimes listening, at other times they are talking or discussing, and at still other moments they are doing something. The reason novel activities engage students more is because they trigger the novelty-seeking aspect of the brain's normal functioning.

The reason this belief remains intelligent speculation and is not yet well established is because some knowledge is indeed achieved through simple linear rehearsal. Take vocabulary memorization, for example, or the multiplication tables. Both are basically learned through rote memorization. This means that certain types of knowledge, what Wiggins and McTighe (1998) call "superficial" because they barely scratch the complexity of the topic, can be learned (and tested) through simple linear instruction. That is, the teacher gives the vocabulary or multiplication table to students and asks them to memorize it. In real life (but not in the world of standardized tests), the actual use of this knowledge goes beyond sheer memorization. If the teacher has students write a story with the vocabulary words or use the multiplication tables to find all the ways to make up the number 12, for example, then he is elevating the thinking level of his students and offering them an activity that is more useful in life. Higher-order thinking does not occur linearly but rather in those great "aha!" moments. This belief will likely be moved to the well-established category when the distinction between levels of thinking and learning are clearer in education. It is not yet well established because levels of thinking processes are not universally understood, documentation in classroom contexts using neuroscientific criteria is sparse, and the individual nature of sensory preferences is hard to study.

Complex Concepts and Sensory Stimuli

> The brain learns complex concepts best when they are taught and experienced through various sensory stimuli. (Tokuhama-Espinosa, 2008b, p. 280)

People can and do learn through single sensory channels, but the probability of significant learning and subsequent recall is enhanced when new information is presented in a variety of formats. This means that a lecture, for example, is not as effective as a lecture plus an activity plus reading, or reading plus discussion, and so on. We mentioned earlier that the brain does not work in a linear function in terms of clear and logical processes, but this concept is more concerned with the variety of senses that can be used to teach a new concept. This is shown by neuroscientific studies indicating that different types of memories are stored in slightly different (though often overlapping) areas of the brain. This effectively means that by inputting the same information through various sensory channels, we are storing it through various neural pathways. This is like putting a reminder to ourselves all over the house, pointing us toward the object we don't want to forget. When we go to look for the object (or information), it will be easier to find if it has been experienced through different sensory channels.

This is intelligent speculation because of the word *best*. It has not yet been proven that learning through multiple senses is superior to learning through a single sense. To move this belief from the intelligent speculation to the well-established category, experiments in neuroscience should be conducted in which half of an experimental age group is taught a novel concept using a single sensory input channel, such as purely auditory stimulus, and the other half is taught the same concept using various sensory input channels, such as auditory plus visual stimuli. A comparison of student recall and learning could be measured and compared to determine once and for all whether learning is enhanced through multiple sensory stimuli.

Time on Task and "Good" Homework

> There is a positive correlation between instructional time (including homework) and student achievement. (Tokuhama-Espinosa, 2008b, p. 282; Ramos-Voigt, 2007)

Student review, rehearsal, and practice of new information take time, but the investment is well worth it because of the increased learning that is achieved. This is only intelligent speculation, however, because different students require different amounts of time to process concepts, so it is very difficult to measure, and harder to generalize. Having said this, the more time a person spends learning something, the more proficient she becomes at that task. The reason this is intelligent speculation, not well established, is that while laboratory time trials of learning seem to show that time-on-task helps learning, some educational experts have noted that this is not true in school. For example, one way time-on-task is extended in our educational system is through homework. However, some believe this extra time is wasted. Duke University's Harris Cooper, for example, "concluded that homework does not measurably improve academic achievement for kids in grade school" (Wallis, 2006, p. 57). Opponents of this view, who have seen the evidence from psychology and neurology, say that the reason some feel homework does not help is because it is often not well designed.

Busywork is not the same as homework. Homework that is well designed complements classroom practice in innovative ways and does not tax students beyond normal attention spans. Ill-designed assignments risk giving students nonproductive work, which only causes family strife and student distress. If teachers do not take the time to correct homework or provide feedback, students can rebel against it. To plan well, some teachers apply the 1-1-1 rule: A teacher should spend one-third of her time actually teaching in the classroom; one-third of it planning, which includes constructing good homework assignments; and one-third of it assessing learning, which means grading homework. This belief will move to the well-established category when guidelines for quality homework become better documented. While proven in education and psychology, this concept is not yet well established because documentation using neuroscientific methods in classroom contexts is sparse.

MODES OF LEARNING

Humans can and do learn in a variety of ways or modes. This category of concepts refers to just how people construct knowledge through different experiences.

Building Skills Through Actions

Humans build knowledge and skills through actions. (Tokuhama-Espinosa, 2008b, p. 281)

While some learning can and does take place solely in our minds, most learning is based on an action (reading, discussion, teaching others, writing, etc.). It can be argued that "thinking" itself is an action. The reason this is mere intelligent speculation, not yet well established, is because *actions* need to be better defined, as does the way we measure what *building knowledge and skills* implies. Is it possible to develop a skill (which normally implies doing something, as in an action) just by thinking about it? For example, can I learn how to bake a cake or fix a car by watching someone else do this, or by reading how to do this, or do I need to actually practice the action before mastering it? This means that while *knowledge* may be gained from passive activity, it is likely that *skills* require action.

One way to move this belief from the intelligent speculation to the well-established category would be to separate out the goals of *knowledge building* from *skills building*. If we can do this, we could say, based on well-established information in MBE Science, that "humans build *skills* through actions (or active processes)" and probably meet little opposition.

Learning Styles

> All people use kinesthetic, visual and auditory pathways to take in new information, and there is strong evidence that different people use different processing strategies at different times depending on the context of the learning. (Tokuhama-Espinosa, 2008b, p. 367)

All humans learn through sensory input. This sensory input can be through feeling or action, through visual, auditory, or olfactory pathways. Different people prefer different sensory pathways depending on the content and context of the learning. That is, people may tend to show a preference for visual stimuli, but this will depend on what is being learned. For example, say we go to a musical concert. Though we may perceive ourselves as "visual learners," when we are at the concert we may focus on our auditory ability. Different types of experiences call on different modes of learning. Many teachers have observed, however, that some students who consider themselves to be "kinesthetic learners" learn to adapt to classrooms that tend to be more visually or auditorily oriented, but others may not make this adjustment. The argument here is that while humans can learn outside of their preferred mode, they may not do as well. Neuroscientific studies show that gifted math students actually use visual pathways in a different way than normal learning peers (O'Boyle, 2008). This suggests that maximizing potential in a skill area may be dependent on using preferred learning styles. Psychological studies also show that people with different learning styles have different preferences for evaluation techniques (Furnham, Christopher, Garwood, & Martin, 2008). While it is well established that all people use kinesthetic, visual, and auditory pathways to take in new information, there is less evidence that we actually strategize about which pathways to use, therefore making this belief intelligent speculation. To move this belief into the well-established category, researchers from education, psychology, and neuroscience will need to collaborate on designing studies to determine whether students consciously choose sensory pathways (to see, hear, feel, taste, or smell input) as they are exposed to different types of learning activities. While logical, this concept is not yet well-established because documentation in classroom contexts is sparse or nonexistent.

Unconscious Learning

> Humans can learn new information while sleeping. (Tokuhama-Espinosa, 2008b, p. 281)

Sleep experts note that some individuals are capable of problem solving while they sleep. This is not to say that novel (never before experienced) information can be learned in unconscious states but rather that old problems can be reviewed and resolved during sleep or hypnosis. The research does *not* support the idea that playing tape-recorded messages of physics formulas, the periodic table, or verb conjugations in foreign languages while sleeping enhances new learning. It may be possible, however, as proponents of productive sleep such as Hobson at Harvard University (2004) claim, that reviewing (not learning for the first time) a physics formula, the periodic table, or verb conjugations can be posed as a problem and tackled while sleeping.

Sleep research laboratories have invested significant resources into determining why humans sleep and what exactly they achieve by sleeping. As reviewed in another part of this book, the rejuvenation of the mind and body, the consolidation of long-term memories, and the rehearsal of appropriate emotional responses to social situations have been proposed as answers to these questions, with numerous credible studies behind them. However, sleep time as a time for new learning is not among the better-researched areas. This means either that no evidence exists or that the field needs to be explored further, which is why this belief remains in the intelligent speculation category for the time being. This concept is not yet well established because documentation is sparse in neuroscience and psychology and is missing entirely in school contexts.

Music

> Music can influence learning (though it is as of yet unclear how and why this occurs and varies by individuals). (Tokuhama-Espinosa, 2008b, p. 281)

Music changes the neural pathways of the brain and influences the way other information is perceived when presented simultaneously. This may be due in part to the emotional reactions or the spatial-temporal variations people experience while listening to different types of music. The reason this belief is intelligent speculation, not well established, is because music affects different people in different ways to such an extent that it is nearly immeasurable. For example, the same piece of music can elicit shock, passion, excitement, joy, sadness, or disgust in different people due to their emotional interpretations. Because reactions to different musical genres are neither universal nor culture-bound, it is nearly impossible to study the effects of music on learning.

A term that often comes up when discussing music and learning is the "Mozart effect." This is based on the idea that there are certain rhythms that are more conducive to learning. This is intelligent speculation, as there are as many studies both supporting as well as rejecting the Mozart effect. Many proponents explain how Mozart's music enhances relaxation and healing and may even soothe epileptic patients. Alfred Tomatis, who is credited with coining the term *Mozart effect*, is a music therapist who has noted the soothing effects of Mozart's melodies on his patients. Raucher, Shaw, and Ky (1995) conducted what was probably the first structured experiment, in which they found a temporary enhancement of spatial-temporal reasoning, as measured by the Stanford-Binet IQ test, after a 10-minute exposure to Mozart's *Sonata for Two Pianos in D Major*. However, on the other side of the fence are numerous studies devoted to debunking the Mozart effect (Dowd, 2008). Large meta-analysis reviews of attempts to replicate Raucher, Shaw, and Ky's work, one conducted by Harvard University (Cromie, 1999) and the other by the German Ministry of Education, failed to find any link between listening to Mozart and enhanced intelligence (Dowd, 2008; McCutcheon, 2000).

Despite this, many people swear that studying with music allows the information they are reviewing to enter neural pathways that would have otherwise gone unused, thus enhancing the probability of recall. Many writers capitalized on the potential psychological benefits of the Mozart effect (e.g., Campbell, 1997), but their work was never proven beyond a doubt. The Mozart debate should not detract from the belief that some music may help some students increase learning at some level, however. This question remains open and subject to better studies. This concept is not yet well established because documentation in classroom contexts using neuroscientific criteria is sparse and controversial.

Movement

> Movement can enhance learning of academic subjects (though it is unclear exactly what the mind-body mechanism is that influences this). (Tokuhama-Espinosa, 2008b, p. 281)

Movement, including exercise classes, acting out information, teaching others, and even changing seats, can impact learning by increasing oxygen to the brain and/or refocusing attention. Active and passive brains display different blood flow and chemistry, as Gazzaniga (2005b) has demonstrated. The physiology of active brains is more conducive to better attention and long-term memory. Several studies document that physical exercise can actually enhance memory and recall due to different neurotransmitters that are released in the process. The brain uses roughly a fifth of the body's oxygen. Moss and Scholey (1995) supply "evidence demonstrating that oxygen administration improves memory formation" (p. 255) and that oxygenation is increased via both exercise and simple movements. Several studies show the relationship between physical education and improved student test scores. It is not yet clear whether the improvement occurs because when bodies are in better shape, so is the mind, as the studies claim, or whether changes in hormones or oxygen levels enhance learning.

Movement can also be interpreted in terms of simple actions, like changing seats, working in pairs, or simply providing moments for *brain breaks,* a series of physical movements used to theoretically help students refocus on their work (Michigan Department of Education, 2006). While the proponents of brain breaks make no claim that these exercises are neuroscientifically proven, their users give them high praise. One brain break involves standing up (first movement), then grabbing your left ear with your right hand (second movement) and your nose with your left hand (third movement), then switching hands and targets (the right hand now goes for the nose and the left hand to the right ear) (fourth movement). The participants repeat this two or three times, generally laughing all the while, and after either punching themselves in the eye or mastering the trick, they are told to return to work. This takes about 2 minutes, but many claim it refocuses the attention and refreshes the mind.

It is mere intelligent speculation that these types of movement help learning, however. There are few, if any, neuroscientific studies testing the effect of brain breaks on learning achievement. While there is well-established information about the role of oxygenation, there is little or no evidence for brain breaks. There are two ways that this belief could be moved into the well-established category. Either the word *movement* should be changed to *oxygenation* or far more studies should be conducted to monitor the neural effects of brain breaks and learning. While proven in physiology and education, this concept is not yet well established because documentation in neuroscience and psychology is sparse.

ACTIVITIES, ENVIRONMENTS, AND ENRICHMENT

A controversial category of concepts within intelligent speculation relates to the types of learning activities that are undertaken, the environments in which they occur, and the debate as to what "enrichment" really means.

Concepts in this category are often defined by terms that have individual interpretations. For example, a "best-practice" activity or a "good learning environment" is vital for effective teaching, but the exact definition of these terms often differs by individual.

Best-Practice Activities

> Best practice activities in education are activities that are student-centered, experiential, holistic, authentic, expressive, reflective, social, collaborative, democratic, cognitive, developmental, constructivist, and /or challenging. Students learn better and faster using best practice activities. (Tokuhama-Espinosa, 2008b, p. 281)

This belief, based on criteria set by Zemelman, Daniels, and Hyde (1998), suggests specific parameters for effective learning activities. While learning can take place in the absence of the characteristics mentioned above, it is more likely when at least one of them is present. Based on the documentation of hundreds of teachers who have testified to the importance of designing classroom activities that embody these characteristics, Zemelman and colleagues also found that when several characteristics are combined in a single activity, student retention is higher and learning is more significant (1998). They suggest that best-practice activities can take place at all grade levels and are effective with learners at all ability levels.

For example, an activity that includes many of the best-practice characteristics listed above is debate. Teachers who use debate techniques know that they are student-centered (the student is the main actor), experiential (the student must actively participate), holistic (debates tend to transcend disciplinary lines), authentic (they are often based in a student's own worldview), expressive (students must articulate their arguments clearly), reflective (debates demand that students anticipate each other's arguments), social (debates contemplate real social dilemmas), collaborative (the debate team must work together in order to win), democratic (the debate structure demands that everyone take a turn or have a specific role), cognitive (they require research and higher-order thinking skills), developmental (debates are best conducted among peers at a similar developmental level), constructivist (debates require the student to build on past knowledge), and challenging (they are not easy due to the organization, time constraints, group work issues, complexity of themes, and other reasons).

In contrast, one could think of lecture-based classrooms. Lectures are not student-centered (the attention is focused on the teacher), experiential (the experience is more passive than active), holistic (a lecture is usually one-dimensional in focus), authentic (lectures may or may not speak to a student's personal life experiences), expressive (students are not meant to express themselves in the lecture format), reflective (though students may reflect on the content, their short attention spans suggest otherwise), social (there is normally little social interaction during a lecture), collaborative (unless asked to share during the lecture, students do not collaborate), democratic (there is no shared responsibility in the lecture format), cognitive (while lectures are meant to stimulate higher-order thinking, this depends on the individual abilities of the learner), developmental (if well-prepared, the lecture addresses the learner's appropriate level of understanding, but this is not guaranteed), constructivist (only if students take the initiative can they build new knowledge from the content of the lecture), or challenging (because the lecture format requires very little from the audience, it is not considered challenging).

Education has embraced best practices, and it would probably not take too much digging to find support for them in psychology as well. However, this belief has not yet stood up to neuroscientific scrutiny. In order to be moved from the intelligent speculation to the well-established category, each of the 13 best practice characteristics would need to be scientifically defined, then tested in lab settings to confirm neurological enhancement reflective of better learning. This is not likely to occur soon, and this belief may remain elusive to MBE Science, despite the overwhelming support in education.

Good Learning Environments

> Good learning environments—defined within this book as being those which are safe, offer intellectual freedom, paced challenges, ample feedback, a level of autonomy, respect, and include active learning activities—are better than learning environments that do not have these characteristics. (Tokuhama-Espinosa, 2008b, p. 281)

Classrooms in which teachers create good learning environments result in optimal psychological well-being for learners. These environments reduce negative stress levels and optimize social learning contexts to the benefit of significant learning experiences. While it is hard to argue that respect, intellectual freedom, paced challenges, feedback, autonomy, and activity are bad for learners, evidence showing that students accelerate when exposed to such environments is more complex. The field of education has accepted these qualities as characteristics of good learning environments, and teacher testimony is readily available to support them. Although substantial evidence from psychology also supports this concept, neuroscience has not produced the same amount of evidence. Therefore, this belief remains in the intelligent speculation rather than the well-established category.

To move into the well-established category, agreed-upon definitions of *safe*, *intellectual freedom*, *paced challenges*, *ample feedback*, *autonomy*, *respect*, and *active* need to be established, followed by studies designed to confirm that each contributes to better learning. This would involve comparing student learning outcomes that have been taught in safe versus unsafe environments, for example. Though there is sufficient evidence in education and psychology to support this claim, there is little evidence in neuroscience, and, because student safety is involved, there might be ethical barriers to testing it.

Enrichment

> Enriched environments make children smarter. (Tokuhama-Espinosa, 2008b, p. 303)

Stimulation is necessary for learning, though enrichment per se is not. However, enriched environments, considered to be those with more stimulation, are logically presumed to lead to better learning experiences (but not necessarily smarter children). Eric Jensen (2006) writes that "enrichment is a positive biological response to a contrasting environment, in which measurable, synergistic, and global changes have occurred" (p. xii). He goes on to explain that this basically means that an enriched environment is measured relative to some less stimulating environment, which in terms of studies with rats means adding twists to the maze, challenging running wheels, and companionship. In human terms, it would be hard to argue with enrichment in these terms, especially since all enrichment exists in contrast to a less-stimulating environment. This is merely intelligent speculation, however, because the actual definition of enriched environments makes them hard to design or measure because they are relative to the learner. That is, studies can and have been done on groups, but as enrichment is relative to the learner, unless the learner's previous environment can be documented and compared, and new learning verified, then it is difficult to say that the environment is the cause of the enhanced learning.

Let's look at it this way. Let's say Jane goes to an "early enrichment class" with her mother from the time she is 3 months old. There are nine children in the class. A third of the other children come from home environments that are barren compared to the enrichment classes; they are truly enriched by the classes. A third of the class comes from home environments that have the same stimulus as the classes; they do not gain from the environment but do not lose anything, either. The last third comes from home environments that are far more enriching than the classes; they gain nothing from the classes and are actually losing time that could be spent in a better environment. Depending on the individual's normal environment, the definition of *enriched* will vary. This statement can be moved from intelligent speculation to well established if a phrase is added: "relative to the learner." That is, "enriched environments (relative to the learner) make children smarter." However, the belief as currently stated suggests that the enriched environments are provided by school design. Can one school enrich all its diverse students? Only if all the students share the same home environment used for comparison, or if teachers differentiate instruction substantially. This concept is not yet "well established" because documentation in classroom contexts using neuroscientific criteria is sparse and the concept of enrichment is based primarily on nonhuman studies.

Differentiated Instruction

> Differentiation (allowing students to learn at different levels and paces) in classroom practice can be justified by the fact that students have different intelligences and cognitive preferences. (Tokuhama-Espinosa, 2008b, p. 187)

Teaching students at their own paces maximizes learning potential, according to educators such as Carol Ann Tomlinson (1999; Tomlinson & Kalbfleisch, 1998; Tomlinson & McTighe, 2006). The main reason this is "intelligent speculation" is that adjusting curriculum expectations to individual students makes neuroscientific comparison impossible. Additionally, different intelligences and learning styles are not yet neurologically verifiable, meaning that it is extremely difficult to justify differentiation based on neuroscience. While it appears that some students may say they have a preference for hearing (or seeing or acting out) information, it is clear that all humans use all sensory channels to take in information, using different modes depending on different contexts.

In order for differentiation to be moved into the well-established category, more evidence needs to be presented that explains *why* differentiation appears to work based on neurological evidence. After all, instructional differentiation takes a great deal more time to plan and execute than instruction aimed at meeting the needs of the average student. Perhaps differentiation works because differentiated classrooms normally employ a wider variety of methodologies. The likelihood that one of these methodologies resonates with students is higher than in nondifferentiated classrooms. If and when different intelligences and cognitive preferences are found to be based on neuroscientific evidence and a subsequent link can be made between the methodologies, then this belief can be moved to the well-established category. For the time being, despite its success in classrooms, differentiation based on different intelligences and cognitive preferences remains intelligent speculation.

PHYSICAL VERSUS FUNCTIONAL WORKINGS OF THE BRAIN

This category of concepts in intelligent speculation is concerned with the complexities of weeding out which functions of the brain relate to which areas of the brain. These concepts relate to separating the physical areas of the brain from the systems they represent.

Memory Systems

> Different memory systems (i.e., short term-, long term-, working-, spatial-, motor-, modality-specific-, rote-, etc.), receive and process information in different ways and are retrieved through distinct, though sometimes overlapping, neural pathways. (Tokuhama-Espinosa, 2008b, p. 190)

It is well established that human memory is a complex system that is vital for learning. However, it is intelligent speculation that different memory systems (long-term memory, short-term memory, etc.) are located in distinct, but often overlapping, neural pathways in the brain. It stands to reason that if information could be put into long-term memory through several pathways (long-term auditory, long-term visual, long-term motor, etc.), instead of just one, it would be easier to find where the brain goes to retrieve that information. The brain, as a unit, receives different sensory stimuli. While all memories-in-the-making pass through the hippocampus, thalamus, and amygdala, long-term storage occurs in the cortex. The auditory cortex works in concert with the hippocampus when we retrieve auditory memories; the occipital (visual) cortex works in concert with the hippocampus when we retrieve visual memories, and so forth. Some evidence in favor of this idea comes from teachers' classroom experiences. This belief implies that if teachers vary their methods of instruction, they would create a variety of pathways through which that information can be retrieved. For example, despite the fact that Howard Gardner's theory of multiple intelligences is not substantiated by neuroscientific studies, it is logical to presume that if new information is taught through a variety of sensory channels it will be easier to recoup. In order for this to be moved from the intelligent speculation to the well-established category, more evidence is needed that establishes how multiple neural pathways for memory serve as complementary recall functions.

Survival Needs

> The brain learns best when content information responds to survival needs (social, emotional, economic, and physical). (Tokuhama-Espinosa, 2008b, p. 273)

People learn things that give them an edge to survive, an edge in social situations, or an economic advantage. This concept comes from evolutionary biology and the belief that the main, if not sole, purpose of the brain is to preserve the body for further reproductive purposes.

This basically means the brain is programmed to learn in order to avoid extinction of the species. To do this, the brain protects the organism by acquiring knowledge. In the survival sense related to the physical body, the brain quickly learns not to let us put our hand in the lion's cage lest it be bitten off. It eventually learns to tell us not to cross the street on a red light because a car might hit us. In the social and emotional sense, the brain learns to protect the organism by seeking out relationships that offer support. In the economic sense, the brain seeks out stability in the modern world through a steady income.

In terms of classroom learning, the brain continues to function at this "survival" level. In psychological terms, perhaps Maslow's (1943) hierarchy of needs expresses this concept best. Though over 60 years old, Maslow's theory explains some basic concepts of human motivation in terms that are still accepted today. Maslow proposed six levels of motivation. At the most basic level, humans must satisfy physical needs (shelter, enough food to eat) before moving toward higher-level needs. After securing physiological needs, humans are concerned with security; only after achieving security can they worry about affect needs, such as the need for meaningful relationships. Once affect needs are fulfilled, humans can move up the hierarchical chain to seek respect from others and, eventually, self-actualization. In the classroom setting, it is vital for teachers to recognize that a student who has not eaten or slept well (physiological needs) will be unable to engage in higher-order thinking. Survival acts in the brain can also be seen in unconscious states. When deprived of sleep, for example, the brain develops a "REM sleep debt" (Mignot, 2008), in which there are increased attempts to enter REM and where recovery rates, once allowed to go into REM, are 140% above the baseline (Endo, Roh, Landolt, Werth, & Aeschbacj, 1998). REM is associated both with dreaming and related to memory consolidation (Stickgold, 2006). Maslow's hierarchy also explains why some students are so motivated to "go with the crowd" as they seek affection. In biological psychology (Wagner, 2009) and neuroscience (Calvin, 1996), the brain first meets survival needs before moving on to higher-order social and thinking skills. In education, the evidence for learning based on survival is less compelling, which partially explains why this is merely intelligent speculation, not well-established. Further evidence from education is needed to join the neuroscientific and psychological support for this belief to change categories.

Synaptic Growth

In terms of synaptic growth, the most active synapses are strengthened, while relatively less active synapses are weakened. Over time, this shapes brain organization. This has been referred to as the "use it or lose it model." (Tokuhama-Espinosa, 2008b, p. 280)

The brain is an efficient organ that allocates its resources well. It is has been well established for about the past 70 years that if two neurons are active at the same time, the connection between them will grow stronger (Hebb, 1949). This means that when the brain is exposed to a stimulus that causes new links between neurons (synapses) to be formed, then the bond between them is reinforced. The links between neurons that are repeatedly strengthened develop a myelin sheath, which speeds up the links between neurons and therefore the speed of responses. It is well established that rehearsal of concepts makes recall faster and that recall becomes faster because the links between chunks of information in the brain stored by different groups of neurons become stronger.

What is not so well established in this statement (and as a consequence is mere "intelligent speculation") is the reason for synaptic die-out. Many think that lack of use causes cell die-off; others speculate that cell die-off is a natural process (see Steen, 2007, for a good summary of this dilemma). The "use it or lose it" idea is based on human experience. We have all had the unfortunate experience of "forgetting" something we once knew. Is this because we did not use the information and the cells died out? Or is the memory irretrievable because it is misattributed and "cataloged" in the wrong area? Or could it be that it is blocked somehow, as Daniel Schacter (2007) suggests? For the time being, we must interpret "lose it" to mean "lose access to it," due either to cell die-off or to inaccessibility. More studies documenting the correlation between cell die-off and forgetting are needed to move this concept from intelligent speculation to well established, but this is probably just a matter of time.

DIFFERENT POPULATIONS

The final group of concepts in this category of intelligent speculation relate to ideas about learning for specific populations, specifically that of children versus adults and males versus females.

Effortless Learning in Children

Children learn certain skills (such as language) effortlessly. (Tokuhama-Espinosa, 2008b, p. 281)

The belief that children learn some skills effortlessly is based on the observations of millions of parents as they watch their small children learn their first and sometimes a second and third language within the first few years of life with what appears to be very little effort. This is supported by modern linguistic views that consider at least some aspects of language to be "hardwired" into human brains. Cultural linguistic studies, such as those conducted by Slobin (1992) at the University of California at Berkeley, demonstrate that all humans around the world develop language in the same order at roughly the same time, from monosyllabic utterings to single words, to two- and three-word sentences, and finally to the ability to speak with nearly perfect grammar by about the age of 5. Most literate societies teach their children to read and write by the age of 8. Each of these language advances is contingent on feedback from people in the surroundings, however. Feedback implies that there are errors, and errors imply corrections, and corrections imply work. This would seem to indicate that children do not learn skills like language "effortlessly."

While humans appear to be hardwired to learn certain skills, such as how to talk, these skills cannot develop in isolation. A human who does not receive the right stimuli may not learn the most basic of skills, such as language. There are just under a hundred documented cases of feral children who were brought up isolated from society—normally nurtured by other animals, as seen in the study documented by Bruno Bettelheim (1959). All these children had great difficulties acquiring human language, and some never achieved more than a few basic words and signs. These are rare cases and a striking example of one of the skills for which there appears to be a critical (as opposed to sensitive) period.

Genetic research is on the verge of deciphering the genes for language and psycholinguists and educational speech pathologists have contributed some studies that both support and reject the belief that language is learned effortlessly. One way to change this belief from the intelligent speculation category would be if the word *relatively* was added before *effortlessly*; that is, language is learned relatively effortlessly, as compared with adults, though in terms of childhood achievements it is still a great deal of work. This is not yet well established because there are only a few studies of dubious quality and because *effortlessly* is a relative term.

Gender Differences and the Brain

Male and female brains learn differently. (Tokuhama-Espinosa, 2008b, p. 281)

It is logical to presume that because men and women's bodies differ in terms of physical size and genitalia, parts of their brains would also differ. Neuroscientists have offered the most information in this area, while psychologists have debated the origin of differences between the genders and educators have worked hard to eliminate them. Neuroscientists have noted that a small area of the prefrontal cortex (related to logic), a part of the limbic system (the hypothalamus, related to emotions), and the corpus callosum (responsible for communication between the two hemispheres of the brain) are larger in women. On the other hand, a small area of the amygdala (related to arousal and threat response) is larger in men (Kimura, 2002). There is also a difference is overall weight and size, with men's brains, on average, being slightly larger than women's. These are documented physical differences in the brain, which could make this belief well established. However, there are inconclusive studies showing that these physical differences translate into different learning abilities, meaning this statement remains intelligent speculation.

There is a great deal of information in psychology on differences between men's and women's behaviors (learning being a behavior). Do boys and girls act the way they do because their brains are different, or do they act differently because of societal expectations? Do boys choose to play with cars and guns more than with dolls (and girls vice versa) due to the structure of their brains, or is the difference due to the gifts our children receive based on their sex? These questions remain hot for debate.

In education the focus is slightly different. There is some evidence that boys and girls do appear to take in information in different ways in our classrooms, though it is not clear how and why this occurs. Some educators have made a point of noting these differences. Michael Gurian and Kathy Stevens (2007) hypothesize that a combination of nature and nurture are responsible for the gender differences in school achievement but ultimately believe that schools could do more to close the gap between the sexes. There is a difference in how boys and girls score on school achievement tests (girls almost always score higher in all areas), but these score differences do not explain how the brain is wired. Until we are able to determine exactly whether and how the physical differences between male and female brains parallel the differences in behavior, this belief will remain merely intelligent speculation. This is not yet well established because correlations among physiology, learning, and academic achievement by gender are sparse.

The information in the intelligent speculation category is important to watch because it is dangerously overapplied in educational practice. These concepts may seem logical but in all cases there is a dearth of scientific evidence behind them and in several cases evidence from one of the parent fields is missing. This is not to say the concepts will never be proven, but for the time being they should be viewed cautiously.

CHAPTER 5

Weeding Out Neuromyths and Misunderstandings

The experts in the Delphi panel were asked to list as many neuromyths as they could think of. This list was compared with a list of neuromyths generated by the OECD (2007) study *The Brain and Learning*. According to the OECD and Briggs's criteria, a concept should be categorized as a neuromyth if there is "[n]o affirmative evidence of effects" or if it has potentially negative effects as demonstrated by research. Because they are completely discredited by a lack of insufficient evidence, such concepts should not be applied in classroom settings. It should be remembered, however, that none of the beliefs or neuromyths is set in stone in the categories found in this book and may indeed be moved to other categories if new evidence is found. For the time being, any application of neuromyths should be avoided in classroom practice.

The information in the neuromyths category is chunked into the following seven groups (see Figure 5.1):

1. Myths About and Misinterpretations of Data
2. Misunderstandings About How the Brain Works
3. Myths About Memory and Learning
4. Myths About Brain Processes
5. Folk Myths About the Brain
6. Unsubstantiated Beliefs
7. Myth About Where Learning Takes Place

MYTHS ABOUT AND MISINTERPRETATIONS OF DATA

There is a large category of concepts related to myths and misinterpretations of data about the brain. Most of these myths are found in unsubstantiated newspaper columns, magazines, or other elements of the popular press. Neuromyths in this category are particularly harmful because they have been repeated so many times that people think they are true simply because they have seen a wide variety of sources repeat the same misinformation.

Figure 5.1. Neuromyths in MBE Science

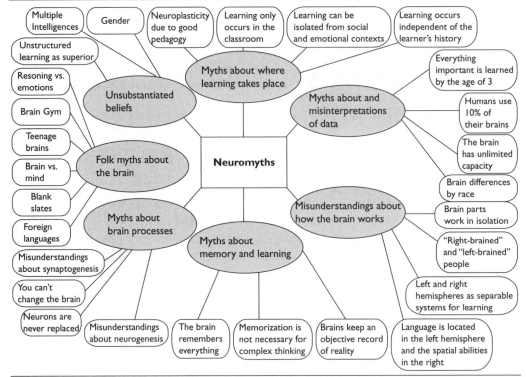

Source: Bramwell, 2009.

Humans Use 10% of Their Brains

No exact percentage can be assigned to brain usage; nonetheless, the more we learn about the brain, the less it appears we are using! Brain use can be measured through imagery, which shows how certain parts of the brain, or clusters of neurons, "light up" when in use. The idea that humans use 10% of their brain is based on the estimated number of synapses in the brain (which neurons are connected to which). However, it is now known that not all areas of the brain are meant to be linked to one another in the first place, so suggesting that lack of use is a reflection of unused potential is unreasonable. Additionally, what can be measured in one moment of brain use changes with the task (for example, brain images of people learning to read and images of accomplished readers reading show different areas in use). A specific percentage of brain use is also noted to be a "neuromyth" by the OECD (2007). This neuromyth influences both students' and teachers' perceptions about potential. Students feel naturally limited by being told incorrectly that they are able to use only a small part of their brains.

The Brain Has an Unlimited Capacity

At the other extreme from beliefs about the brain's percentage of use is the idea that the brain has unlimited capacity. This is also a neuromyth. Although the brain is perhaps the most amazing machine in the world, it has a finite capacity. Placing the brain in the wondrous magical category of entities with infinite abilities is not realistic. Students should know about the amazing plasticity of the brain and the potential to learn throughout life—but within the realistic confines of its physical bounds.

There Are Brain Differences by Race

No studies exist documenting differences in brains based on race. In a controversial twist, however, there are studies documenting differences in intelligence by race. These differences have been debated widely and have been attributed to culture, socioeconomic factors, test preparation, and previous schooling. These studies have also called into question how intelligence is measured. However, race is not reflected in brain structure.

Everything Important About the Brain Is Determined by the Age of 3

There are sensitive periods, *not* critical periods, in human brain development during which certain skills are learned with greater ease than at other times. The large body of evidence related to neuroplasticity also provides evidence debunking this myth. Having said this, good nutrition and health in the early years is correlated to better-functioning brains. This is also noted to be a neuromyth by the OECD (2007).

MISUNDERSTANDINGS ABOUT HOW THE BRAIN WORKS

A second category of neuromyths relates to misunderstandings about actual brain structures and how the brain works. These myths are normally overgeneralizations or oversimplifications about the complex nature of the brain. These neuromyths are dangerous because they undermine our understanding of the complicated structure of the brain.

Brain Parts Work in Isolation

Brain areas do not work independently; they work as systems. During the 1990s, it was popular to think of the brain as divided into compartments. Localizationism claimed that language function occupied the left hemisphere of the brain, for example. It is now clear that it is easier to identify which areas of the brain are *not* involved in language functioning than to identify which are. The current view is that the entire brain works to develop systems among different areas of the brain for different skills.

Some People Are More "Right-Brained" and Others Are More "Left-Brained"

Humans have only one brain, comprised of a right and left hemisphere. Ninety-five percent of right-handed people and 70% of left-handed people have similarly structured brains, in which, for example, certain language areas (Broca's and Wernicke's areas) are located in the left frontal and parietal lobes. However, as discussed in the chapter on well-established information, no two brains are identical. This is also noted to be a neuromyth by the OECD (2007).

Left and Right Hemispheres Are Separable Systems for Learning

There are many learning systems in the brain, most based on human skills, not on left- and right-hemisphere division. In the popular press, right-hemisphere learners are said to be more creative, for example. While there is evidence that most people have certain spatial orientation systems in the right hemisphere, there is no evidence that the right-hemisphere learning systems exist and are in contradiction to left-hemisphere learning systems. It is misleading to tell children they can "stimulate their right brains" by doing certain activities and to sell books purporting to show teachers how to create right-brained classrooms to stimulate creativity.

Language Is Located in the Left Brain and Spatial Abilities Are in the Right Brain

Broca's and Wernicke's areas tend to be located in the left hemisphere of the brain, with some exceptions (in 5% of right-handed people and 30% of left-handed people, these two language systems are either in the right hemisphere or divided between the hemispheres). However, some aspects of language, such as comprehension of metaphors and analogies as well as some aspects of humor and intonation, are typically found in the right hemisphere. These exceptions make this statement a neuromyth.

MYTHS ABOUT MEMORY AND LEARNING

A third category of neuromyths relates to the important role of memory in learning. It is clear that without memory, there is no learning, but the literature is not always clear about exactly how memory systems work in the brain. These neuromyths are normally in the form of good metaphors, but they are not realistic representations of the complex nature of memory.

Brains Objectively Record Reality

This myth suggests that memories are, in essence, objective recordings of situations and that reality exists in a similar form for all to perceive. Individual human memories are not recorded as if stored on a hard drive but are influenced by the experiences of the learner. People's memories of events are clouded by different individual filters that are subject to false recollection and/or misinterpretation.

Memorization Is Unnecessary for Complex Mental Processing

This is a neuromyth because acquisition of declarative knowledge depends on both memory and attention, which means that complex mental processing is impossible without memorization.

Forgetting

There is a myth that the brain remembers everything it has ever experienced and that forgetting is simply an absence of recall ability. While forgetting is an absence of recall, the brain does not necessarily remember everything that it has ever experienced. Only information that has moved from working to long-term memory in its many forms is retrievable and can be remembered.

MYTHS ABOUT BRAIN PROCESSES

Another category of neuromyths relates to how various brain processes work. These myths are typically misunderstandings about how brain cells grow, connect, and die out. These neuromyths are important for teachers to understand because the terms *neurogenesis* (growth of new brain cells), *synaptogenesis* (formation of new links between brain cells), and *cell death* are commonly seen in the popular press but are not always used correctly.

Misunderstandings About Neurogenesis

There is a myth about how new brain cells are formed, or what is known as the process of neurogenesis. This is based on the idea that there are optimal periods for learning that are directly related to neurogenesis. Some popular books tell teachers they should time their lessons with periods of neurogenesis, something that is nearly impossible to predict. There are sensitive periods, not critical periods, in human brain development in which certain skills are learned with greater ease than at other times, but these are not related to neurogenesis. This is also noted to be a neuromyth by the OECD (2007).

Misunderstandings About Synaptogenesis

This is based on the idea that more will be learned if teaching is timed with periods of synaptogenesis, the times at which new synapses are formed. This statement is a myth for two reasons. First, learning causes synaptogenesis, not the other way around. Second, this statement presumes that (1) we can anticipate moments of synaptogenesis and that (2) better learning occurs with "new" brain cells than with older ones. Neither of these statements has been proven to date.

Brain Cell Death

There is a myth that neurons are never replaced (you can't grow new brain cells). This neuromyth is defied by the existence of neurogenesis, which is growth of new brain cells.

Immutability of the Brain

Some say you can't change the brain. This is a neuromyth because not only can you change the brain, it is impossible *not* to do so. This neuromyth is disproved by the fact that the brain is a complex, dynamic, and integrated system that is constantly changed by experience.

FOLK MYTHS ABOUT THE BRAIN

There are some neuromyths that have been promoted for so long that they have been passed on from one generation to another. These folk myths about the brain are particularly dangerous because they incorrectly suggest limitations on the brain's potential.

Learning Foreign Languages Disrupts Knowledge of Students' Native Language

This neuromyth, propounded in the 1960s, was based on the belief that there was one area for language and the brain, and that if that area were to be "divided" between two (or more) languages, then overall language potential would be separated between a first and second language. This has since been refuted by numerous studies in linguistics and education (see, e.g., Tokuhama-Espinosa, 2008a) that show the overall mental benefits of both simultaneous and subsequent bilingualism. This is noted to be a neuromyth by the OECD (2007).

Children Are Blank Slates

The belief that a child is born as a blank slate upon which parents and educators write the experiences of his life was popularized by John Locke in the 17th century but has since been refuted. Modern psychology and neuroscience demonstrate how skills as basic to human survival as language may be "preprogrammed" in the genetic makeup.

Brain and Mind Are Separate

There is a controversial myth that the mind and the brain are separate. The brain is a physical organ, while the mind is an intangible representation of self; the brain generates the concept of the mind, without which it would not exist.

Incomplete Brain Development Explains Teenagers' Behavior

This myth is based on the idea that teens act out and are irresponsible because the prefrontal cortex doesn't develop fully until the mid-20s. While it is true that the prefrontal lobe (which is partially responsible for executive function) is still developing in teenagers, teenagers act out for a great number of reasons, which include poor parenting and the influence of hormones, as well as the influence of their social networks.

Reasoning Is Contrary to Emotion

This is based on the idea that reasoning and decision making can be divorced from emotion and feeling and that doing so improves the quality of one's thought. In fact, however, emotions are critical to decision making. Although reasoning and emotions appear to be on different ends of the rationality spectrum, they are actually complementary processes.

Brain Gym

Brain Gym ("a series of simple body movements to integrate all areas of the brain to enhance learning" [Goswami, 2006, pp. 406–413]) is said to be an effective way to enhance young children's learning potential. Brain Gym is a nonprofit organization committed to the principle of "educational kinesiology," the belief that specific physical movements enhance cognition. This is a neuromyth because Brain Gym replicates, albeit in an innovative way, normal human movements and in some cases may take advantage of the placebo effect, but it is not grounded in neuroscience. That is, some children who do Brain Gym activities report positive results, but this is due to the parents' and children's desire to believe in the activities and their promised effects, not because of the movements themselves. It is marketed as a way to stimulate children through whole-body activities, which are claimed to stimulate both hemispheres of the brain, but there is no evidence that Brain Gym activities enhance potential any more than normal play does.

UNSUBSTANTIATED BELIEFS

There is a category of neuromyths that are based in an overgeneralization of a partial fact. Many of these myths relate to teaching methods and need to be understood because they directly impact classroom activities.

Unstructured Learning Is Superior to Structured Learning for Neurological Functioning

This myth is based on the idea that unstructured discovery learning is preferable to structured, teacher-centered instruction because the former improves neurological functioning. The definition of *unstructured discovery* learning makes this statement hard to judge. However, modern pedagogy acknowledges that student-centered learning activities are preferred over teacher-centered activities. This statement is a neuromyth because unstructured learning benefits are due not to neurological functioning but to student self-efficacy and active learning principles.

The Theory of Multiple Intelligences Is Neuroscientifically Verifiable

Howard Gardner, the creator of this theory, acknowledges that it is not supported by neuroscience research but rather by psychological and pedagogical research.

MYTHS ABOUT WHERE LEARNING TAKES PLACE

There is a final category of neuromyths about where learning takes place. These myths sometimes elevate the classroom to an unnecessarily high status. While the role of the teacher is indisputable, exactly where and how learning occurs is often confused in popular books.

Plasticity and Pedagogy

There is a myth that neuroplasticity is due to good pedagogy. Neural plasticity is based on the natural neuroanatomical structure of the brain and occurs with or without good pedagogy (though it is likely enhanced by stimulation).

Learning Occurs Only in the Classroom

There is an unsubstantiated belief that teaching and learning are limited to classroom experiences. As most of us know from our own lives, learning occurs both inside and outside the classroom—and does so lifelong.

A Student's History Does Not Affect His Learning

A learner's past experiences always influence his learning. It is vital that teachers know that a student's potential to learn is heavily impacted by what he already knows or has experienced.

Learning Can Be Isolated from Social and Emotional Content

Learning is always influenced by the social and emotional context in which it occurs.

KEEPING THE DATA HONEST

Many experts believe that some of the concepts listed here might end up being moved from the neuromyth category based on new evidence and research in the coming years. We all must monitor these myths so as to add, delete, or move them among categories based on the most state-of-the-art evidence. This means that the field is dynamic and will most likely change, and this should be welcomed by practitioners because better information means better teaching. For the time being, however, concepts categorized as neuromyths should be avoided in order to ensure good teaching practice.

We now turn to the tenets, principles, and instructional guidelines in MBE Science that we can draw from the current research, expert commentary, and the continuum from well-established concepts to neuromyths.

Part II

Applying
Mind, Brain, Education Science
in the Classroom

CHAPTER 6

Tenets:
Applying Knowledge About
the Individual Nature of Learning
to Classroom Teaching

Based on the categorization system that separates neuromyths from more substantiated beliefs, the main tenets and principles of MBE Science become clear. Together, the tenets and principles are the skeleton of the MBE Science body, without which there would be no form or substance. The important thing to remember is that the tenets are relative to each individual learner, while the principles are important in the same way for all learners. The tenets are primarily concerned with aspects of learning that are individualized, such as how and what *motivates* teaching and learning experiences. The principles, on the other hand, are concepts about learning that are true for all learners, such as the fact that *learning is based in part on the brain's ability to self-correct*. Each of the 12 tenets and 21 principles contribute to the 10 instructional guidelines. In all of these tenets, readers will find echoes of the foregoing assignment of information into the trusted categories of what is well-established and probably so, with reference here to relevant research. In this chapter, we will first look at the tenets.

There are three large groupings of tenets. First, there are tenets that relate to emotions and learning. Second, there are tenets that relate to the physical way that the body impacts the mind and its potential to learn. And third, there are tenets that correspond to the way the individual student as a whole approaches learning (see Figure 6.1). Each tenet is explained below and chunked into one of these three groups.

Figure 6.1. The Tenets in MBE Science.

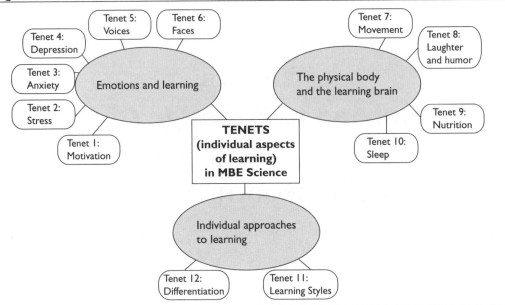

Source: Bramwell, 2009.

EMOTIONS AND LEARNING

Tenet 1: Motivation. *Motivation Impacts How Teachers Teach and How Students Learn*

This tenet is supported by the well-established belief that all brains are not equal in their ability to solve all problems. Context as well as ability influence learning. Context includes the learning environment, motivation for the topic of new learning, and prior knowledge. This is also supported by the intelligent speculation that self-esteem impacts learning and academic achievement. The research in this group claims, in some form or another, that people learn better when they are highly motivated than when they have no motivation (Reeve, 2004). This should come as no surprise, since positive motivation and interest levels are linked (Halpern & Hakel, 2002). As McCann and Garcia (1999) and Smith (2004) have shown, students who are interested in a subject tend to devote more time to pursuing knowledge about it.

There are two caveats to this general claim about motivation, however. Motivation can be either positive or negative. This means that people can learn things because they feel pushed or threatened to do so, but they can also learn things because they *want* to do so. Second, motivating factors are regulated in a highly individualized fashion; what is motivating to one individual may not be motivating to another. This is why one child might be quiet in class, as the teacher requests, in order to stay in class, and another might be loud because he actually *wants* to be sent out into the hallway. Studies on the physical areas of the brain or the neurotransmitters involved in motivation indicate how different areas of the brain are actually activated when a learner has high or low motivation for a task (Depue & Collins, 1999), meaning that motivation is not only a psychological state of mind but also a physical need. An understanding of how motivation works in this physical sense has implications for instructional guidelines; no matter what level of motivation a student brings to class, the teacher, for good or for ill, impacts it. This tenet also has policy implications because it forces teachers to realize that they, not only students themselves, are responsible for student motivation.

Tenet 2: Stress. *Stress Impacts Learning*

This is supported by the belief that "good" stress (eustress) heightens attention and helps learning, while "bad" stress detracts from learning potential. This is also supported by analyzing the literature, which includes hundreds of articles on stress. The basic premise behind this tenet is that moderate stress (eustress) is positive and excessive stress is negative. Eustress can enhance learning by putting the body in a prepared state through the release of hormones (Berk, 2001). Negative stress can detract from learning because the excess of certain hormones actually blocks the uptake of new information, according to the Society for Neuroscience (2007c). The literature on this topic has also considered how to manage stress, tame stress, or as Sapolsky's work (2003) has shown, use stress to one's advantage. Other work has tracked the correlation between the deterioration of certain brain areas with high-level stress and the neurotransmitters involved in stress, making it clear that stress is physiologically as well as psychologically damaging.

An understanding of stress has major implications for teachers, who have direct control over the stress level in learning environments. This tenet also has policy implications because teachers have been known to achieve good standardized test results through teaching methods that evoke negative stress. Does the end justify the means? Is it worth putting students through "a little stress" in order to get higher test scores? On the flip side, "good" stress environments do not guarantee learning—only a more pleasant setting. Finally and most controversially, we now know that what causes one person's good stress may cause another's bad stress. It is important that we as teachers and emerging MBE scientists understand the ways stress impacts motivation and learning, how we can control stress, and how to manage stress elements in the classroom.

Tenet 3: Anxiety. *Anxiety Blocks Learning Opportunities*

This tenet is supported by the belief that emotions are critical to decision making. It is also supported by hundreds of animal studies and dozens of human studies that attest to the negative role anxiety can play in learning. Studies in this subfield relate to the psychological, neurological, and educational results of high-anxiety situations, including classroom stress. Some of the studies in this field relate to the neurobiological effects of anxiety on student outcomes (e.g., Kalueff, 2007; Kilts, Kelsey, Knight, & Ely, 2006). These studies show how the state of the mind can change bodily functions and even cause them to deteriorate. Other studies explain how physical areas of the brain are impacted by excessive anxiety (e.g., Rauch, Shin, & Wright, 2003; Walker, Toufexis, & Davis, 2003), resulting in long-term learning problems. Perhaps most interesting to teachers are the vast number of articles related to the way anxiety manifests itself during test situations, as in work done by Hong (1999), in which he explains how students feel a sense of "blockage" when stress arises and, as a result, how their test scores are affected.

Knowledge about anxiety is vital for teacher preparedness and has important policy implications. Should anxiety management techniques be explicitly taught in classroom settings? That is, should "math anxiety" or general "test anxiety" be addressed in classrooms? Some studies supporting this tenet (e.g., De Raedt, 2006) testify to the benefits of such instruction. We teachers need to be aware of anxiety reduction techniques, and further research should be conducted to determine whether they should be taught in all classrooms so as to maximize learning potential.

Tenet 4: Depression. *Depressive States Can Impede Learning*

This tenet is supported by the belief that emotions are critical to decision making and by thousands of studies in the literature, which show how depressive states can impede learning both for psychological and neurological reasons. Some of these studies explain the physical effects of depression on areas of the brain. For example, Sapolsky (2001) noted that the hippocampus, an area of the brain related to long-term memory, is impacted by long-term depression and use of antidepressants, the drugs that help people out of depressive states. Other studies relate to hormonal changes during depressive states, showing, for example, how depression and mood swings are related (Society for Neuroscience, 2007a).

These studies are important for teachers to consider because students' (and teachers') frames of mind are influenced by class settings. Even if a teacher doesn't cause a student's depressive state (though in some cases she may indeed do so), she needs to be aware of the influence that such depression can have on student learning potential.

Tenet 5: Voices. *Other People's Tones of Voices Are Quickly Judged in the Brain.*

The literature supports the idea that the human brain judges others' faces and tones of voices for threat levels in a rapid and often unconscious way, influencing the way information from these sources is perceived (e.g., as valid, invalid, trustworthy, untrustworthy, etc.). Some of these studies show how the human perception of voice tones influences learning. It has been well documented that infants recognize their mother's voices from birth (Purhonen, Kilpelainen-Lees, Valkonen-Korhonen, Karhu, & Lehtonen, 2004), which indicates that tones of voice are probably an innate or early-learned perception of the brain. Some research in this area relates to how the brain processes emotional speech or how the brain perceives anger through the sound of a voice (e.g., Sander and colleagues, 2005). Other studies consider how men's and women's tones of voice are perceived by gender (Schrimer, 2003). All these studies point to the fact that the brain perceives and judges tones of voices in an almost unconscious way.

This tenet has implications for teachers because, whether consciously or not, they may be sending out signals to their students, both negative and positive, based on their tone of voice. Good MBE scientists know how to use their voices (including levels of intonation) to draw students into classroom discussions, not to repulse or bore them.

Tenet 6: Faces. *People's Faces Are Judged Nearly Instantaneously in the Brain*

As with Tenet 5, a meta-analysis of the literature supports the idea that the human brain judges others' faces and tones of voices for threat levels in a rapid and often unconscious way, influencing the way information from these sources is perceived (e.g., as valid, invalid, trustworthy, untrustworthy, etc.). Face perception is better established than voice perception in human brain studies, though, similar to voices, faces are recognized nearly from birth (deHaan, Pascalis, & Johnson, 2002). The area of the brain most often mentioned in research on face recognition is the fusiform "face area," which is most active when the brain studies the unique traits of faces (Gauthier et al., 2000; Kanwisher & Yovel, 2006). It is important to realize that while artificial intelligence computers have managed to do many things, the one thing they can't do is recognize a human face. According to some researchers, faces are quickly analyzed and categorized in the human brain (Smith, Gosselin, & Schyns, 2007) not only by traits but also by our personal preferences. Face preferences are developed early in the human repertoire of skills (Benar & Miikkulainen, 2003). This has implications for teaching. Students perceive their teacher and his intentions based on the signals sent by his facial expressions. Although none of us can change the way we look, we can be more conscious of our facial expressions as we interact with students.

A remarkable study by Ambady and Rosenthal (1993) demonstrated that students could actually judge the quality of a teacher—his knowledge of the subject and how to teach it—within seconds of viewing him on video (without sound) based on his body language, including facial expressions. The way teachers express themselves to their students (in part through their facial expressions) influences learning. Since what students believe their teachers think about them impacts their learning, the way faces are perceived is important to learning. Teachers are rarely taught how to manage their facial expressions and body language. This has implications for overall communication skills in the classroom and teachers' initial and continuing training.

THE PHYSICAL BODY AND THE LEARNING BRAIN

Tenet 7: Movement. *Movement Can Enhance Learning*

There are three primary findings that support the positive impact of movement on learning. First there are studies on the use of *brain breaks*. These are short moments between lessons or parts of lessons dedicated to the body in order to refresh the mind. Such breaks can be as simple as changing seats in a class (Keuler & Safer, 1998). There is no conclusive evidence as to whether brain breaks work because they increase oxygenation or simply because they refocus attention. Second, there are studies showing how movement helps to reorient attention. It was found that when students alternated movement activities with thinking activities, they were able to maintain better attention for longer periods (Chatterjee, 2004). Third, other studies have shown how movement and physical exercise increase oxygenation and, therefore, concentration and memory. It stands to reason that the more physical activities students engage in, the more oxygen is flowing through their bloodstreams.

The research in this category focuses on the way movement influences learning (Leppo & Davis, 2005). This is a controversial area, however, and several studies consider just how much of the fanfare over movement is actually based on evidence; the greatest "black hole" surrounding discussion of the benefits (or lack thereof) of movement is due to the relative nature of the benefits of movement. Several brain-based learning books promote the concept of movement to enhance learning, though the studies behind the claim should be further substantiated. It stands to reason that brain breaks, refocusing attention, and oxygenation logically stem from movement. Conscientious teachers should keep this in mind as they plan classes. All learners can recall bad classroom experiences in which boredom set in; movement should be considered as a solution to such fatigue.

Tenet 8: Laughter and Humor. *Humor Can Enhance Learning Opportunities Through Laughter*

This tenet is supported by the belief that laughter can enhance learning (though it is unclear as to exactly what the mind–body mechanism is that influences this). It is also supported by dozens of examples in the literature. Some studies on humor and learning show the impact of laughter on neural mechanisms related to memory and attention. Laughter triggers the release of endorphins and enhances oxygenation in the brain, both of which aid in learning. Some of these studies relate to the changes in hormones during laughter, as demonstrated by Berk (2001) and reported by the Society for Neuroscience (2007b). Many teachers have reported the results of using humor in classroom settings, including Bain (2004), Bonwell (1993), Filipowicz (2003), Garner (2006), and Littleton (1998). Since humor is highly individualized, good teachers not only need to stimulate laughter in order to enjoy its learning benefits but also must understand what type of humor triggers laughter for individual learners.

Tenet 9: Nutrition. *Nutrition Impacts Learning*

This tenet is supported by the belief that good eating habits contribute to learning and poor eating habits detract from the brain's ability to maximize its learning potential. Several of the studies in this field are related to the impact of nutrition on learning (Liu, 2004) or its impact on states of mind (Lesser, 2003). Marcason's (2005) studies, for example, demonstrated how diet might have an impact on neural tissues that affect executive function and attention. In laymen's terms, this means that our ability to pay attention is directly related to what we eat and drink. Specifically, Molteni (2002) showed that "a high-fat, refined sugar diet reduces hippocampal brain-derived neurotrophic factor, neuronal plasticity, and learning" (p. 803). This means that fatty foods or high-sugar soft drinks, which often make up part of teenage diets in the United States, may be a contributing factor not only to obesity but also to learning problems. Other studies relate to how diet might impact certain learning deficits.

This tenet has implications for school policy (e.g., cafeteria options) as well as national health policies. Again, as with all the other tenets, the difficult aspects of nutrition issues lie in their relative nature. To a certain extent, different people have different nutritional needs and will react differently to specified diets. What is clear is that what happens to the body impacts the brain's potential to learn. At a minimum, MBE scientists should be aware of the link between nutrition and learning and perhaps even be responsible for teaching students about it.

Tenet 10: Sleep. *Sleep Is Important for Memory Consolidation*

This tenet is supported by the belief that sleep is vital for declarative memory consolidation (though other types of memories, such as emotional memories, can be achieved without sleep). Conversely, sleep deprivation has a negative impact on memory; people who do not get enough rest can neither pay attention nor consolidate memories effectively. Much of the work in this subfield explains the importance of sleep for school success (Carskadon, Wolfson, Acebo, Tzischinsky, & Seifer, 1998). Sleep not only rests the body and mind; it is also fundamental to the consolidation of long-term memory (Hobson, 2004; Mednick, Nakayama, & Stickgold, 2003). Sleep patterns are highly individual, however, meaning that they can be difficult to regulate who receives enough sleep and who does not. Though sleep specialists such as Hobson (2004) acknowledge that "normal" sleep patterns for students can range from between 5 to 12 hours nightly, it is agreed that adolescents require more hours of sleep than adults (Carskadon, Acebo, & Jenni, 2004; Taylor, Jenni, Acebo, & Carskadon, 2005). The concept of "chrono-education" is a new and exciting area of MBE Science (Golombek & Cardinali, 2007). This fact has huge policy implications; several school systems are experimenting with later school starting times to accommodate the sleep needs of adolescents. Sleep, which occupies approximately one-third of a person's lifetime, is a central area for further MBE Science research since there are grave implications for health and learning.

INDIVIDUAL APPROACHES TO LEARNING

Tenet 11: Learning Styles. *Learning Styles (Cognitive Preferences) Are Due to the Unique Structure of Individual Brains*

Experts note that all people use kinesthetic, visual, and auditory pathways to take in new information, and there is strong evidence that different people use different processing strategies at different times depending on the context of the learning. However, the experts do not think there is enough evidence to say that some people are "kinesthetic learners" as opposed to "auditory learners" or "visual learners" because this depends greatly on the subject being learned, the stage of learning (new concepts versus rehearsal), and the intrinsic motivation of the learner for the topic at hand. Learning styles are also supported by a well-substantiated belief that human brains are as unique as faces; while the basic structure is the same, no two are identical. Although there are general patterns of organization in how different people learn and which brain areas are involved, each brain is unique and uniquely organized. Rita Smilkstein and colleagues (Gunn, Richburg, & Smilkstein, 2007) believe learning styles relate to the basic idea that when we experience information through preferential cognitive modes, we grow better and faster as learners. It should be noted that the belief in the existence of different learning styles is supported by hundreds of studies in the literature (e.g., Van Der Jagt, Ramasamy, Jacobs, Ghose, & Lindsey, 2003) that look at learning style preferences combined with environmental factors. Analyses that combined cognitive preferences with the stages of learning and student motivation are helpful in determining how to reach students and make one's teaching more effective.

Learning styles and cognitive preferences are often confused with the theory of multiple intelligences. Over the years, several writers have tried to unravel the crossover areas between multiple intelligences and learning styles (e.g., Guild & Chock-Eng, 1998). Levine (2000) offers a third perspective. Levine's *neurodevelopmental constructs* divide up human potential into systems, or what he calls "constructs." Levine believes that just as the body has seven systems (digestive, reproductive, respiratory, circulatory, nervous, skeletal, and muscular), the brain has eight: memory, attention, temporal sequential ordering, spatial ordering, language, neuromotor function, social cognition, and higher-order cognition. We all know that if any one of the body's systems is not functioning properly, then the entire body suffers. In a similar way, the brain's potential can be limited if one of its systems is not functioning fully. For example, Levine argues that memory and attention are the driving constructs in learning. If a child has a problem with any aspect of memory (working, short-term, or long-term) or suffers from attention deficits at any level, learning is impaired. Similarly, if a student has a poor temporal sequential ordering system, she is challenged in comprehending mathematical formulas or grammatical rules since sequential ordering relates to formulas and rules. A deficit in any one of the constructs impacts the entire learner and effectively impacts his potential intellectual abilities. Levine's work is different from, though not in opposition to, Gardner's theory of multiple intelligences. According to Levine,

> If anything, our models complement each other and certainly are not diametrically opposed. One difference is that he is a psychologist and I'm a clinician. A clinician's model naturally identifies where breakdowns are occurring. When Gardner talks about musical intelligence, I can talk about some of the brain functions—sequencing ability and motor-rhythmic abilities—that would contribute to musical intelligence. Various neurodevelopmental functions in a sense are the ingredients of each of his intelligences. (quoted in Scherer, 2006)

Levine's work bridges the gap between purely psychological models of intelligence and biologically based ones. Though less well known than Gardner's multiple intelligences, Levine's neurodevelopmental constructs finds support from MBE Science. Questions about the way intelligence is defined invite many challenges, however. What seems clear is that learning styles and the theory of multiple intelligences share the recognition that people have different preferences for different types of sensory inputs depending on the subject being learned. It stands to reason, then, that if no two brains are identical, then different learning styles probably exist. At a minimum, MBE Science should recognize that information could be delivered in different forms—kinesthetic, visual, and auditory, and so on—to maximize possible retention.

Tenet 12: Differentiation. *Teaching Students Individually Enhances Learning*

Students' different intelligences and cognitive preferences, combined with their varying levels of knowledge and skills, justify differentiation in classroom practices. There are also hundreds of research articles that offer evidence in the literature analysis. A large number of the studies related to this tenet explain the importance of designing learning plans based on individual learner potential (Levine, 2000; Tomlinson, 1999). The vast majority of these studies come from the field of education (not neuroscience or psychology), though the premise of differentiation rests in the idea that no two brains are alike. Therefore, teaching and assessing students based on their potential is a basic tenet of MBE scientists.

It must be acknowledged, however, that most support for differentiation is practice-based rather than evidence-based, though it is convincing all the same and deserving of future research. Some very credible authors in education, such as Tomlinson and McTighe (2006), have joined forces to begin to explain how differentiated practice can be seen in design, in teaching, and in assessment of student learning, and their work points to important changes in the way we teach. For example, differentiation calls into question whether assessment and evaluation practices should change from the traditionally *product*-focused plan (an end test result), to a balance of *product, process,* and *progress* as suggested by Tucker and Strong (2005). This is an important evolution in evaluation.

SUMMARY OF THE TENETS

The 12 tenets found in the meta-analysis of the literature and supported by basic beliefs in MBE Science reflect highly individualized aspects of learning. Each tenet impacts learning but does so in different ways for each learner. What motivates (Tenet 1), stresses (Tenet 2), causes anxiety (Tenet 3) or depression (Tenet 4) is individual in nature but impacts all learners. How students react to their teachers' faces (Tenet 6) and voices (Tenet 5) is also individualized to a certain extent, but it is clear that these reactions impact learning. Physical movement (Tenet 7), laughter (Tenet 8), nutrition habits (Tenet 9), and sleep patterns (Tenet 10) are all related to physiological changes in the body that impact learning. Finally, an individual's learning style (Tenet 11) and the teacher's ability to differentiate planning, teaching, and assessment for different students (Tenet 12) can impact the quality of the learning experience. The 12 tenets are complemented by the 21 principles of MBE Science, which are described next.

CHAPTER 7

Principles:
Applying Universal Concepts
About the Brain and Learning
to Classroom Teaching

Principles are fundamental concepts upon which all activities and methodologies should be designed. In the best cases, all classes that adhere to MBE Science should apply the following principles. For the most part, the foundational principles of MBE Science are related to concepts that were deemed to be "well-established" or "probably so" and received vast support from the meta-analysis of the literature. Unlike the tenets, the principles are "universals"—that is, they are true for all learners and express fundamental aspects of the learning brain.

There are 21 principles in all, covering the gamut of human learning (see Figure 7.1). The principles can be divided into five broad categories:

1. Core beliefs
2. Survival skills of the brain
3. Attention and social cognition
4. Memory and learning processes
5. The mind versus the brain in the teaching and learning process

CORE BELIEFS

Principle 1: Each Brain is Unique and Uniquely Organized

This is based on the well-established belief that human brains are as unique as faces; while the basic structure is the same, no two brains are identical. Despite general patterns of organization in how different people learn and which brain areas are involved, each brain is unique and uniquely organized.

Figure 7.1. Principles in MBE Science

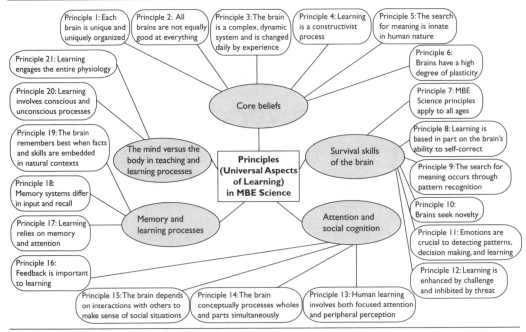

Source: Bramwell, 2009.

Some studies in this field are related to which aspects of learning are easy to generalize and appear to involve similar mechanisms across all learners. Some of the studies—such as those by McCann and Garcia (1999); Pelegrina, Bajo, and Justicia (1999); Thompson (1999); and Sohn, Doane, and Garrison (2006)—delve into the individual strategies used by learners to approach problems. The journal *Learning and Individual Differences* is a major source of information in this field. There are several studies that demonstrate how different people learn different skills, such as Korenman and Peynircioglu's (2007) work documenting differences in how people learn music. It should be noted that Principle 1 is elementary in the foundations of MBE Science, which justify a more individualized approach to teaching.

Principle 2: All Brains Are Not Equally Good at Everything

This is based on the well-established belief that all brains are not equal in their ability to solve all problems. Both context and ability influence learning. Context includes the learning environment, motivation for the topic of new learning, and prior knowledge. This means that expecting the same results for all students may be unreasonable. The idea that all brains are not equally good at everything goes against the optimistic ideals of the 1970s and 1980s, when teachers were taught that, with the right instruction (behavioral guidance), all children could reach the same levels of achievement (Skinner, 1974). Rather, this principle means that each child is born with a certain genetic learning potential, which can be maximized by good teaching techniques. In this sense, a teacher's role changes from being a behavioral modifier to being a professional who must diagnose the potential of each student and then design an individualized learning program to help that student understand his own strengths and weaknesses (Levine, 2000).

Other studies related to Principle 2 seek to confirm parameters set for "normal" versus "delayed" growth curves for certain skill acquisition. Among others, Miller and colleagues (2002) as well as Voelkle, Wittmann, and Ackerman (2006) have helped determine the broad parameters of "normal" from a neurological perspective, confirming observations in education and psychology. Principle 2 has strong implications for policies, especially those related to standardized teaching and grading as compared with individualized learning practices. Based on this principle, teachers are encouraged to know their students better and to apply differentiated teaching methods.

Principle 3: The Brain Is a Complex, Dynamic System and Is Changed Daily by Experiences

This is based on the well-established belief that the brain is a complex, dynamic, and integrated system that is constantly changed by experience, though most of this change is evident only at a microscopic level. The brain's complexity and the constant changes it experiences refute beliefs, prominent in the 1970s, that personality and intelligence are fixed by a certain age, instead supporting the current belief that learning can and should be a lifelong process.

This also confirms the dictum "Use it or lose it." This is supported by the belief that in terms of synaptic growth, the most active synapses are strengthened, while relatively less active synapses are weakened. Over time, this process shapes brain organization, as is extensively documented in the literature (e.g., LeDoux, 2003; Ortega-Perez, Murray, & Lledo, 2007). Neurons that are linked by continual firings demonstrate greater synaptic growth. Unused neural links may be pruned away (Sylwester, 1985). In this sense, the brain is extremely efficient in managing its resources. The areas that are used more get more in terms of building blocks, and the areas that are used less are reduced. This is important for learners of all ages because it reminds us that if knowledge is left unused, it will be lost. For example, many students go through mandatory foreign-language classes in high school yet find, as adults, that they can't recall a word they learned because the language has gone unused for so many years. The flip side is that continual training of the brain results in continued synaptic growth, even into old age, as Goldberg (2006) has shown. This principle has implications for lifelong learning guidelines.

Some work in this field (e.g., Fischer, 2007) make the link among physical brain changes, behavioral changes, and the implications for education. Other work establishes how and what changes occur in the brain based on new experiences (OCED, 2007). All these studies attest to the ever-changing state of the human brain and the physical changes that occur with new learning across the life span. Principle 3 influences instructional guidelines in that it reinforces both the developmental and constructivist approaches to teaching.

Principle 4: Learning Is a Constructivist Process, and the Ability to Learn Goes Through Developmental Stages as an Individual Matures

This is supported by the idea that a learner who actively constructs knowledge will be motivated and engaged in learning. This is also supported by the educational belief that humans construct meaning from existing knowledge structures. Such existing knowledge structures are individually defined. Additional evidence is found in thousands of studies in the literature. An understanding of the developmental construction of the world by children was introduced in the 1950s in the psychological context (Piaget, 1955) and the neuropsychological context (Berninger & Abbott, 1992), then expanded in the context of neuroscience (e.g., Mareschal et al., 2007; Restak, 2008). Some studies in this field relate to the linkage of constructivist processes and memory (e.g., Schacter & Addis, 2007). This principle illustrates the move away from behavioral theories of learning to the current cognitive-constructivist approach.

Constructivist processes have been linked to learning in educational circles for decades but have been very distant from the neuroscience literature. Good MBE scientists apply this principle by ensuring that new information is embedded in context and can be related to knowledge that the students already possess.

Principle 5: The Search for Meaning Is Innate in Human Nature

Humans are born to learn. The search for meaning is an inborn human need. This is supported by hundreds of works in the literature analysis showing that learning was necessary to survival in the evolutionary processes. If humans did not learn, the species would not survive. Human brain development demonstrates that learning is based on adaptation (e.g., Linden, 2007a; Maloney, 2004) and that the human brain is naturally programmed to learn as a survival function (Calvin, 1996). This principle has led some educators, such as Gunn and colleagues (2007), to promote the idea that there is a "natural" way to teach that is more in synch with ways the brain learns best, which may be contrary to some formal classroom structured learning.

This principle is important because it calls attention to the disconnect between traditional (passive, teacher-centered) classrooms and more modern pedagogical practices that celebrate student-centered, active learning. More research is needed to determine whether "natural" learning processes are antithetical to today's classroom settings and, if so, which aspects of formal classroom structure need changing. This principle has major implications for instructional guidelines, since maximizing student learning should probably be as "natural" as possible. Whether "innate" is equal to "natural" is a point for future research in MBE Science.

Principle 6: Brains Have a High Degree of Plasticity and Develop Throughout the Life Span

Though similar to Principle 3, Principle 6 emphasizes the physiological aspect of plasticity rather than the experiential aspect. Studies in this area explain plasticity, neurogenesis, and physical changes in the brain caused by aging; hormonal and physical changes in development; and what learning looks like in terms of synaptogenesis or neurogenesis (e.g., Benfenati, 2007; Bourgeois, 2001; Huttenlocher & Dabholkar, 1997; Martin & Morris, 2002). This is an important group of studies that reminds teachers that factors extraneous to classroom activities, such as aging processes, impact learning. Principle 6 both supports the idea of developmental learning processes and reminds teachers of learning factors that are invisible to the naked eye. Principle 6 has implications for policy structures related to lifelong learning programs. It also reminds teachers that the order of learning steps is more important than the age at which a skill is learned.

Principle 7: MBE Science Principles Apply to All Ages

This is supported by the well-established belief that human brains have a high degree of plasticity and develop throughout the life span, though there are major limits on this plasticity and these limits increase with age. It is further supported by the refutation of the idea that everything important in the brain is determined by the age of 3. That is, MBE Science principles are not restricted to the early years, or even to school-age learners, but apply across the life span. While all the principles are modified and/or have different limitations based on the age of the individual, in general learning should be viewed as a lifelong process.

Some of the studies in this category relate to differences in executive functions based on age (e.g., Holtzer, Stern, & Rakitin, 2004). Others show how early detection of certain structural malformations in the brain can predict learning problems (e.g., Molfese, 2003). Yet others have to do with the relationship between age and learning mechanisms or physical brain structures. This has clear social implications because people around the world are living longer and educational implications because older and older degree-seeking students are returning to the classroom. Good MBE scientists also use the principle that learning is a lifelong process to guide curriculum design. While there may be *sensitive* periods for learning some skills, there are no *critical* periods that limit opportunities to do so.

SURVIVAL SKILLS OF THE BRAIN

Principle 8: Learning Is Based in Part on the Brain's Ability to Self-Correct

The brain learns from experience through the analysis of data and self-reflection. This is based on the well-established belief that connecting new information to prior knowledge facilitates learning. In an interesting twist, this occurs because of both self-preservation (Calvin, 1996) and self-reflection (Bransford, Brown, & Cocking, 2003). Self-preservation means the brain corrects the actions it produces when the results of the actions are undesirable. Self-reflection means the brain self-corrects when it deems its actions emotionally or morally challenging or opposed to its belief systems. In both self-preservation and self-reflection, the brain learns as it corrects itself. Teachers need to be fully aware of the learning process that students go through so they can maximize their students' potential. The brain's ability to self-correct has strong implications for instruction and especially for assessment practices. Using a variety of assessment tools to evaluate students (as opposed to relying on a single grade) is one of the best methods teachers can apply in classroom, according to well-known authors in the area of evaluation such as Ronis (2007) and Wiggins & McTighe (2005). To take advantage of the brain's ability to self-correct, evaluations should be ongoing, basically formative, based on extensive feedback, and aimed at enhancing metacognitive learning processes (Popham, 2001).

Principle 9: The Search for Meaning Occurs Through Pattern Recognition

This principle means that the brain's continual comparison between what it senses and what it already knows aids learning. This is based on the belief that human brains seek patterns upon which they predict outcomes and that neural systems form responses to repeated patterns of activation (patterns being individually defined). This is also supported by examples and evidence from the meta-analysis. Pattern recognition is achieved by continually comparing new information with what the brain already knows. The brain then makes predictions about what it expects based on past experiences.

Some of the studies in this field relate to the physical changes that occur in the brain related to patterning (e.g., Fisher, 2005; Yan & Fischer, 2007) or how normal patterning can be interrupted (Japikse, 2002). Others relate to longitudinal studies demonstrating the overall growth pattern of brains, such as research on growing teenage brains (Thompson et al., 2000). This principle has vital implications for classroom learning. Most classroom practices are based on the belief that the brain learns from past experience. Principle 9 is fundamentally grounded in the constructivist philosophy; learners build their own knowledge by continually building new conceptual understanding on previously learned concepts.

Principle 10: Brains Seek Novelty

This is based on the belief that human brains seek and often quickly detect novelty (which is individually defined). This is also backed by thousands of studies in the literature analysis. According to research by Calvin (1996), Siegel (1999), and others, brains have evolved to detect fluctuations and change. This may seem contradictory to Principle 9—the idea that the brain seeks patterns—though they are actually complementary processes. While the brain searches for patterns, it is alerted to change by its thirst for novelty.

Some of the studies in this field have noted how early childhood experiences can influence the way novelty is interpreted in adulthood (e.g., Schwartz, Wright, Shin, Kagan, & Rauch, 2003). For example, Touyarot, Venero, and Sandi (2004) reviewed how stress can impact individual reactions to novelty. This principle has implications for classroom instruction. While some students may be positively stimulated by novelty, others may react fearfully and shut down their learning processes. Teachers who know that brains seek novelty can use this information to their advantage by varying classroom routines to create significant learning experiences.

Principle 11: Emotions Are Crucial to Detecting Patterns, Decision Making, and Learning

This is based on the well-established belief that emotions are critical to decision making and evidence from thousands of studies in the literature. Emotions are vital in learning as a whole. Descartes' belief that "I think, therefore I am" is modified by Principle 11 to be closer to "I feel, therefore I know" or, as Immordino-Yang and Damasio (2008) posited, "We feel, therefore we learn."

This principle challenges the belief that learning is primarily a rational and cerebral undertaking. Many of the works in this field are related to the neural mechanisms of emotion, both normal and abnormal. The impact of emotions on learning has only recently entered the evidence-based category of knowledge for teaching, as LeDoux (2008), a longtime expert in the field on emotions and learning, acknowledges. Some of the studies in this field are related to the normal development of emotions in human beings, while others consider the impact of emotions on self-regulation. Despite this principle's newness, the implications for the classroom are tremendous. The belief that when an emotion competes with a concept, the emotion almost always wins, as expressed by Sousa (2000), makes it clear that how students feel about what they experience in the classroom affects what they are able to learn. Instructional practice should be improved to take emotions into greater considerations.

Principle 12: Learning Is Enhanced by Challenge and Inhibited by Threat

This is supported by the belief that learning is enhanced by challenge and is typically inhibited by threat (in which threat is individually defined) and by a substantial amount of literature from the meta-analysis. Though this concept is logical at first blush—few people enjoy threatening situations or find them conducive to learning—what constitutes "threat" or "challenge" is relative to the individual, making the principle more difficult to apply. The basic premise relates to the definition of "good" learning environments, which are presumed to be filled with personal challenges and low threat levels. Research in this field studies the physical changes in the brain when it is under threat, as in the study by Compton, Heller, Banich, Palmieri, and Miller (2000) on changes in different hemispheres of the brain or the work on understanding how the amygdala identifies and labels different emotions by Fitzgerald, Angstadt, Jelsone, Nathan, and Phan (2006). Other studies relate to the link between threat perception and social interactions (e.g., Muris, Merckelbach, & Damsma, 2000). This principle has implications for teacher–student interactions in that it calls on teachers to reflect on their exchanges with students and to measure their perceived level of threat to the student. To apply this principle successfully, a teacher must know each student's individual measure of challenge and threat. To do this, a teacher must take the time to know her students well through dialogue and observation. Principle 12 is related to the pedagogical practices of differentiation in instruction and assessment.

ATTENTION AND SOCIAL COGNITION

Principle 13: Human Learning Involves Both Focused Attention and Peripheral Perception

The literature review documented thousands of studies to support this principle. Teachers demand that their students stay on task (focused attention), but they rarely take into account how students' peripheral perception is also constantly in play, dividing the brain's attention. Some of the research in this field is concerned with how attention itself is achieved by the brain, as with Holcombe and Johnson's (2005) work. Other studies, such as that of Rueda and colleagues (2004) explain the developmental process of attention. Many key studies relate to the overall consideration of attention and the brain (Posner, 2004) and the distinctions among varying attention pathways (Raz & Buhle, 2006). The majority of the studies in this field relate to the role of attention in learning or the role of attention during specific skill learning. Several studies relate to the way in which emotional states impact attention (e.g., Vuilleumier, Harmony, & Dolan, 2003) and the subsequent effects of attention on memory. Fernandes and Moscovitch (2000) looked at how attention and memory can become divided and how this disturbs information encoding, all of which makes long-term memory impossible and subsequently impedes learning. There are also a great number of studies related to abnormalities in attention mechanisms, as with attention-deficit disorder (ADD). Nigg (2005) has been a prolific writer in this field, concentrating on the link between neurology and psychology in tracking the roots of attention-deficit/hyperactivity disorder.

An understanding of the different aspects of attention has important implications for instructional practice. From the brain's perspective, what happens around a student is just as important as what is happening directly in front of her. In evolutionary terms, without peripheral perception (vision, sound, smell), human beings as a species might not have survived. When a child drifts off at the sound of voices behind him or gazes through an open window in the room, he is actually paying attention, just not the right kind for a classroom setting. It is important that teachers who apply good MBE Science practice take all the types of attention in the human repertoire into account.

Principle 14: The Brain Conceptually Processes Wholes and Parts Simultaneously

The literature strongly supports this principle. The basic idea is that the mind does not process input linearly in an orderly, first-come first-served fashion but rather is capable of processing whole concepts simultaneously. This has implications for teacher practices. Teachers need to be aware that students do not capture concepts in a step-by-step fashion; rather, they do so in epiphanies of linked concepts. Teachers should be aware that great insights, so called "aha!" moments, occur most frequently when all the pieces fall into place as a whole rather than as each individual step is completed.

Several studies supporting this principle relate to mental processing and larger learning concepts (e.g., Barsalou, Breazeal, & Smith, 2007; Yordanova, Falkenstein, Hohnsbein, & Kolev, 2004) and how the brain physically processes them. Other studies consider developmental processes and subject-specific conceptual processing. The greatest number of studies in this area concern whole and part conceptual processing of specific skills, such as reading and writing. A smaller number of studies focus on other skill areas, such as spatial learning, face recognition, musical processing, or how the bilingual mind processes information. Others relate to developmental processes of concept development.

A growing number of studies, related to the impact of normal processing time and instructional practices (Poppel, 2004), support the belief that giving students time to reflect on new concepts increases their ability to make more intelligent connections to concepts they already know. For example, a math instructor usually teaches the steps to a new formula in stages. However, the concept becomes clear to the student not as he processes the steps individually (parts) but rather when the larger concept the math formula represents is revealed (whole). Teachers should always keep in mind that it takes time to process all of the pieces into a larger whole. This processing produces those "aha!" moments when students "get it."

Principle 15: The Brain Depends on Interactions from Others to Make Sense of Social Situations

This principle is supported by the belief that is probably so according to the experts: Support (academic, moral, or otherwise) from others (often teachers, peers, or parents) is critical for optimal academic performance, which includes learning. Learning *cannot* be isolated from social contexts. There are thousands of studies in the literature providing evidence in favor of this principle.

For example, a significant number of studies have demonstrated how social support impacts learning, as illustrated by Bjorkman's work (2007), which examines the relationships among academic stress, social support, and internalizing and externalizing behavior in adolescence. This principle supports pedagogical concepts such as active, peer, or collaborative learning activities. Some studies relate to how social interactions can be structured within good school environments (Armstrong, 2006; Sylwester, 2003). Other studies focus on the broader concept of socialization and learning (Borich, 2006) or look at the connections among social cognition, neuroscience, and psychological principles of learning (e.g., Lieberman, 2007; Meltzoff & Decety, 2003). Some studies establish a clear link between what people think or believe about one another's intelligence and how that impacts what they are capable of learning (e.g., Levine, 2000; Mangels, Butterfield, & Lamb, 2006). Still other research looks at the learning of specific skills, such as math or reading, and how instructional practices can be influenced by social context. Other studies consider the developmental processes of social-cognitive growth and the physical structure of the brain and social cognition, including neural pathways and genetic makeup. Finally, there are numerous studies linking the function of mirror neurons and social cognition, as with Meltzoff's (2009) work on the foundations of social cognition. Research on mirror neurons as they relate to social cognition is sure to grow in the future.

This principle is based on the premise that humans are social creatures and that social interaction facilitates learning. When individuals share perceptions, they often change how or what they think. This has important implications for teaching because it encourages instructional practices that are adapted to integrate space for shared conceptual learning. In a historical sense, it is interesting to note that in practice this is fundamentally what the Socratic method is based upon—iterative questioning, or the constant "back and forth" between individuals, facilitates learning. Formal learning inherently takes place as a social exchange. More teachers need to be aware of this principle in order to enhance learning among their students.

Principle 16: Feedback Is Important to Learning

This is supported by the concept that feedback and meaningful assessment is important to human learning, though the importance and role of feedback vary greatly across domains and processes. This is also supported by hundreds of studies in the literature. The term *feedback* is used differently in educational circles than in neuroscience. In neuroscience, *feedback* or *feedback loops* refer to automated neural responses to stimuli, which lead to predictable actions (e.g., Jehee, Rothkopf, Beck, & Ballard, 2006). In neuroscience, some of the studies relate to the physical feedback mechanisms in the brain connected to sensory input. Other studies consider the operation of neural mechanisms during feedback (Willoughby, 2005).

In education, feedback is based on the premise that in order to improve learning, students need to know what they do not yet know. That is, when a student is guided toward recognition of her errors and is then given implicit or explicit direction as to how to correct them, she learns better: Moments of evaluation become moments of teaching. Many of the studies in this category make it clear that feedback is important for all age groups, not just for children. Adults, too, can benefit from formative evaluation. This has implications for teacher training, where the art of giving feedback is not usually taught.

MEMORY AND LEARNING PROCESSES

Principle 17: Learning Relies on Memory and Attention

This is supported by the belief that acquisition of declarative knowledge depends on both memory and attention. It is also supported by numerous studies in the meta-analysis and the formula that Memory + Attention = Learning. Though overly simple, this formula makes it clear that there is no learning without both memory and attention (*memory* is defined as in Principle 18 and *attention* is defined as in Principle 13).

Many of the supporting studies relate to the interactions between attention and memory, as shown in the work by Iidaka, Aderson, Kapur, Cabeza, and Craik (2000). This principle means that if either memory systems (e.g., long-term, short-term, emotional, social, etc.) or attention systems (focused or peripheral) malfunction, learning will be inhibited. This explains why students with ADD have such a hard time learning in traditional school systems (Denckla, 2005). This has important implications for instruction. Good MBE scientists are able to diagnose whether a student has trouble learning because of attention or memory problems—or for reasons directly related to the subject matter. Once this is diagnosed, good MBE scientists help students manage their learning challenges through appropriate methods.

Principle 18: Memory Systems Differ in Input and Recall

Different memory systems (short-term, working, long-term, emotional, spatial, rote) receive and process information in different ways, and that information can be retrieved through different neural pathways. This is supported by the beliefs that the rehearsal of retrieval cues aids in declarative memory processes and that the acquisition of declarative knowledge depends on both memory and attention. This is also supported by thousands of studies reviewed in the literature analysis. Because all declarative learning depends on long-term memory, this principle is key for MBE scientists.

For example, middle school language teachers may notice that some students have a great ability for creating metaphors but a poor ability for spelling. Both metaphors and spelling are aspects of language, but they occur in the brain through distinct neural pathways and therefore are learned, stored, and retrieved in often overlapping, but distinct, ways (see Kacinik & Chiarello, 2007; Tainturier, Schiemenz, & Leek, 2006). Similarly, Johnny may be great at geometry but miserably poor at algebra, as these skills share overlapping but distinct neural pathways. This means that a student may have strikingly different aptitudes in different sub-areas of different skills. Good MBE scientists know that if they achieve the input of information through several memory neural pathways, the likelihood of retrieval of that information is higher in the future.

The great majority of the studies relate to working memory, or how the brain moves information from short-term storage to long-term memory, where it can be used to build learning (e.g., Funahashi, Takeda, & Watanabe, 2004; Jonides & Nee, 2006). This is a vital group of studies for MBE scientists as processing time during working memory is often short-changed in the classroom setting. Teachers need to give students more time in class to reflect on new concepts. Other studies in this category relate to how infants store their first memories (e.g., Morasch, 2007) and how childhood memories are created (e.g., Edin, Macoveanu, Olesen, Tegnér, & Klingberg, 2007). Child and infant learning potentially impact future learning, and good MBE scientists should have an understanding how and why this occurs. Other studies relate to the improvement of memory, including mnemonic devises or exercises for classroom learning (e.g., Edin et al., 2007).

Some studies in this category are concerned with the neurotransmitters involved in memory, and others relate to the physical structures involved in memory, including the amygdala and hippocampus. Kalueff (2007) considered some global theories on how memories create our selves and the exact impact that biology and experience have on this process. Finally, there are significant contributions making the link among mind, memory, and learning, as in the works of Pickering and Phye (2006), Sylwester (1985), Walker Tileston (2003), and Wolfe (1996). All these studies are important for MBE scientists and have implications for instructional guidelines, which we will review in the next chapter.

Principle 19: The Brain Remembers Best When Facts and Skills Are Embedded in Natural Contexts

This is based on the belief that the human brain learns best when facts and skills are embedded in natural contexts or concrete examples in which the learner understands the problems she faces and recognizes how the facts and/or skills might play a role in solving that problem. It is also supported by evidence and examples found in the educational literature (e.g., in Fink, 2003).

Memory is improved by proper learning contexts, or contexts that are closer to "real life," as suggested by Given (2002). For example, students remember Newton's law of gravity better if an apple is dropped in front of their eyes than if a formula is written on a chalkboard. Placing facts and skills in context facilitates memory processes, as these memories are embedded in real-life experiences. While this sounds like a logical assumption, there are many concepts that must be learned out of context. For example, the order of the planets in the solar system is difficult to teach in its natural context. Despite this, students learn the planet order, usually by means of rote memorization. This demonstrates that while brains may learn best when facts and skills are embedded in natural contexts, this is not imperative for learning to occur. This principle seems logical to good teachers, and it should also be more widely taught in teacher training programs.

THE MIND VERSUS THE BRAIN IN THE TEACHING AND LEARNING PROCESS

Principle 20: Learning Involves Conscious and Unconscious Processes

Sometime we are aware (conscious) of our learning, and at other times we are unaware (unconscious) of our learning. While all teachers know that learning involves conscious processes, the mechanisms of unconscious processes are much less clear to most. Two ways that learning occurs unconsciously are in the unconscious perceptions of voices and faces and during sleep.

As mentioned earlier, the human brain judges others' faces and tones of voices for threat levels in a rapid and often unconscious way, influencing the way information from these sources is perceived (e.g., valid, invalid, trustworthy, untrustworthy, etc.). This was explained in an earlier part of the book and will not be repeated here (for details, see Chapter 3).

Second, sleep is important for declarative memory consolidation (though other types of memories, such as emotional memories, can be achieved without sleep). This means that sleep deprivation has a negative impact on memory. Studies in the literature related to sleep and to different levels of consciousness and learning mechanisms, such as those by Hobson and colleagues (Hobson, 2004; Hobson & Pace-Schott, 2002; Hobson, Pace-Schott, & Stickgold, 2000), show that learning does indeed occur at different levels of consciousness. While none of the studies in the meta-analysis suggest that people learn new knowledge in their sleep or while hypnotized, several clearly define the role of REM (rapid eye movement) sleep in the consolidation of both declarative and procedural memory (e.g., Stickgold, 2005). That is, sleep plays an important role in attention (through a rested mind and body) as well as memory (through the release of certain neurotransmitters), both fundamental elements in learning.

Some of the studies focus on specific age groups, their sleep patterns, and the impact of sleep on learning, such as with adolescents (e.g., Carskadon et al., 2004). Other studies relate to the neurobiology of sleep (e.g., Hobson & Pace-Schott, 2002) as well as the physical structures involved in the sleep–memory link, especially the hippocampus (Best, Diniz Behn, Poe, & Booth, 2007). Yet other studies consider changes in the brain that affect the body as a result of sleep deprivation (e.g., Copinschi, 2005; Durmer & Dinges, 2005; Miller, 2004). Other studies related to sleep deprivation show its link to poor decision making and its potential impact on both social and academic functioning (e.g., Killgore, Blakin, & Wesensten, 2005).

Sleep research related to learning is a relatively new area of study and calls attention to the way the brain uses different levels of consciousness in its learning processes. Teachers should be aware that students who pull all-nighters to study for an exam are less likely to remember the information in the long term than those who pace their studying and get a good night's sleep (Pace-Schott &

Hobson, 2002). Because many of the numerous learning processes are outside of the influence of teachers, a close alignment of home practices and school expectations is imperative to maximize a child's learning potential.

The conscious and unconscious processes of learning demand further research. It is apparent that learning is, indeed, impacted by various levels of consciousness. This has tremendous implications for policy. Should teachers be trained to control facial expressions and voice inflections? Should schooldays begin later for adolescents? Should schooldays be rearranged to meet human learning needs rather than the social demand to get students to school before parents have to go to work? These questions and more must be addressed by administrators if we are to maximize student learning.

Principle 21: Learning Engages the Entire Physiology (the Body Influences the Brain and the Brain Controls the Body)

This is supported by four beliefs: Nutrition, sleep, stress, and water intake all impact learning. It is also supported by thousands of articles in the literature review, including evidence that nutrition (e.g., Liu, 2004), sleep (e.g., Stickgold, 2005), and exercise (e.g., King, 1999) all influence the brain's potential to learn.

Some studies are related to the impact of exercise on specific skills, such as reading (e.g., Reynolds, Nicolson, & Hambly, 2003). Other studies look at the overall general benefit of exercise on learning in formal academic programs (e.g., Dwyer, Sallis, Blizzard, Lazzarus, & Dean, 2001). Additional studies relate to the long-term impact that exercise can have on brain plasticity (e.g., Cotman & Berchtold, 2002) and the overall health of the brain. This principle has implications for educational policy as well as for parental monitoring roles in education. Though nutrition, sleep, and exercise originate in the home, their impact is felt in the classroom. The evidence in this category makes it imperative that good MBE scientists help parents and students understand the devastating impact that poor nutrition, bad sleeping habits, and/or lack of exercise can have on learning potential.

SUMMARY OF THE PRINCIPLES

All 21 principles have important implications for classroom instruction. These 21 core concepts of MBE Science point to fundamental elements that define the parameters of the new learning model. All the principles are firmly and equally rooted in neuroscience and pedagogical research, and most also have significant psychological studies behind them. While this and preceding chapters have offered numerous examples of the implications of scientific findings for teaching, in the next chapter we turn to what is perhaps the most practical section for new and old teachers alike: how the tenets and principles translate into clear instructional guidelines.

CHAPTER 8

Ten Instructional Guidelines in MBE Science

Combined, the literature, the expert survey, the tenets, and the principles point to ten explicit instructional guidelines. These instructional guidelines should be evident in all MBE Science activities and can serve as a reference point for scientifically substantiated practice (see Figure 8.1). Each of these guidelines is described briefly below.

INSTRUCTIONAL GUIDELINE 1: ENVIRONMENTS

Broadly defined, good learning environments in education are those with physical and mental security, respect, intellectual freedom, self-regulation, paced challenges, feedback, and active learning (Billington, 1997). *Physical and mental security* means that students feel that their classrooms and schools are protected and that they have no fear of humiliation from peers or teachers. *Respect* should be mutual between teachers and students, students and students, teachers and teachers, as well as between all members of the school's support staff. *Intellectual freedom* implies a learning environment in which all students feel free to share beliefs without fear of ridicule or reprimand. *Self-regulation* means that at least some of the activities are student-directed or chosen by the student. *Paced challenges* are new tasks that are introduced gradually and ensure stages of success along the way to final completion. *Feedback* means constant formative assessment to and from teachers and students. *Active learning* includes activities in which the students participate in lively discussion and are given the chance to structure aspects of their own knowledge discovery. Good learning environments also include what Geoffrey and Renate Caine (2001) call "relaxed alertness." Incorporating relaxed alertness into instruction means creating "good stress," whereby students are paying attention but do not feel anxiety.

Figure 8.1. Instructional guidelines in MBE Science

Source: Bramwell, 2009.

Experienced teachers know that good learning environments are made, not found. MBE scientists acknowledge the importance of creating good learning environments and thus design their classroom interactions around this knowledge. This begins with modeling and requiring respectful exchanges between students and the teacher, a class assessment of what students already know, a clear vision of what they need to know to learn the material well, and the design of learning activities that are student-centered and dynamic.

Over 17,000 documents on learning environments can be found in an educational journal search, over 5,000 in a psychology journal search, and over 2,700 in a medical journal search. (It should be noted that good learning environments are not the same as "enriched environments," but rather relate to the impact that different types of settings have on the brain and learning.) This group of studies considers the relationship between environments and the ensuing changes in brain structure based on effective classroom practices. Some of the studies supporting this instructional guideline also relate to learning environments and the individual nature of how environments are perceived (e.g., Lindblom-Ylänne & Lonka, 1999).

This guideline means that the elements of good environments should be evident in every classroom activity. Many teachers begin the schoolyear by asking their students to come up with their own list of rules that would create a good environment, and it is surprising how many students will identify *security, respect, intellectual freedom*, and *self-regulation* on their own. Teachers can then focus on creating learning experiences that are neither too easy nor too hard (*paced challenges*), offering constant formative assessment (*feedback*), and designing work that is student-centered and dynamic (*active learning*). Once teachers have designed good learning environments, they can turn their attention to designing coursework that has both sense and meaning.

INSTRUCTIONAL GUIDELINE 2: SENSE, MEANING, AND TRANSFER

Many of the documents in this field relate to the pedagogical concept of "sense and meaning," which Sousa (2000) describes as putting learning into context within the learner's world—a concept that others simply call "transfer." That is, students learn best when what they learn makes sense, has a logical order, and has some meaning in their lives. It is hard to convince students to learn things they feel are irrelevant to their lives. This piggybacks on the principle that the brain remembers information best when facts and skills are embedded in authentic experiences (natural contexts).

A focus on sense, meaning, and transfer means good MBE scientists make the attempt to link school knowledge with life experiences. For example, a sixth-grade math class can examine "shapes" from real-life contexts before launching into geometric terms. The students can first create geometric shapes with construction paper, and then use them to build a replica of their neighborhood. The teacher can then ask how many squares (cubes), triangles (cones), rectangles (cubes), and circles (cylinders) they can find. After these shapes are clear, she can then ask how much building material they would need based on the calculation of area and how much living and commercial space is in each building based on the calculation of volume. The children grasp the basic concepts of geometric shapes, area, and volume as they contemplate the architecture of their own neighborhood.

Teachers who try to link what is taught in class with applications to the students' lives are more successful. This requires not only knowing the subject matter but also knowing the students. Understanding student needs can be achieved only through a clear assessment of prior knowledge and appreciation of the culturally based neural network (knowledge) they bring with them to class. Teachers can also think of this guideline as the "so what?" principle: The teacher thinks about the activity he has planned and imagines the entire class looking back at him and asking, "So what?" When the teacher can respond with a reason for doing the activity that resonates with the students, then he has achieved both sense and meaning and thus potential transfer.

INSTRUCTIONAL GUIDELINE 3: DIFFERENT TYPES OF MEMORY PATHWAYS

MBE scientists are aware of the different types of memory and use this knowledge to design learning experiences that store memories in a variety of ways in order to increase the likelihood of recall.

Much of the research in MBE Science relates to differing memory systems and their impact on learning. Good MBE Science teachers appreciate the complex nature of memory and understand the vital link between memory and learning. One way to take advantage of the different memory systems is to vary classroom activities. Different modes of instruction take advantage of different sensory pathways in the brain. Teachers should teach to auditory, visual, and kinesthetic pathways as well as allow for both individual and group work in order to improve the chances of recall.

Additionally, MBE scientists acknowledge that long-term memory can take one of three basic forms. Long-term memory is associative, is emotionally important (value-laden), or has survival value. Associative learning activities link past knowledge with new information. For example, a teacher can help students understand new information about the structure of a question in French by associating it with the structure of a question in English. Likewise, an instructor can teach division by reminding students of how it relates to multiplication. Emotionally important, or value-laden, memory is highly individualized; it is what the student himself gives importance to. For example, rather than teaching a history lesson full of dates and facts about far-off characters, a teacher might play on students' values about "loyalty" or "honesty" to explain choices made in history. Finally, humans learn things that help them survive. People remember not to put forks into electric sockets because they risk a shock. In the school context, "survival" may also take the form of avoiding failure by passing an exam.

It is important for teachers to remember that they can facilitate the development of long-term memory by instigating forced recall sessions. In the old days, these took the form of "pop quizzes," and students either passed or failed. A more modern version is to give the pop quiz (full of questions about the key concepts of prior classes) and then to correct it in class with the whole group. This fulfills several objectives. First, it gives students a form of immediate feedback about their level of conceptual understanding in the course. Second, it reminds students of what key concepts they are responsible for knowing. Third, it means the teacher does not need to take time to grade the work. Most importantly, "jarring" a student's memory in this way leads the student himself to begin to develop a "habit of mind" about how to store and retrieve important information. As we have seen throughout this book, memory and attention are close allies in learning.

The next instructional guideline relates to how teachers can help students pay better attention in class.

INSTRUCTIONAL GUIDELINE 4: ATTENTION SPANS

Thousands of studies in the field relate to attention spans. Many teachers can attest to the fact that the average student has an attention span between 10 and 20 minutes. This implies that students learn best when there is a change of person (from teacher to student, for example), place (a change of seat, for example), or topic (a conceptual refocus, for example) at least every 20 minutes. Unless students are highly intrinsically motivated, it is difficult for them to stay focused for long. This can be remedied to a certain extent if the teacher allows students to raise their hands and ask questions during the lecture, but even this is often discouraged by some who request that students "save questions until the end." The lecture format is convenient for the presenter, but it is not necessarily efficient for the receiver. There are many theories about why student attention spans are so short, some of which were discussed in the section on plasticity in an earlier chapter. One modern theory relates to how the plastic brain adjusts itself to what it is exposed to most; short attention spans may be related to the rapid changes in video games, which take up the majority of some children's time. These games "prime" the brain for shorter attention blocks, making attention in school settings weak. Many MBE scientists recognize that attention spans are likely related to the amount of energy needed to concentrate, which is finite. Experienced teachers know that students also need "downtime" to reflect on new information in order to maximize memory consolidation. This downtime is directly related to improved metacognitive abilities. This means it is imperative that moments of intense concentration be balanced with reflection time about the content knowledge. One way to allow for reflection is by asking students to write down questions at the end of a new information period. Other teachers ask different students to contribute to a summary of the information they were just exposed to. These activities create the space for reassessing the information, identifying gaps in content, giving clarifications, and allowing the students to make their own links to the information.

Interest impacts attention spans and, consequently, the motivation for learning. Teachers can improve attention spans by taking the time to get to know their students and by playing on their interests. For example, a computer teacher can take advantage of her eighth-grade students' entrepreneurial spirit by having them create an Excel spreadsheet for a business rather than simply testing them on a series of commands. The adage "time flies when you're having fun" is based on attention spans. Students who enjoy their work stay focused for longer periods of time.

Attention spans are also related to what is known as primacy-recency. Humans remember best what occurs first, second best what occurs last, and least what occurs in the middle. Attention as an instructional guideline means good MBE scientists teach within the attention spans of their students. These teachers understand that students have limited attention spans, which vary by individual, subject matter, and activity. To take advantage of attention spans, teachers should minimize passive activities, which can easily bore students.

Teachers are faced with a student body that appears to have shorter and shorter attention spans. Whether television, the "I want it now" generation, or video games cause this, student attention is at a premium. It is harder to be a teacher than it used to be because we now know that grabbing a set of notes from last year and lecturing for an hour is an inefficient way to teach. We now know that we need to spend time designing classroom experiences that engage the learners. Though it is harder to do this, it is also far more satisfying, because we now have the assurance that students are retaining more knowledge when we respond to their attention spans. Another way we can improve our instructional practice is to take advantage of the social nature of learning.

INSTRUCTIONAL GUIDELINE 5: THE SOCIAL NATURE OF LEARNING

The brain is a social organ, and people learn best when they are able to "grow" ideas and "bounce" concepts off of others. There are hundreds of documents in the field related to the social nature of learning. Teachers who understand that learning often occurs in social contexts, such as classrooms, realize that it can often be enhanced through social interaction, as in student group work or discussions. Good MBE professionals structure teaching activities that encourage active exchanges of perceptions and information. As mentioned earlier, debate, which has been popular since the time of the ancient Greeks, is one of the most effective teaching methods. Debate forces students to think critically and to interact with each other; it also prepares them to deal with countering opinions. All of these skills are useful not only for exploring concepts in the school context but also for surviving in the world.

Another social activity is small-group work, which requires a few students to interact collaboratively to produce new findings. Sometimes both students and teachers bemoan this process, as it is inevitably inequitable— one person always ends up doing more work than others. One way to look at this is that managing differing ability levels is important in life, and school is a safe environment for this type of experimentation. Another way to look at this is that teachers can facilitate a better balance of student contributions through creative assessment tools through which all group members are given the chance to grade each other. This gives learners the chance to make it clear who has contributed what to the group process.

The social nature of learning means that teachers should structure classroom activities that encourage social interactions, orchestrating them in such a way as to encourage maximum participation and thus allow students to construct their own learning. This can be a challenge, since it always takes less work to prepare a lecture class than it does to design an interactive activity. However, students retain more new information and learn better when they engage in social learning.

Teachers who apply the social nature of learning instructional guidelines realize that the various personalities we come across in class should be seen as an opportunity to trigger new learning experiences by combining these personalities in the right way. Teachers are often tempted to let students choose their partners for group activities. However, managing the groups is part of the teaching process. Depending on the objectives of the lesson, the teacher may want to have similar-ability learners working together. In other cases, the teacher may want to group learners of different ability levels in order to encourage peer teaching.

> Peer teaching involves students learning from and with each other in ways which are mutually beneficial and involve sharing knowledge, ideas and experience between participants. The emphasis is on the learning process, including the emotional support that learners offer each other, as much as the learning itself. (Boud, Cohen, & Sampson, 2001)

There is evidence that when learners of different ability levels are grouped together, all benefit. Ironically, the one who benefits the most is the student who knows the most. This is due to the fact that the best way to learn is to teach.

INSTRUCTIONAL GUIDELINE 6: THE MIND–BODY CONNECTION

The basic premise of this instructional guideline is that students' brains learn best when the needs of the body are met, as we saw in earlier chapters. Many of the documents in this field relate to the mind–body connection. The body impacts the mind, and the mind controls the body. This includes active learning techniques and a reminder to students about the importance of sleep, nutrition, and physical exercise.

In practical terms, this means that teachers themselves should be well versed in the ways that nutrition, sleep, and exercise impact learning and should try to serve as examples to their students. This is a complicated guideline to implement because many choices, such as what to eat or what time to go to bed, are in the hands of parents, not teachers. Teachers should call both student and parent attention to lapses of concentration that might be due to poor mind–body balance. Administrators and policy makers who have an influence on school start times and on cafeteria choices should also seriously consider this guideline.

Teachers can apply knowledge of the mind–body connection to their instructional practice by explicitly teaching students about how certain food choices or bedtimes can give them an edge. Many students are unaware that their choice of beverage can lead to peaks and valleys in their attention spans, for example. And while many students might feel the effects of staying up late to study, few actually understand that they are not really doing themselves any favors because the information is not being consolidated for long-term recall. Armed with this knowledge, many students self-correct damaging behaviors.

INSTRUCTIONAL GUIDELINE 7: ORCHESTRATION AND "MIDWIFING"

A significant number of the documents in the field relate to the concept of "orchestrated immersion," a term coined by the Caines (Nummela-Caine & Caine, 1994; Nummela-Caine, Caine, McClintic, & Klimek, 2008), or "midwifing," first suggested by Socrates (470 B.C.–399 B.C.). In orchestrated immersion, teachers in MBE Science are similar to an orchestra director who immerses students in complex experiences that support learning by calling on individuals one by one to bring out their voices and then weaving them into a single class experience. Teachers must integrate different gifts and help each player perform to their best abilities for the good of the group. MBE scientists understand the social nature of learning and not only allow but also encourage students to work together and exchange ideas. Teachers who carefully plan the structure and form of each class in a way that takes advantage of each student's knowledge and that compensates for student weaknesses are more successful in their practice. Socrates suggested that teachers are like midwives, whose job is essentially to help students give birth to their own understanding.

Teachers who accept that their classrooms will be filled with different types of students, with different brain content from different past experiences, and with different preferences for ways to receive new information will be not only more productive but also less frustrated. Successful teachers will consider these differences to be an opportunity and will create interactions that integrate the strengths and weaknesses of the learners. It is impossible to integrate the abilities of different learners if you don't know them. This means picking up on all of the cues students provide us in class. When given the chance, students are normally very eager to let us know who they are.

INSTRUCTIONAL GUIDELINE 8: ACTIVE PROCESSES

This is one of the oldest educational concepts: Human brains learn best when they are active (i.e., "I hear and I forget. I listen and I understand. I do and I remember"). In the pursuit of active learning, teachers do not rely on passive experiences but rather design learning experiences that demand the active participation of the students. Good MBE Science professionals understand that to be engaged, learners need to be involved. Such involvement often combines activity with reflective processing. Teachers who know when and how to integrate active learning experiences in the classroom enhance learning potential.

Active learning techniques have progressed from being a fad (Best, 2006) to experiencing decades of results, which are now confirmed by some studies in neuroscience and psychology. Several characteristics are associated with students in active learning classrooms: Students are involved in more than passive listening, display higher-order thinking skills, engage in activities that put less emphasis on information transmission and greater emphasis on developing student skills, are encouraged to explore attitudes and values, and receive immediate feedback from their instructors (Bonwell & Eison, 1991). Teachers who apply active processes take the time to design significant learning experiences that require students to act on their own knowledge. This means teachers not only help students acquire knowledge of their subject; they also show them how to put that knowledge into action in order to develop skills. Students cannot "own" knowledge without clearly seeing how it is applied.

INSTRUCTIONAL GUIDELINE 9: METACOGNITION AND SELF-REFLECTION

Teachers who incorporate activities that stimulate metacognition increase the overall conceptual grasp of new knowledge. This means teachers allow time for reflection about the concepts being taught and create spaces to "think about thinking." There are thousands of psychological and educational articles and hundreds of documents in neuroscience on metacognition. Part of metacognition is based in reflection. While students need to be active, they also need the "downtime" provided by metacognitive reflection to consider new information in order to maximize memory consolidation. This means teachers need to allow time for metacognition during class and to assign homework that requires the use of metacognitive skills. One example of such an activity is to reserve the last five minutes of class for a metacognitive activity, such as journal writing or end-of-class reflections or questions about the subject matter, both of which encourage higher-order thinking skills. Teachers can help students improve their metacognitive skills by guiding their development of habits of mind that encourage reflection.

Barbara Presseisen (1999) suggests that one way to encourage meta-cognition and higher-order thinking skills is to develop a "habit of skepticism." This means that teachers should cultivate in students a questioning attitude about information and guide them to become critical consumers of data. This is done by constantly asking students, "Where did the information come from?" Students should constantly ask themselves: What biases could the source of the information have? How credible is this source? What other viewpoints are there on this topic? These types of questions guide students toward a better understanding of what they consider "good" information and why. Such reflection elevates general thinking skills and creates meta-cognitive practices, which mean students become more critical thinkers.

The final instructional guideline relates to learning throughout the life span. All of the previous tenets, principles, and instructional guidelines apply to all ages.

INSTRUCTIONAL GUIDELINE 10: LEARNING THROUGHOUT THE LIFE SPAN

As proven in the meta-analysis of the literature through thousands of articles in neuroscience, psychology, and education, people can and do learn throughout the life span. It is useful for teachers to know about "normal" skill achievements at different ages, though this should not become an impediment: Developmentally appropriate age-related activities should be milestones and benchmarks, not roadblocks. Sensitive periods in brain development mean that some skills are learned more easily at certain times, but these are not critical periods during which windows of opportunity close if they are not taken advantage of.

Teachers should view learners as lifelong candidates for new knowledge. Human brains have a high degree of plasticity and continue to develop throughout the life span. Teachers in MBE Science also know that human learning is achieved through developmental processes, which follow a universal pattern for most skills, including academic skills shared across literate cultures, such as reading, writing, and math. This means that there are sensitive periods (*not* critical periods) in human brain development during which certain skills are learned with greater ease than at other times.

Teachers can take advantage of this instructional guideline to teach skills at an appropriate time, based on the characteristics of the learner. Nonetheless teachers should understand that there are wider windows for learning than previously thought. In practice, this means that teachers should resist the temptation to label students who don't meet the standard developmental milestones. Rather, they should provide remedial activities to help the student fill in the gaps in knowledge that may exist in order to help the student advance and fulfill his own potential.

For example, if a student is reading below grade level, a teacher can take several steps to help. First, in order to preserve the student's self-esteem, the teacher should let that student know that different people advance in different skills at different paces. Second, the teacher should diagnose which aspect of reading is slowing the student down. (Does he have adequate phonemic awareness? Does he understand the basic grammatical structure? Is he missing key vocabulary? Can he read haltingly or fluently? Does he understand what he is reading, or is his comprehension of the content weak?) Third, once both the teacher and the student understand the area of reading that is pulling the student down, then they can begin to work together on improving that subelement of reading through extra exercises. The teacher needs to be sure the student understands that he can improve, but only with effort; the student's willingness to do better is crucial to improvement.

Learning throughout the life span also means that knowledge can be acquired into old age. People can and do go back to school later in life and have been very successful. Nola Ochs became the world's oldest college graduate at age 95, and at age 96 Bernard Herzberg is the oldest living student in England (he is pursuing a doctorate degree). Kenya's Kimani Nganga Maruge was 84 when he became the world's oldest student to enroll in primary school. These examples are testament to the human ability to continue to learn into old age given proper stimulation. All of these older students attributed their healthy mental states to leading active lives in which they always kept their minds busy. They are an inspiration as well as a source of evidence for this instructional guideline.

SUMMARY OF THE INSTRUCTIONAL GUIDELINES

The ten instructional guidelines, in the context of the tenets and principles explained earlier, form the parameters around which MBE Science is constructed. Unlike brain-based learning as represented in the popular press, all of these foundations are built on solid evidence and teachers can have full confidence in them. To explore how teachers can continue to scrutinize information in the most efficient way possible, we turn to some tools to help us evaluate the quality of new sources of information.

CHAPTER 9

How Do We Distinguish Good Information from Bad in MBE Science?

The speed with which knowledge is produced these days makes it impossible for anyone to know all there is to know in his or her field or profession, especially a new one like MBE Science. Individuals can only hope to learn how to think critically in order to gather as much information as possible, analyze it, make the necessary inferences, and act accordingly. According to Hurd (1960, Introduction), society today is characterized by "too many facts, too little conceptualizing, too much memorizing, and too little thinking." A definition of critical thinking can be constructed as follows: "Critical thinking is the ability to analyze facts, opinions, presentations and manifestations; synthesize, generate, organize and express complex ideas; defend opinions, perspectives and beliefs; make comparisons and references; evaluate arguments; and resolve problems in creative and thoughtful ways" (Chance, 1986, p. x).

In its highest form, critical thinking is fundamental to the development of the individual as well as to his contributions in society. Without citizens prepared to think critically, unscrupulous media sources can manipulate opinions, charismatic but unintelligent leaders can convince the masses of wrongs, and society stagnates. Critical thinking is also fundamental to human learning. Not all learners are critical thinkers, but all critical thinkers are learners. Critical thinking is perhaps one of the most prized individual qualities in today's world.

The primary way that teachers can judge proven information from unproven is by applying critical thinking skills. Tools exist that can support critical thinking skills. We will first look at the steps involved in thinking critically and then look at tools that facilitate judgment about the quality of information in MBE Science.

CHARACTERISTICS OF A CRITICAL THINKER

Every critical thinker embodies certain basic characteristics. Nine of these characteristics are described below, as suggested by Paul (1992), Facione (2004), and Tokuhama-Espinosa, Sanguinetti, & Guerra (in press).

Intellectual Curiosity

Intellectual curiosity is an unending sense of wonder and awe at the world, which is evidenced by ceaseless questioning of oneself and one's surroundings. This is something that small children innately demonstrate and that adults must maintain if they are to seek out new opportunities, challenges, and ideas over the course of their lives in order to grow. Facione calls this the trait of inquisitiveness and the concern to become and remain well informed.

Intellectual Courage

Intellectual courage is the same as challenging norms, questioning authority, and knowing when to doubt. Adolescents do this as they defy authority figures in order to define their own thinking. Unfortunately, adults sometimes lose their willingness to challenge ideas with which they disagree. Intellectual courage requires fair-mindedness on the part of the learner, tempered with prudence in judgment about when and how to express this doubt to authority figures.

Intellectual Humility

Intellectual humility is the ability to say, "I don't know the answer." The acknowledgment that no one is owner of the truth is a vital trait of a critical thinker. Facione calls this open-mindedness—the consideration of all options before forming a decisive opinion.

Intellectual Empathy

Intellectual empathy is the ability to see issues from a variety of perspectives and to understand and appreciate others' reasoning, without feeling obliged to agree with them. Children are often asked, "What would *you* feel like if you were Johnny and someone hit you?" However, adults lose this facility unless it became habitual during childhood and often do not take the time to consider contrasting views or contradictory opinions. The most convincing arguments are those formed with opposing views taken into consideration.

Intellectual Integrity

Intellectual integrity is honesty with oneself and others. When individuals fail to hold themselves or others to a high degree of truthfulness, then acts of dishonesty occur. In the academic world, this can manifest as plagiarism; in politics, as corruption; and in everyday discourse, as half-truths or lies.

Intellectual Generosity

Intellectual generosity is the willingness to share knowledge with others. Colleagues who pass on interesting articles to each other know that the dictum "knowledge is power" has been exchanged for the formula "1 + 1 = 3"; sharing ideas breeds greater insights than does hoarding.

Intellectual Perseverance

Intellectual perseverance is refraining from the temptation to stop at the first available source that agrees with your perception. To truly exhaust all possible resources when seeking information about a topic, one must display tenacity of spirit. In practical terms, this means sticking with the critical thinking process even though it might seem tiresome or overwhelming. If perseverance is not learned as a child, it is a challenge to acquire as an adult.

Faith in Reason

Faith in reason is a belief in a methodological or scientific process that will yield results with credibility. This means adopting a process of gathering and analyzing information and retrieving and accepting the results, even if they are not what one expected to find. This does not mean blindly accepting information, but it does mean being critically tolerant of unexpected results. This implies self-confidence in one's ability to reason.

Just Action

Acting justly is the willingness to act on findings while having the disposition necessity to consider unexpected or unanticipated outcomes. For example: *If* humans cause global warming, what can one do to contribute to a solution? *If* we see child learning does not differ from adult learning except in degree of critical thinking, then how can we guarantee that we exploit all levels of learning to their greatest extent? This implies a willingness to revise. Action must follow analysis: Without it, critical thinking is a philosophical exercise with little pragmatic application.

Individuals who display intellectual curiosity, courage, humility, empathy, integrity, generosity, and perseverance, while demonstrating a faith in reason and acting justly by displaying the disposition to consider improbable outcomes, embody the characteristics of critical thinkers. If as MBE scientists we display each of these characteristics, then we are closer to ensuring that we use quality information. But each characteristic presumes certain actions, and for this reason we now turn to the process of critical thinking itself.

THE CRITICAL THINKING PROCESS

Critical thinkers always use at least eight steps in processing new information.

Step 1. Unite All the Information

Gather all of the information possible to make necessary choices. To a small child playing house, this means knowing who else is playing and what other people's priorities will be, acknowledging the problem of the day, and being able to identify the available props and resources. This is also what the leader of a country does before making decisions about budget priorities, the waging of war, and other national decisions of major consequence.

Step 2. Understand All the Concepts

Once the other players and resources are gathered, a critical thinker ensures he understands all the terms being employed. This includes defining core concepts, as in defining "playing house" to mean acting out scenarios of how real people relate when they live together, which can involve a myriad of activities, including shopping, cleaning, cooking, sleeping, going to school, and so on. A world leader needs to do much the same: He must assess all the other players involved, their roles, and the resources he has available to make decisions.

Step 3. Ask Where the Information Comes From (Biases)

A good critical thinker understands where information comes from in order to know whose perspective influences the accompanying values and thinking. A child will take a comment from the "daddy" in a different way than he would from the "baby sister," just as a world leader would take the opinion of a factory worker in a different way from a lawyer when contemplating a new labor law.

Step 4. Analyze the Source of Information (Credibility)

Strong critical thinkers assess the sources of the information before they believe it. The "robber" who tells the child to "lend" him the television set will be treated differently from the "best friend" who asks the same, just as the world leader will believe one head of state more than another, depending on the history of their relationships.

Step 5. Doubt the Conclusions

Independent of the end result, a good critical thinker contemplates alternatives. The small child whose "mother" says there is no money to buy candy will ask why she can't go to the bank or what she spent the money on instead. In a similar vein, the world leader will seek out alternatives to the recommendation of "inevitable" choices, like going to war or cutting certain budgets, if he is a good critical thinker.

Step 6. Accustom Oneself to Uncertainty

Good critical thinkers entertain new possibilities and do not limit themselves to scripted outcomes. Children playing house are often overheard saying, "OK, let's say you did this instead, OK?" World leaders who apply critical thinking take advice from a variety of sources and are prepared to entertain unexpected ideas in order to achieve the best possible outcome.

Step 7. Examine the Whole

After all the information is gathered, biases checked, credibility verified, and options analyzed one by one, good critical thinkers take a step back and judge whether or not they are missing anything. The child playing house who is preparing for her "daughter's" birthday party will see that the house is clean, the guests invited, the gifts bought, and the cake made. The world leader examining the whole will review the problem and its likeliest solution and then ask himself whether the solution is still appropriate after all has been considered.

Step 8. Generate New or Distinct Ideas/Information

Good critical thinkers produce novel approaches to old problems. The small child who is told by "daddy," "mommy," "brother," and "sister" that there is no money for a new bike "builds" one from available resources. The world leader who is advised to do A or B takes the best of these two options and chooses to do C instead. Creativity is part of critical thinking at all levels, in all degrees, and is evident from small children to adults.

The various steps in the critical thinking process—uniting all the information, understanding all the concepts, asking where the information came from (biases), analyzing the source of information (credibility), doubting the conclusions, accustoming oneself to uncertainty, examining the whole, and then generating new or distinct ideas/information—are habits of mind that small children become familiar with and adults should refine throughout their lifetimes. This is especially needed of MBE professionals if we are to ensure that we are using high-quality information.

THE ROLE OF REFLECTIVE SKEPTICISM IN CRITICAL THINKING

All levels of critical thinking can and should be enhanced by what Brookfield (2005) calls "reflective skepticism" (p. 7). Reflective skepticism calls for all information to pass through the filter of doubt, independent of how good the source of the information appears. Reflection enhances the quality of thinking, but it is a process that takes time, which is often the reason it is skipped in many people's thinking. Those who manage to incorporate reflective skepticism into their thinking patterns are rewarded by exceptional insight, including transformative learning.

Mezirow (1991) considers reflection to be an integral part of transforming the learner. He breaks down reflection into that which occurs in the world, that which occurs on a metacognitive level, and, perhaps most importantly, that which is associated with our assumptions and their origins in past experiences. By understanding where, how, and why we assume certain things, we are able to identify our own biases in information as well as those of others. This is a call to being conscious of the habits of mind we help children form.

Critical reflection is essential in the classroom. For example, teachers often give a test to evaluate whether students have mastered a certain type of information. When the exams are corrected and returned, the teacher usually moves on to the next topic. A more effective way to teach would involve the missing step of reflection. Students need to know what they don't already know. By asking students to return to the problems that were originally answered incorrectly and to correct them in class or, better yet, by asking them to determine themselves which answers were wrong (e.g., "Two of your answers are incorrect. Can you figure out which ones were wrong?"), then correct them, we encourage them to reflect and deepen their learning through critical thinking.

Reflection is "downtime" away from explicit teaching, which allows for better processing of concepts. Teachers who cultivate critical thinking in their students explain new concepts and then provide the space and time for reflection, resulting in greater student recall of those concepts in the future. Such a guided activity hopefully becomes self-regulated over time. This is a crucial piece of the critical thinking puzzle—and an important one for teachers who are evaluating claims of brain-based teaching.

How does skeptical reflection apply to the MBE practitioner? As teachers face choices about which information to believe, they should think not only reflectively but also skeptically. Why should I believe this? What is it about my own experiences that give me reason to believe (or reject) this information? Good MBE scientists quickly progress through the stages of critical thinking, using their perspective as advanced or master thinkers to evaluate information. These stages are explained below.

THE STAGES OF CRITICAL THINKING

Elders and Paul (1996) suggest that critical thinking progresses in six stages:

Stage 1: The Unreflective Thinker
Stage 2: The Challenged Thinker
Stage 3: The Beginning Thinker
Stage 4: The Practicing Thinker
Stage 5: The Advanced Thinker
Stage 6: The Master Thinker

Unreflective Thinkers are unaware of the role that thinking plays in their own decisions. Challenged Thinkers are aware of thinking in their own decision making but do not yet know how to improve it. Beginning Thinkers start to explicitly take charge of improving their own thinking. Practicing Thinkers have a sense of how to improve their thinking and work toward its improvement. Advanced Thinkers have good thinking processes and habits and continually improve their own decision-making abilities. Master Thinkers have not only mastered their own thinking processes but are continually refining these processes and improving them.

Critical thinking is more like writing than speaking: Whereas speaking is a natural human skill that some argue is innate (Hauser, Chomsky, & Fitch, 2002), writing develops only with explicit teaching and practice. Unlike learning to speak, critical thinking skills must be cultivated, if not taught outright. Elder and Paul (1996, p. 40) believe that "the thinking of students will remain 'invisible' to them unless they are supportively challenged to discover the problems in their thinking"—that is, unless they arrive at a metacognitive understanding of their own levels of thinking, they do not advance from one stage to the next. Their view is that these stages are best achieved when led by reflective questioning. Elder and Paul's stage theory has strong implications for the view that human learning occurs on a continuum, from novices to experts in critical thinking.

The steps to critical thinking are vital for judging information in the field of MBE Science. Aside from the activities mentioned above, there are two specific tools that can facilitate critical thinking.

TOOLS TO JUDGE THE INFORMATION

The simplest way to judge the quality of information in the new field of MBE Science is to remind ourselves to think critically when we hear of a new methodology. In addition to critical thinking, there are at least two other ways that proven and unproven information can be distinguished in MBE Science. The first tool was introduced in Chapter 2 when we talked about the beliefs and neuromyths table. If we remember to adhere only to concepts that are "well established" or "probably so," and avoid those that are "neuromyths," then we are also assuring ourselves of quality information. Additionally, we can remember to apply the tenets, principles, and instructional guidelines at all times.

Second, on an institutional level, societies and organizations are entrusted to publish quality information in their peer-reviewed journals and to sponsor teacher training forums and conferences in which good information is shared. According to the Delphi panel members, there are only a handful of organizations that are qualified to judge the information in MBE Science at present. If teachers find that they are under too much time pressure to sift through the information themselves, then they should look for seals of approval from organizations that are charged with judging the quality of information in the new discipline. According to Figure 9.1, there are few organizations that are prepared to judge the quality of information in MBE Science because such organizations should have cross-disciplinary training, be formed by professionals from the new field or the three parent fields (neuroscience, psychology, or education), and have formal society rules and a peer-reviewed journal to back them.

According to the Delphi expert panel, the organizations that can be entrusted with generating good information include the following:

The American Educational Research Association (AERA)
Australia's Neurosciences Australia Ltd (NSA)
British Oxford Cognitive Neuroscience Education Forum
France's INSERM (French National Institute of Health and Medical
    Research)
Japan Research Institute of Science and Technology
The British Neuroscience Association
The Dutch Science Council (NWO)
The International MBE Society (IMBES)

Figure 9.1. Who should judge the information in the emerging field of MBE Science?

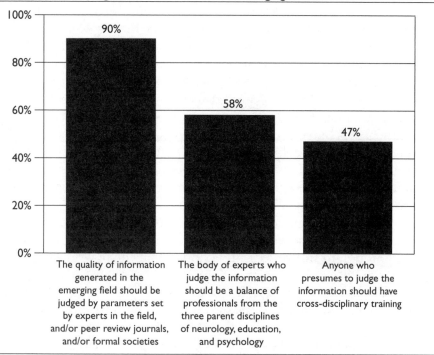

The Mexican Society for the Neurosciences
The National Institute of Child Health and Human Development
The Oxford University Institute for the Future of the Mind
The Pontifical Academy of Sciences
The RIKEN Institute in Japan
The Society for Neuroscience

Further research, plus the simple test of time, will determine which other organizations are qualified to judge the quality of the information in the emerging field. For now, we know that information published or produced by the organizations listed above will most likely be of high quality. It also means that these organizations can be counted on to pass good judgment on the quality of information from journals, Internet sources, and books in the popular press.

SUMMARY OF THE TOOLS

Proven information can be distinguished from unproven in MBE Science with at least three different tools. First, teachers should remember to apply good critical thinking skills when considering new information and to maintain a habit of skepticism as they consider new methods. Second, the four-point continuum of information that is "well established" to "probably so" to "intelligent speculation" to "neuromyths" should be used as a guide, as should be the instructional guidelines found in this book. The people who research, produce, and use the information from the emerging field should be armed with this basic set of guidelines. Finally, information can be judged on an institutional level. There are organizations and societies that can be trusted to give (or take away) the seal of approval on claims about teaching methods. Thought leaders in MBE Science who use strict criteria by which they judge the information run these societies and organizations. This means that the teaching methods they approve of are most likely of quality.

Determining proven information from unproven in MBE Science is a complex task. Individuals have to be vigilant, and organizations must be thorough in this process. It is hoped that the new tools presented here will provide a useful structure for judging the quality of information in the new discipline. To find quality information often requires tenacity and the ability to resist the promises of brain-training miracles that are marketed to teachers. Each professional in MBE Science is responsible for helping teachers identify the best sources possible as well as for denouncing false claims. For example, it is important to note that websites rarely identify the primary sources for their claims. This leaves judgment about the quality of the information up to the individual web surfer. The great majority of websites are managed by private individuals, not by credible organizations, schools, or universities (though these do exist). This means that it is nearly impossible to check the credibility of online information. About half of websites were found to offer good information, while the other half often offer "easy fix" methods, which are claimed to be "brain-based" but which do not provide evidence to back this. Easy-to-access sources, such as the Internet and books in the popular press, provide a mixed bag of resources, some of which stand up to the tough criteria of MBE Science and others of which fail miserably. Each teacher has a responsibility to elevate the level of information used in our field.

Having looked at ways in which we can become more critical consumers of information, we will now look at ways the field of MBE Science can continue to grow and improve.

CHAPTER 10

Improving the Field and Moving Forward

The new field of MBE Science is intriguing, dynamic, and full of promise. It is clear that the information in MBE Science helps teaching, but there are still many ways to improve the field. This chapter will consider ways in which this can occur and offer suggestions to guide each of us in gauging our own contributions in this movement.

WHAT CAN YOU DO?

Institutions as well as individuals can help to improve the new academic discipline of MBE Science and, in doing so, improve teaching as a whole. What can you and I work on, starting today, that will help move the field forward as well as improve our practice? We return back to some of the core concepts shared in Chapter 1 to explore steps that we each can take to better our practice as teachers willing to become MBE scientists.

Improve Transdisciplinary Thinking

To move the field forward, it would be helpful if each teacher would agree to approach education from a multidisciplinary angle. Thinking across disciplines is a key quality of MBE specialists. This means looking not only to neuroscience and psychology to nurture education but to other academic disciplines as well. As teachers, we should always seek evidence from as many other fields as possible to create scientifically substantiated support for our art of teaching. Related to transdisciplinary thinking is the power of synthesis. Synthesis is the ability to take ideas that come from many different fields and perspectives and to understand how they are related. Gardner (2007) writes about the need for the mind of the future to be able to synthesize and judge the quality of information that currently exists in the world. There is so much information that bombards individuals on a daily basis (in MBE Science and otherwise) that teacher training should include explicitly taught skills about how to "sort the wheat from the chaff," as suggested by the James S. McDonnell Foundation (2005). Eisenhart and DeHaan (2005) build on this idea by explaining how doctoral learners should be trained to become scientifically based educational researchers. To do this, teachers need to learn to identify quality information.

Remember that "everything that can be counted does not necessarily count; everything that counts cannot necessarily be counted" —Albert Einstein

Einstein's comment is a reminder that simply reducing the art of teaching to a cold, clinical science, or "biologizing" educational practice, is not the solution, as Brown and Bjorklund (1998) noted in their own research. Using measurable scientific data is not the only way to gauge student learning or evaluate successful teaching. Moving forward in MBE Science does not mean rejecting teacher intuition; rather it means finding ways to explain it in empirical form. Some of the best practices in classroom settings have yet to be confirmed by science (Howard-Jones, 2007). MBE scientists' role is not to reject these practices but to help establish where such practices fall on the OECD continuum and to communicate this to teachers. How can this be done? If all professionals in MBE Science always remembered the maxim *do no harm* before undertaking research, practicing their trade in classrooms, or designing policy, then the field would be in better hands. It may, indeed *do harm* if MBE scientists "throw out the baby with the bathwater" by rejecting everything in educational practice that cannot be proven by neuroscience.

Avoid Overgeneralization of Findings

In many cases, "breakthroughs" about the brain are refuted almost immediately by "exceptions" found by other scientists. For example, in the early years of MBE Science, it was popular to talk about right-brain and left-brain activities, only to have dozens of studies published shortly thereafter demonstrating that such oversimplification was shortsighted and full of exceptions, meaning that we as teachers have work to do to match our peers in other respected professions. Irresponsible communicators tend to overgeneralize a single fact (e.g., no two brains are alike), and promote neuromyths (e.g., right- and left-brain learners). It is disconcerting that over generalizations are found most commonly in books in the education field, not in psychology or neuroscience. We are all responsible for the quality of information in the field, and this begins with teacher training institutions that should not accept questionable sources of information as the basis for thesis work.

This points to important implications for education programs and teacher training: All educators need to be acquainted with the tenets, principles, and instructional practices of MBE Science as well as the beliefs and myths continuum, not only those who are affiliated with the new discipline. This is not presumptuous; it is simply being responsible to students. To work on all of the areas mentioned above, it is clear that teachers, neuroscientists, and psychologists need to share more information and communicate better. This can be done in a number of ways.

Improved Communication and Research

By working together and exchanging viewpoints on topics, individuals can promote interdisciplinary communication as well as identify greater areas of common ground. Teachers need to reach out to psychology and neuroscience, and vice versa, to create better dialogue. As demonstrated in the literature review, only about half of the websites that are easily found through search engines are valid sources of information. Individuals should take it upon themselves to improve the level of quality information easily available to teachers.

MBE Science is a new and imperfect field. To grow and improve—including a continual refinement of the field's goals and its eventual contributions to improvements in society—the leaders in the emerging field need to be active advocates. This includes keeping a critical eye on the balance between learning and teaching sciences and the balance among neuroscience, psychology, and education in research. This hinges on improved communication among the parent fields.

But each of us has a job as well. We must each remember to think in a transdisciplinary way, never forgetting that both the art and the science of teaching have merit. We also have to harness our own enthusiasm for findings and avoid overgeneralizations by maintaining a healthy level of skeptical criticism. We need to improve teacher training and better document our own practice through action research. We need to seek out opportunities to publish our findings and, at a minimum, share them within our own school districts in order to encourage debate and discussion. In this way, we will continually raise the bar for others and ourselves and improve the level of education available to our students.

NEXT STEPS IN THE FUTURE OF MBE SCIENCE

The Teacher Practitioner

In a thoughtful letter to the editor of *Nature*, Daniel Ansari (2005b) applauded the introduction of neuroscience into the classroom and made specific recommendations for how this should occur: "it is now essential to begin integrating the teaching of scientific evidence from cognitive neuroscience into teacher training and further education programmes. This would facilitate the creation of a 'research-practitioner' model of the field of education" (p. 26). Such a model is beginning to emerge, as exemplified by the National Science Foundation initiative in which the actual application of neuroscience to classrooms is considered. This is also seen in the structure of formal teacher education programs in MBE Science, such as that of the University of Texas at Austin, Harvard University, Oxford University, Cambridge University, and similar programs at the University of Southern California and Dartmouth. It is predicted that these types of programs will grow exponentially as parts of educational programs around the world. Hopefully, this will also expand to educational psychology programs and educational neuroscience programs around the world as well.

Curriculum

The ultimate utility of MBE Science will be measured by its successful application in real classrooms with real students. Therefore, the immediate future of MBE Science rests on an evaluation of programs that claim to adhere to principles and instructional guidelines in the field. Specifically, reading programs such as Fast ForWord (Scientific Learning Corp, n.d.) and RAVE-O (Wolfe, Barzillai, Gottwald, Miller, Spencer, Norton, Lovett, & Morris, 2009), which were developed by neuroscientists and have been applied in classrooms, should also be placed on a continuum similar to the beliefs and neuromyths table in order to be judged for quality and adherence to MBE Science standards. This also means that specific curriculum suggestions for math during "neuronal recycling" (Dehaene, 2004) as well as other topics are rich areas for future comparative research. Finally, global learning theories, such the Universal Design for Learning (UDL), which is based in research on diversity, brain-based learning, multiple intelligences, and the flexibility of digital media (Rose & Meyer, 2006), should also be measured against the criteria of standards in MBE Science. One possible tool to achieve this could be use of the table aligning the OECD categories with the Best Evidence Encyclopedia and the What Works Clearinghouse, as suggested by Briggs (2008) in Chapter 2.

Neuroethics

Combined with acceptance of the new field of MBE Science will come more words of caution. Calls for neuroethical decisions will increase as the proper use of information about individual brains becomes more publicly available. There will be increased calls for stands to be taken about memory-enhancing drugs, the benefits and potential drawbacks of scanning students' brains for "defects," and the responsibilities that teachers and parents have for the proper care of children's brains (Illes, 2005; Sheridan, Zinchenko, & Gardner, 2005). All of these ethical issues will pose challenges to practitioners in the future. The fields as a whole will have to reflect on these issues, as will each individual professional in the discipline.

Consultancy and Training

In the future there will be a proliferation of new and improved teacher training programs based on MBE Science concepts. Unlike many previous programs, however, these will be held to higher levels of scrutiny and judged by the empirical evidence supporting their tenets, principles, and instructional guidelines. Training that is not backed by science will fall into oblivion. The field of MBE Science itself will begin to self-regulate and will rein in false prophets, and the general level of common knowledge shared in the field will grow.

Practice

The "easier" aspects of MBE Science, including the timing of classroom activities to maximize attention, physical reminders to parents about diet and sleep, and attempts at differentiation, will soon be applied in many classrooms. Soon to follow will be the "harder" aspects, including planning that takes advantage of the brain's plasticity and conscious learning to link new concepts to learners' past experiences. It is likely that more progressive private institutions or maverick public institutions will take the lead, since they have greater autonomy in their teacher training and curriculum designs.

FUTURE DEVELOPMENT

In a visionary statement over a decade ago, Robert Sylwester (1997) said, "I think . . . there will some day be a new researcher who will translate all of this into educational theory that will affect teaching and learning, and I think it will support such practices as integrative and cooperative learning, the arts in education, and the importance of the humanities" (p. 3). Others in MBE Science acknowledge that the movement toward better classroom practice is already under way. This is a shift away from traditional strategies toward classroom activities that are based on MBE Science concepts.

In terms of development, in the near future the field will mature as better imaging techniques become available and methods for studying the brain improve. Currently, the young field of MBE Science is sprinkled with studies on how the brain best learns to read, do math, conceive of music, and conduct higher-order thinking, among other skills. These sparse testimonies will grow in number as well as quality as technology evolves and becomes less costly. Neuroimaging will become common, even in low-budget universities, instead of being reserved for prestigious research institutions. As a result, there will be a proliferation of graduate studies, which will add quantity to quality in MBE Science studies.

It is anticipated that better brain-imaging techniques will allow for improvements in many areas. Some of these developments include (1) more personalized reading and writing strategies, which will become available as a larger number of studies document individual differences; (2) increased differentiated assessment in schools based on evidence that each child's brain is unique; (3) increased educational software production, which will take advantage of knowledge related to attention spans; and (4) parental insistence on better teacher management of positive school learning environments. The next 5 years will likely be decisive for the field.

FINAL THOUGHTS

Over 20 years ago, after writing a treatise establishing the foundations of the cognitive sciences, Howard Gardner wrote the conclusion to *A Mind's New Science*. If the word *cognitive* is replaced with *Mind, Brain, and Education*, Gardner's conclusions mirror the state of MBE science in 2010:

> How much further [MBE] science can proceed, and which of the competing visions it will choose to pursue, are issues that remain open. All who style ourselves as [MBE] scientists are on the spot. If we heed the lessons entailed in our scientific history and lurking in our philosophical backgrounds, if we attend to but are not stymied by the reservations aired by shrewd skeptics, if we recognize the limitations of all inquiry but do not thereby encounter a failure of nerve, there are clear grounds for optimism. (Gardner, 1987, p. 392)

We must approach the future of MBE Science with this same optimism. Every one of us who envisions being a part of MBE Science is on the spot at this point in history. If we can remember that "everything that can be counted does not necessarily count; everything that counts cannot necessarily be counted" when we conduct research, and remind ourselves to *do no harm* as we teach our classes and design our research policy, we will inch forward in fulfilling the goals of the new discipline. If we continually encourage the pursuit of neuroscientifically substantiated beliefs founded in educationally inspired research questions, the results of which have potential application to educational practice, we will become more responsible members of this learning community. If we can increase our intellectual humility as individuals as well as members of different parent disciplines, then we will enhance the communication among fields and be able to work toward the common goal to reciprocally connect research with practice on processes of learning and teaching. If we can learn to broaden our appreciation of studies found across academic fields and to "connect the dots" between ideas, we will be able to see the larger concepts and establish a working understanding of the dynamic relationships among how we learn, how we educate, how the brain constructs new learning, and how the brain organizes and processes information.

There are a lot of *ifs* in the future of MBE Science. The future of the emerging field depends on a great many variables, but it also enjoys the benefits of an enthusiastic membership. MBE Science is an internationally conceived, interdisciplinary science. As such, it is privy to an intellectual base that is broader than that of any branch of neuroscience, psychology, or education in existence today. MBE Science also enjoys a leadership that not only fulfills the entire *if* scenarios above but established them in the first place. Many of these leaders participated in the Delphi panel that helped construct the parameters offered here. This leadership will provide the guidance necessary for the field's maturation, which will in turn inspire further membership that shares the goals of the field.

Finally, the greatest predictor of success lies in the motivation for the field's conception in the first place: the student. A day does not pass in which we are not reminded of the role of education in human economic, social, and intellectual development. There is no greater impetus for research, practice, or policy than the students in our classrooms. How can we teach to maximize each learner's potential? Better teaching is the single greatest reason for MBE Science, and it provides the crucial energy and optimism needed to advance the field.

Terms That May Be Encountered in Further Reading in Mind, Brain, and Education Science

Acetylcholine: A neurotransmitter associated with memory that activates muscles; a major neurotransmitter in the autonomic nervous system.

Action potential: A measure in excitable cells that indicates the transfer of knowledge; often referred to as a nerve impulse, spike, or the "firing" of the membrane.

Active learning: Discovery learning in which the proponent of the learning is the learner herself (as opposed to the teacher); often includes physical movement.

Affect and learning: The interaction between feeling or emotion and learning.

Amygdala: Almond-shaped groups of neurons (one in each hemisphere) located in the medial temporal lobes and part of the limbic system; related to the processing of emotional memory.

Angular gyrus: Brodmann area 39 located in the parietal lobe; involved in language and cognition.

Anxiety and learning: The interactions among the physiological, cognitive, somatic, emotional, and behavioral states that impact on learning.

Attention and learning: The cognitive process of selectively concentrating on a single aspect of one's surroundings while ignoring other things.

Authentic assessment: Evaluation methods that measure significant learning experiences; often mentioned in contrast to typical multiple-choice tests.

Axon: A long, slender projection of a nerve cell, or neuron, that conducts electrical impulses away from the neuron's cell body.

Basal ganglia: A group of nuclei in the brain interconnected with the brainstem, thalamus, and cerebral cortex; related to motor control, cognition, emotions, and learning.

Behaviorism: A philosophy of psychology in which learners are analyzed through the experimental analysis of their behaviors.

Brain development: The cellular and molecular mechanisms by which the nervous system emerges throughout life.

Brainstem: The lower part of the brain, adjoining and structurally continuous with the spinal cord.

Broca's area: Area in the brain associated with language processing, speech or sign production, and comprehension; located in the inferior frontal gyrus of the left frontal lobe.

Cerebellum: Area of the brain related to sensory perception, motor control, equilibrium, attention, and motor learning; located in the inferior posterior portion of the head.

Cerebral cortex: Gray matter of the brain enveloping its surface that plays a role in memory, attention, perceptual awareness, thought, language, and consciousness.

Cerebral hemispheres: The two regions of the brain that are united by the corpus callosum and delineated by the body's median plane (left hemisphere and right hemisphere).

Chunking of information: Strategy in cognitive psychology and mnemonics in which more efficient use of short-term memory is achieved through recording of information.

Cingulate gyrus: An integral part of the limbic system in the medial part of the brain; involved with emotion formation and processing, learning, memory, and executive control.

Cognition: Thinking: Information processing.

Cognitive development: A theory in cognitive psychology that concerns the growth of intelligence, which for some means the ability to accurately represent the world and to perform logical operations on representations of concepts, grounded in interactions with one's surroundings.

Cognitivism: A psychological approach to understanding the mind that supposes that mental functions can be understood through scientific methods.

Consciousness: A state of subjective experience that involves thoughts, sensations, perceptions, moods, emotions, dreams, and an awareness of self.

Constructivism: A theory of learning in which new knowledge is built on past experiences.

Cooperative learning activities: The purposeful mixing of often-heterogeneous groups of students for the purposes of enhanced learning experiences.

Corpus callosum: A structure connecting the right and left cerebral hemispheres that is the largest white-matter structure in the brain; responsible for interhemispheric communication.

Cortex: The outermost layer of the brain, divided into motor, prefrontal, visual, and cerebellar regions.

Cortisol: A hormone normally associated with stress.

Critical period: A limited time during which an event can occur, usually resulting in transformations or changes in behavior.

Critical thinking (higher-order thinking skills): Mental processes of analysis, evaluation, discernment, interpretation, inferences, and self-regulation; considered by many to be one of the most important goals of education.

Declarative knowledge: Awareness and understanding of factual information about the world; often considered knowing *what* in contrast to knowing *how*.

Dendrites: The branched projections of a neuron that conduct the electrical stimulation received from one neural cell to the cell body of another.

Differentiated instruction: Individual instructional strategies based on the needs of diverse learners.

Direct instruction: Explicit teaching methods, including lectures.

Divergent thinking: Thought processes or a method of thinking resulting in idea generation, creativity, problem solving, or innovation.

Dopamine: A hormone and neurotransmitter related to cognition, motor activity, motivation and reward, inhibition, sleep, mood, attention, and learning.

Ecological validity: A form of validity in a study or experiment in which the methods, materials, subjects, and settings of an experiment must approximate the real-life situation that is under study.

EEG (electroencephalograph): A brain-imaging device to measure the electrical activity produced by the brain, which is recorded by electrodes placed on the scalp.

Emotional intelligence: The ability, capacity, or skills to perceive, assess, and manage one's emotions.

Emotions and learning: See *Affect and learning*.

Encoding: The process of transforming information from one format to another.

Endorphins: Polypeptides (resembling opiates) produced in the pituitary gland during exercise, excitement, and orgasms that result in a feeling of happiness.

Episodic memory: Memories that refer to events, times, places, and their associated emotions.

Equilibrium/disequilibrium: Systems in which competing influences are balanced or in which a dynamic working balance exists among interdependent parts.

Event-related potentials (ERPs): Brain-imaging technique that measures the electrophysiological response to a stimulus related to thought or perception.

Executive functions: Cognitive control in which the brain processes thought and behavior in accordance with internally generated goals; often known as the "control center" of the brain.

Experiential learning (hands-on learning/discovery learning): Inquiry-based learning.

Explicit learning: Making meaning from direct experience.

Explicit memory: The conscious, intentional recollection of previous experiences and information.

fMRI (functional magnetic resonance imaging): Brain-imaging technique that measures the hemodynamic (blood flow and oxygenation) responses related to neural activity in the brain or spinal fluid.

Formative assessment: A self-reflective process in which feedback is used by the learner for improvement.

Frontal lobe: Part of the brain located at the front of each cerebral hemisphere; related to executive functions.

Good learning environments: Situations in which a student feels secure and respected, has a degree of self-regulation, experiences paced challenge, and active learning, and receives feedback.

Gray matter: See *Cerebral cortex.*

Habituation: A type of nonassociative learning in which increased repetition of a stimulus results in a progressive decline of behavioral response.

Hippocampus: Part of the forebrain located in the medial temporal lobe and belonging to the limbic system; plays a role in short-term and working memory as well as spatial navigation. Also associated with long-term memory consolidation.

Hormones: Chemical messengers that carry signals from one cell to another.

Imagery: The invention or development of mental representations in the mind to reflect experience.

Imitation: A behavior in which an individual replicates another's actions.

Impact of self-efficacy on learning: An understanding of how a teacher's belief that he is able to execute the actions required to teach impacts his learning.

Implicit learning: Unannounced and sometimes passive learning experiences in which exposure to information results in learning (as opposed to overt, explicit, or active learning processes).

Inhibition, memory: The ability not to remember irrelevant information, which is an effective aspect of functional memory.

Innate: Inborn.

Interference theory: A theory of forgetting; certain things interfere with the recall of others.

Learning by teaching: Classroom activity in which the student-as-teacher structure improves the learning process. Based on Seneca's idea that "by teaching we are learning."

Learning styles: Methods of teaching in which an individual's particular learning preferences are taken into account.

Levels-of-processing framework: Memory recall of stimuli as a function of the depth of mental processing.

Limbic system: The name for the joint reference to the hippocampus, amygdala, anterior thalamic nuclei, and limbic cortex; related to emotions, behavior, and long-term memory.

Long-term memory: Memory stored as meaning that can last from a few days to decades, differing structurally and functionally from working memory and short-term memory; related to the natural forgetting process.

Long-term potentiation: The long-lasting enhancement in communication between neurons that results from simultaneous stimulation.

Memory consolidation and learning: The process by which information, which enters short-term or working memory, is crystallized into long-term memory.

Metacognition: Awareness or knowledge of one's own cognitive processes and the use of self-awareness to self-regulate these cognitive processes.

Mind, Brain, and Education Science: The scientifically substantiated art of teaching, or the confirmation of best pedagogical practices with studies on the human brain. It has roots in cognitive neuroscience and is sometimes called educational neuroscience, neuroeducation, and, in the popular press, brain-based learning.

Mirror neurons: Neurons that fire both when a human or an animal acts and when it observes the same action performed by another.

Motivation: The reason(s) for engaging in a particular behavior.

Motor cortex: Area of the cerebral cortex involved in planning, control, and execution of voluntary motor functions.

Myelin: An electrically insulating layer that surrounds the axons of many neurons and is responsible for the increased speed with which impulses propagate.

Negative transfer of knowledge: The applicability of knowledge to a new domain in an incorrect fashion.

Neural network: Circuits of neurons.

Neurobiology: The study of cells of the nervous system and the organization of these cells into functional circuits that process information and mediate behavior.

Neurochemistry: A branch of neuroscience devoted to the study of chemicals.

Neuroeducation: See *Mind, Brain, and Education Science*.

Neuroethics: A subcategory of bioethics related to neuroscience.

Neurogenesis: The process by which neurons are created.

Neuron: Excitable cells in the nervous system that process and transmit information.

Neuroplasticity: Refers to the changes that occur in the organization of the brain as a result of experience.

Neurotransmitter: Chemicals that are used to relay, amplify, and modulate signals between neurons.

Occipital lobe: The visual processing center of the brain located in Brodmann area 17.

Optimal tomography: The newest brain-imaging technique that uses light to measure brain activity.

Parallel processing: The ability of the brain to simultaneously process incoming stimuli.

Parietal lobes: Area of the brain superior to the occipital lobe and posterior to the frontal lobe that is responsible for sensory information related to spatial sense and navigation.

Peptides: The links between amino acids.

PET (positron emission tomography) scan: A nuclear medicine imaging technique that produces a three-dimensional image or map of functional processes in the body or brain.

Prefrontal cortex: The anterior part of the frontal lobes of the brain, lying in front of the motor and premotor areas implicated in planning complex cognitive behaviors, personality expression, and moderating correct social behavior.

Primacy-recency effect (serial position effect): Recall accuracy is highest for items presented first and last, then for those presented in the middle.

Priming: A teaching technique by which a stimulus is used to sensitize students to a later presentation of the same stimulus.

Problem-based learning activities: A student-centered instructional strategy in which students work together to find a collaborative solution to a common problem.

Procedural knowledge (memory): The knowledge of how to perform some task.

Reasoning: The cognitive process of looking for beliefs, conclusions, actions, or feelings, often by using introspection.

Retrieval, information: Memory recall.

Scaffolding: Helpful interactions between instructors and learners, or between children who have different levels of knowledge about a topic, that provide sufficient support for achievement.

Schema: A mental structure that represents an individual's view of the world; an organized network of knowledge devised in abstract mental structures.

Self-concept: The way in which one views oneself, based in terms of self-assessment of feelings.

Self-directed learning: An instructional practice in which the learner is given latitude to structure (in part) his own didactic experiences.

Self-efficacy: Belief that one is capable of performing in a certain way and/or of attaining certain goals.

Self-empowerment: Personal self-image or transformation in which one feels capable.

Semantic memory: Memory of meanings, understandings, and other concept-based knowledge unrelated to specific experiences.

Sensitive period: Important periods in childhood development related to the acquisition of certain abilities.

Sensory store (short-term store): See *Short-term memory*.

Serotonin: A neurotransmitter in the central nervous system that plays an important role modulating anger, aggression, body temperature, mood, sleep, sexuality, and appetite.

Short-term memory: Memory that holds sensory input for a few seconds.

Social cognition: How people process social information based on existing mental schemas.

Social-emotional learning (SEL): An instructional practice designed to use social interaction and emotional connections to information to enhance learning experiences.

Standards: Parameters that (1) define common terminology accepted in the field; (2) determine the rules for evaluating quality information; (3) confirm how producers, users, and receivers are defined and how they are treated.

Stimulus: Something that incites to action or exertion or quickens action, feeling, or thought.

Student-centered learning: Educational approach in which the student is the protagonist of the learning activity.

Student motivation: Reason(s) behind student behavior, often based on needs (including acceptance, food, desired object, goals, state of being, or ideas).

Summative assessment: Evaluation that refers to assessment of the learning and summarizes the development of learners, normally at the end stage of instruction.

Synapses: Specialized junctions through which neurons signal to each other and to non-neuronal cells, such as those in muscles or glands.

Synaptogenesis: Formation of synapses.

Temporal lobe: Part of the cerebrum, involved in speech, memory, and hearing; located beneath the lateral Sylvian fissure.

Theory of mind: A specific cognitive capacity to attribute mental states to oneself and others in order to understand that others have beliefs, intentions, desires, and so on, different from one's own.

Transcranial magnetic stimulation: A noninvasive method to excite neurons in the brain and measure changing magnetic fields (electromagnetic induction).

Transfer: The application of knowledge to a new domain.

Vigilance: The process of paying close and continuous attention; watchfulness.

Wernicke's area: Area of the brain encircling the auditory cortex on the Sylvian fissure (Brodmann area 22); located in the left hemisphere and related to receptive language comprehension.

White matter: The tissue through which messages pass between different areas of gray matter within the nervous system composed of myelinated nerve cell processes, or axons.

Working memory: Processes used for temporarily storing and manipulating information dependent on the frontal cortex, parietal cortex, anterior cingulate, and parts of the basal ganglia.

Members of the Delphi Panel and Expert Reviewers

Daniel Ansari, Ph.D.: Professor of Psychology and Education at the University of Western Ontario and Research Chair in Developmental Cognitive Neuroscience.

Michael Atherton, Ph.D.: Former head of the American Educational Research Association Special Interest Group on the Brain and Learning.

Virginia Berninger, Ph.D.: Professor of Educational Psychology at the University of Washington.

Jane Bernstein, Ph.D.: Senior Associate in Psychology/Neuropsychology at Children's Hospital, Boston, and on the faculty of the Department of Psychiatry at Harvard Medical School and Faculty Fellow of the Mind/Brain/Behavior Initiative of Harvard University.

Sarah Jayne Blakemore, Ph.D.: Research Fellow at the Institute of Cognitive Neuroscience in London.

John T. Bruer, Ph.D.: President of the James S. McDonnell Foundation.

Donna Coch, Ed.D.: Primary Researcher in the Reading Brain Lab of Dartmouth College.

David Daniel, Ph.D.: Editor of the *Mind, Brain, and Education Journal* and Professor of Psychology at James Madison University.

Stanislas Dehaene, Ph.D.: Professor at the Collège de France, Chairman of the Experimental Cognitive Psychology Department, Director of the Cognitive Neuroimaging Unit.

Marian Diamond, Ph.D.: Head of Integrative Biology at the University of California at Berkeley.

Kurt Fischer, Ph.D.: Founder and Chair of the Mind, Brain and Education Program at Harvard University's Graduate School of Education.

Howard Gardner, Ph.D.: Professor at Harvard University and Director of Project Zero.

John Geake, Ph.D.: Professor of Education at the Westminster Institute of Education, Oxford Brookes University.

Usha Goswami, Ph.D.: Director of the Centre for Neuroscience in Education at the University of Cambridge.

Christina Hinton, Ed.M. (Ed.D. candidate): OECD English editor of *Understanding the brain: Towards a new learning science* (2002).

Paul Howard-Jones, Ph.D.: Professor at the Graduate School of Education at the University of Bristol.

Mary Helen Immordino-Yang, Ed.D.: Director of the Brain & Creativity Institute at the University of Southern California.

Eric Jensen, Ph.D. candidate: Renowned speaker on brain-based education.

Jelle Jolles, Ph.D.: Director of the Brain & Behaviour Institute and the Department of Neuropsychology and head of the Division of Cognitive Disorders at Maastricht University.

Hideaki Koizumi, Ph.D.: Professor at Tokyo University and lead researcher in neuroimaging for Hitachi.

Renate Nummela-Caine, Ph.D., M.Ed.: Renowned speaker on brain-based education.

Michael Posner, Ph.D.: Adjunct Professor at the Weill Medical College in New York (Sackler Institute).

Marc Schwartz, Ed.D.: Director of the University of Texas Mind, Brain, and Education program and Associate Researcher in the Science Education Department at the Harvard-Smithsonian Center for Astrophysics.

Rita Smilkstein, Ph.D.: Teacher consultant and educational author.

David Sousa, Ed.D.: World-renowned speaker on brain-based education and superintendent of New Providence public schools in New Jersey.

Robert Sylwester, Ph.D.: Emeritus Professor of Education at the University of Oregon.

Judy Willis, M.D., M.Ed.: Board-certified neurologist and middle school teacher in Santa Barbara, California, and renowned speaker on brain-based education.

Patricia Wolfe, Ed.D.: World-renowned teacher trainer on the brain and teaching.

Exemplary Works in the Field

Some of the seminal writers who managed to merge the three disciplines of neuroscience, psychology, and education are noted below by categories.

General Introduction to Mind, Brain, and Education Concepts

Battro, A., Fischer, K. W., & Léna, P. J. (Eds). (2008). *The educated brain: Essays in neuroeducation*. Cambridge, UK: Cambridge University Press.

Bransford, J., Brown, A. L., & Cocking, R. R. (Eds.). (2003). *How people learn: Brain, mind, experience and school*. Washington, DC: National Academy Press.

Byrnes, J. (2001). *Minds, brains, and learning: Understanding the psychological and educational relevance of neuroscientific research*. New York: The Guilford Press.

Byrnes, J. (2007). Some ways in which neuroscientific research can be relevant to education. In D. Coch, K. W. Fischer, & G. Dawson (Eds.), *Human behavior, learning, and the developing brain: Typical development* (pp.30–49). New York: The Guilford Press.

Geake, J. (2005b). The neurological basis of intelligence: Implications for education: An abstract. *Gifted and Talented, 9*(1), 8.

Goswami, U. (2007). *Cognitive development: The learning brain*. London: Taylor & Francis.

Jossey-Bass. (2008). *The Jossey-Bass Reader on the brain and learning*. San Francisco: John Wiley & Sons.

Kandel, E., & Squire, L. R. (2000). Neuroscience: Breaking down scientific barriers to the study of brain and mind. *Science, 290*, 1113–1120.

Levine, M. (2000). *A mind at a time*. New York: Simon & Schuster.

Mind, Brain, and Education Journal (all issues). Available on www.imbes.org

Pickering, S., & Howard-Jones, P. (2007). Educators' views on the role of neuroscience in education: Findings from a study of UK and international perspectives. *Mind, Brain, and Education, 1*(3), 109–113.

Posner, M., & Rothbart, M. K. (2007). *Educating the human brain*. Washington, DC: American Psychological Association.

Wolfe, P. (2001). *Brain Matters: Translating research into classroom practice*. Alexandria, VA: Association for Supervision and Curriculum Development.

Teaching Using MBE Concepts

Crawford, M., & White, M. (1999). Strategies for mathematics: Teaching in context. *Educational Leadership, 57*(3), 34–39.

Doidge, N. (2007). *The brain that changes itself: Stories of personal triumph from the frontiers of brain science.* New York: Penguin.

Harvey, S., & Goudvis, A. (2007). *Strategies that work: Teaching comprehension for understanding and engagement* (2nd edition). Portland, ME: Stenhouse Publishers.

Holcombe, K., & Johnson, M. H. (2005). Educating executive attention. *Proceedings of the National Academy of Science, 102*(41), 14479–14480.

Marsh, R. L., Landau, J. D., & Hicks, J. L. (1997). Contributions of inadequate source monitoring to unconscious plagiarism during idea generation. *Journal of Experimental Psychology: Learning, Memory, and Cognition, 23*(4), 886–897.

Marzano, R. (2007). *The art and science of teaching: A comprehensive framework for effective instruction.* Arlington, VA: Association For Supervision and Curriculum Development.

Ronis, D. (2007). *Brain-compatible assessments* (2nd ed.). Thousand Oaks, CA: Corwin Press.

Sousa, D. (2000). *How the brain learns.* Thousand Oaks, CA: Corwin Press.

Willis, J. (2007a). *Brain-friendly strategies for the inclusion classroom.* Alexandria, VA: Association for Supervision and Curriculum Development.

Neuroethics

Canli, T. (2006). When genes and brain unite: Ethical implications of genomic neuroimaging. In J. Iles (ed.), *Neuroethics* (pp.169–183). Oxford: Oxford University Press.

Coch, D. (2007). Neuroimaging research with children: Ethical issues and case scenarios. *Journal of Moral Education, 36*(1), 1–18.

Farah, M. (2002). Emerging ethical issues in neuroscience. *Nature Neuroscience, 5*(11), 1123–1129.

Farah, M. (2005). Neuroethics: The practical and the philosophical. *Trends in Cognitive Science, 9,* 34–40.

Farah, M. (2007). Social, legal, and ethical implications of cognitive neuroscience: "Neuroethics" for short. *Journal of Cognitive Neuroscience, 19*(3), 363–364.

Farah, M., & Wolfe, P. (2004). Monitoring and manipulating brain function: New neuroscience technologies and their ethical implications. *Hastings Center Report 34,* 34–45.

Farah, M., Noble, K., & Hurt, H. (2006). Poverty, privilege, and brain development: Empirical findings and ethical implications. In Illes, J., ed. *Neuroethics* (chapter 18). Oxford: Oxford University Press.

Gazzaniga, M. S. (2005). *The ethical brain.* New York: Dana Press.

Glannon, W. (2006). *Bioethics and the brain.* New York: Oxford University Press.

Glannon, W. (2006). Neuroethics. *Bioethics, 20*(1), 37–52.

Glannon, W. (Ed.) (2007). *Defining right and wrong in brain science: Essential readings in neuroethics.* New York: Dana Press.

Illes, J. (2002). Brain and cognition: Ethical challenges in advanced neuroimaging. *Brain and Cognition, 50*(3), p. 341–344.

Illes, J. (2003, October 24). Neuroethics in a new era of neuroimaging. *American Journal of Neuroradiology, 24,* 1739–1741.

Illes, J. (2005). *Neuroethics in the 21st century.* Oxford: Oxford University Press.

Illes, J. (2006). *Neuroethics, neurochallenges: A needs-based research agenda.* Based on the David Kopf Annual Lecture on Neuroethics, Society for Neuroscience. Retrieved on May 10, 2007, from http://neuroethics.stanford.edu/documents/Illes. NeuroethicsSFN2006.pdf

Illes, J., (Ed.). (2006). *Neuroethics.* Oxford: Oxford University Press.

Marcus, S. (2004), *Neuroethics: Mapping the field.* New York: Dana Press.

Racine, E., Bar-Ilan, O., Illes J. (2005). fMRI in the public eye. *Nature Reviews Neuroscience, 6*(2), pp.159-64.

Rees, D., & Rose, S. (2004). *New brain sciences: Perils and prospects.* Cambridge University Press.

Riis, P. (2003). Neuroethics. *European Journal of Neurology, 10,* 218–223.

Neuro-Physiological and Neuro-Pharmacological Aspect of Learning

Anderson, M. (2007). Evolution of cognitive function via redeployment of brain areas. *The Neuroscientist: A review journal bringing neurobiology, neurology and psychiatry, 13*(1), 13–21.

Atallah, H., Frank, M. J., & O'Reilly, R. C. (2004). Hippocampus, cortex, and basal ganglia: Insights from computational models of complementary learning systems. *Neurobiology of Learning and Memory, 82*(3), 253–267.

Bear, M., Connors, B. W., & Paradis, M. A. (2007). *Neuroscience: Exploring the brain* (3rd ed). Baltimore, MD: Lippincott, Williams, & Wilkins.

Boecker, H., Sprenger, T., Spilker, M. E., Henriksen, G., Koppenhoefer, M., Wagner, K. J., Valet, M., Berthele, A., & Tolle, T. R. (2008, February). The runner's high: Opioidergic mechanisms in the human brain. *Cerebral Cortex, 18,* 2523.

Gazzaniga, M. (Ed.). (2005b). *The cognitive neuroscience, III.* Cambridge, MA: Massachusetts Institute of Technology Press.

Gibbs, A., Naudts, K. H., Spencer, E. P., & David, A. S. (2007). The role of dopamine in attentional and memory biases for emotional information. *The American Journal of Psychiatry, 164*(10), 1603–1610.

Johnson, C. (1999). Acupuncture works on endorphins. *News in Science, ABC Science Online.* Australian Broadcasting Corporation.

Kitabatake, Y., Sailor, K. A., Ming, G. L., & Song, H. (2007). Adult neurogenesis and hippocampal memory function: New cells, more plasticity, new memories? *Neurosurgery Clinics of North America, 18*(1), 105–113.

Levy, R., & Goldman-Rakic, P. S. (2000). Segregation of working memory functions within the dorsolateral prefrontal cortex. *Experimental Brain Research, 133,* 23–32.

Napadow, V., Ahn, A., Longhurst, J., Lao, L., Stener-Victorin, E., Harris, R., & Langevin, H. M. (2008, September). The status and future of acupuncture clinical research. *Journal of Alternative and Complementary Medicine, 14*(7), 861–869.

Peretz, I., & Zatorre, R. J. (2005). Brain organization for music processing. *Annual Review of Psychology 56,* 89–114.

Poldrack, R., & Wagner, A. D. (2004). What can neuroimaging tell us about the mind? Insights from prefrontal cortex. *Current Directions in Psychological Science, 13,* 177–181.

Pugh, K., Shaywitz, B. A., Shaywitz, S. E., Shankweiler, D. P., Katz, L., & Fletcher, J. M. (1997). Predicting reading performance from neuroimaging profiles: The cerebral basis of phonological effects in printed word identification. *Journal of Experimental Psychology: Human Perception and Performance, 23,* 299–318.

Rauch, S., Shin, L. M., & Wright, C. I. (2003). Neuroimaging studies of amygdala function in anxiety disorders. *Annals of the New York Academy of Sciences, 985,* 389–410.

Sadato, N., Pascual-Leone, A., Rafman, J., Ibanez, V., Deiber, M. P., Dold, G., & Hallett, M. (1996). Activation of the primary visual cortex by Braille reading in blind subjects. *Nature, 380,* 526–528.

Schlaggar, B., & McCandliss, B. D. (2007). Development of neural systems for reading. *Annual Review of Neuroscience, 30,* 475.

Shaywitz, S., Shaywitz, B. A., Fulbright, R. K., Skudlarski, P., Mencl, W. E., Constable, R. T., Pugh, K. R., Loan, J. M., Marchione, K. E., Fletcher, J. M., Lyon, G. R., & Gore J. C. (2003). Neural systems for compensation and persistence: young adult outcome of childhood reading disability. *Biological Psychiatry, 54*(1), 25–33.

Simos, P., Fletcher, J. M., Foorman, B. R., Francis, D. J., Castillo, E. M., Davis, R. N., Fitzgerald, M., Mathes, P. G., Denton, C., & Papanicolaou, A. C. (2002). Brain activation profiles during the early stages of reading acquisition. *Journal of Child Neurology, 17*(3), 159–63.

Society for Neuroscience. (2007). *Depression and stress hormones.* Retrieved on September 11, 2007, from www.sfn.org/index.cfm?pagename=brainbriefings_depressionandstresshormones

Society for Neuroscience. (2007). *Memory enhancers.* Retrieved on September 11, 2007, from http://www.sfn.org/index.cfm?pagename=brainBriefings_memoryEnhancers

Sparling, P. B., Giuffrida, A., Piomelli, D., Rosskopf, L., & Dietrich, A. (2003, December). Exercise activates the endocannabinoid system. *Neuroreport 14*(17), 2209–2211.

Yordanova, J., Falkenstein, M., Hohnsbein, J., & Kolev, V. (2004). Parallel systems of error processing in the brain. *Neuroimage, 22*(2), 590–602.

Social Aspect of Teaching and Learning

Adolphs, R. (2003). Cognitive neuroscience of human social behaviour. *Nature Reviews Neuroscience 4*(3), 165–78.

Adolphs, R. (2006). How do we know the minds of others? Domain-specificity, simulation, and enactive social cognition. *Brain Research, 1079*(1), 25–35.

Cozolino, L. (2006). *The neuroscience of human relationships: Attachment and the developing social brain.* New York: W.W. Norton & Company.

Damasio, A. (2004). The neural basis of social behaviour. In S. Marcus, *Neuroethics. Mapping the field* (pp. 100–107). New York: Dana Press.

Lieberman, M. (2005). Principles, processes, and puzzles of social cognition: An introduction for the special issue on social cognitive neuroscience. *NeuroImage, 28*(4), 745–756.

Meltzoff, A., & Decety, J. (2003). What imitation tells us about social cognition: A rapprochement between developmental psychology and cognitive neuroscience. *Philos Trans R Soc London B Biological Science, 358*(1431), 491–500.

Sander, D., Grandjean, D., Pourtois, G., Schwartz, S., Seghier, M., Scherer, K. R., & Vuilleumier, P. (2005). Emotion and attention interactions in social cognition: Brain regions involved in processing anger prosody. *NeuroImage, 28*, 848–858.

Suslow, T., Ohrmann, P., Bauer, J., Rauch, A. V., Schwindt, W., Arolt, V., Heindel, W., & Kugel, H. (2006). Amygdala activation during masked presentation of emotional faces predicts conscious detection of threat-related faces. *Brain and Cognition, 61*(3), 243–248.

Emotional Aspects of Teaching and Learning

Damasio, A. (2000). *The feeling of what happens: Body and emotion in the making of consciousness.* New York: Harvest Books.

Damasio, A. (2003). *Looking for Spinoza: Joy, sorrow, and the feeling brain.* New York: Harvest Book.

Immordino-Yang, M., & Damasio, A. (2008). We feel, therefore we learn: The relevance of affective and social neuroscience to education. In *The Jossey-Bass Reader on the brain and learning* (pp.183–198). San Francisco: John Wiley & Sons.

LaBar, K., & Cabeza, R. (2006). Cognitive neuroscience of emotional memory. *Nature Reviews Neuroscience 7*(1), 54–66.

LeDoux, J. (1996). *The emotional brain: The mysterious underpinnings of emotional life.* New York: Simon & Schuster.

LeDoux, J. (2000). Emotion circuits in the brain. *Annual Review of Neuroscience, 23*, 155–184.

LeDoux, J. (2003). *Synaptic self: How our brains become who we are.* New York: Penguin Books.

LeDoux, J. (2008). Remembrance of emotions past. In *The Jossey-Bass reader on the brain and learning* (pp. 151–182). San Francisco: John Wiley & Sons.

Panksepp, J. (2003). At the interface of the affective, behavioral, and cognitive neurosciences: Decoding the emotional feelings of the brain. *Brain and Cognition, 52*, 4–14.

Reeve, J. (2004). *Understanding motivation and emotion* (4th ed.). New York: Wiley & Sons.

Rosiek, J. (2003). Emotional scaffolding: An exploration of the teacher knowledge at the intersection of student emotion and the subject matter. *Journal of Teacher Education, 54*, 399–412.

Wismer Fries, A., & Pollack, S. D. (2007). Emotion processing and the developing brain. In D. Coch, K. W. Fischer, & G. Dawson (Eds.), *Human behavior, learning, and the developing brain: Typical development* (pp. 329–361). New York: The Guilford Press.

Memory and MBE Principles

Achim, A., & Lepage, M. (2005). Neural correlates of memory for items and for associations: An event-related functional magnetic resonance imaging study. *Journal of Cognitive Neuroscience, 17*(4), 652–667.

Baddeley, A., & Andrade, J. (2000). Working memory and the vividness of imagery. *Journal of Experimental Psychology, General, 129*(1), 126–145.

Bauer, P. (2004). Getting explicit memory off the ground: Steps forward construction of a neuro-developmental account of changes in the first two years of life. *Developmental Review, 24*, 347–373.

Bauer, P. (2005). Developments in declarative memory. *Psychological Science, 16*(1), 41–47.

Benfenati, F. (2007). Synaptic plasticity and the neurobiology of learning and memory. *Acta Bio-Medica: Atenei Parmensis, 78*(Suppl 1), 58–66.

Bright, P., & Kopelman, M. D. (2001). Learning and memory: Recent findings. *Current Opinion in Neurology, 14*(4), 449–455.

Kandel, E. (2007). *In search of memory: The emergence of a new science of mind.* New York: W.W. Norton & Company.

Linden, D. (2007). The working memory networks of the human brain. *The Neuroscientist, 13*(3), 257–267.

Liston, C., & Kagan, J. (2002). Brain development: Memory enhancement in early childhood. *Nature, 419*, 896.

Schacter, D. (2001). *The seven sins of memory: How the mind forgets and remembers.* New York: Houghton Mifflin Company.

Schacter, D., & Addis, D. R. (2007). The cognitive neuroscience of constructive memory: Remembering the past and imagining the future. *Philosophical Transactions of the Royal Society of London Series B, Biological Sciences, 362*(1481), 773–786.

Squire, L., & Schacter, D. L. (Eds.). (2002). *Neuropsychology of memory* (3rd ed.), New York: Guilford Press.

Attention in MBE Science

Hopfinger, J., Buonocore, M. H., & Mangun, G. R. (2000). The neural mechanisms of top-down attentional control. *Nature Neuroscience, 3*(3), 284–291.

Iidaka, T., Aderson, N., Kapur, S., Cabeza, R., & Craik, F. (2000). The effort of divided attention on encoding and retrieval in episodic memory revealed by positron emission tomography. *Journal of Cognitive Neuroscience, 12*(2), 267–280.

Kok, A., Ridderinkhof, K. R., & Ullsperger, M. (2006). The control of attention and actions: Current research and future developments. *Brain Research, 1105*(1), 1–6.

Lawrence, N., Ross, T. J., Hoffmann, R., Garavan, H., & Stein, E. A. (2003). Multiple neuronal networks mediate sustained attention. *Journal of Cognitive Neuroscience, 15*, 1028–1038.

Martens, S., Munneke, J., Smid, H., & Johnson, A. (2006). Quick minds don't blink: Electrophysiological correlates of individual differences in attentional selection. *Journal of Cognitive Neuroscience, 18*(9), 1423–1438.

Pashler, H., Johnsyon, J. C., & Ruthruff, E. (2001). Attention and performance. *Annual Review of Psychology, 52*, 629–651.

Posner M. (Ed.). (2004). *Cognitive neuroscience of attention.* New York: Guilford.

Posner, M., & Rothbart, M. K. (1998). Developing attention skills. In J. Richards (Ed.), *Cognitive neuroscience of attention: A developmental perspective* (pp. 317–323). Hillsdale, NJ: Lawrence Erlbaum Associates.

Posner, M. & Rothbart, M. K. (2007). Research on attention networks as a model for the integration of psychological science. *Annual Review of Psychology 58*, 1–23.

Vuilleumier, P., & Driver, J. (2007). Modulation of visual processing by attention and emotion: Windows on causal interactions between human brain regions. *Philosophical Transactions of the Royal Society of London Series B, Biological Sciences, 362*(1481), 837–855.

Vuilleumier, P., Harmony, J. & Dolan, R. (2003). Reciprocal links between emotion and attention. In R. S. J. Frackowiak (Ed.), *Human brain function* (pp. 419–444). San Diego: Academic Press.

Math and MBE Principles

Bisanz, J., Sherman, J. L., Rasmussen, C., & Ho, E. (2005). Development of arithmetic skills and knowledge in preschool children. In J. I. D. Campbell (Ed.), *Handbook of mathematical psychology* (pp. 143–162). New York: Psychology Press.

Byrnes, J. (2008). Math skills. In *The Jossey-Bass reader on the brain and learning* (pp. 301–330). San Francisco: John Wiley & Sons.

Dehaene, S. (1999a). Counting on our brains. *Nature, 401*(6749), 114.

Dehaene, S. (1999b). *The number sense: How the mind creates mathematics.* New York: Oxford University Press.

Dehaene, S. (2008a). Small heads for big calculations. In *The Jossey-Bass reader on the brain and learning* (pp. 273–300). San Francisco: John Wiley & Sons.

Dehaene, S. (2008b). Cerebral constraints in reading and arithmetic: Education as a "neuronal recycling" process. In A. Battro, K.W. Fischer, & P.J. Léna (Eds.), *The educated brain* (pp. 232–247). Cambridge, UK: Cambridge University Press.

Dehaene, S., Moiko, N., Cohen, L., & Wilson, A.J. (2004). Arithmetic and the brain. *Current Opinion in Neurobiology, 14*(2), 218–224.

Desoete, A., & Grégoire, J. (2006). Numerical competence in young children and in children with mathematics learning disabilities. *Learning & Individual Differences, 16*(4), 351–367.

Gardner, R., Ansari, D., Reishofer, G., Stern, E., Ebner, F., & Neuper, C. (2007). Individual differences in mathematical competence predict parietal brain activation during mental calculation. *NeuroImage, 38*, 346–356.

Geake, J. (2003). Young mathematical brains. *Primary Mathematics, 7*(1), 14–18.

Hoek, D., Van Den Eeden, P., & Terwel, J. (1999). The effects of integrated social and cognitive strategy instruction on the mathematics achievement in secondary education. *Learning and Instruction, 9*(5), 427–448.

Rourke, B., & Conway, J.A. (1997). Disabilities of arithmetic and mathematical reasoning: Perspectives from neurology and neuropsychology. *Journal of Learning Disabilities, 30*, 34–46.

Reading in MBE Science

Cohen, L., Dehaene, S., Naccache, L., Lehéricy, S., Dehaene-Lambertz, G., Hénaff, M-A., & Michel, F. (2001). The visual word form area: Spatial and temporal characterization of an initial stage of reading in normal subjects and posterior split-brain patients. *Brain, 123*(2), 291–307.

Corina, D., Richards, T. L., Serafín, S., Richards, A. L., Steury, K., Abbott, R. D., Echelard, D. R., Maravilla, K. R. & Berninger, V. W. (2001). MRI auditory language differences between dyslexic and able reading children. *Neuroreport, 12*(6),1195–201.

Fischer, K. W., Bernstein J. H., & Immordino-Yang, M. H. (Eds.). (2007). *Mind, brain and education in reading disorders.* Cambridge UK: Cambridge University Press.

Fowler, A., & Swainson, B. (2004). Relationships of naming skills to reading, memory, and receptive vocabulary: Evidence for imprecise phonological representations of words by poor readers. *Annals of Dislexia, 54*(2), 247–281.

Johnston, P., & Costello, P. (2005). Principles for literacy assessment. *Reading Research Quarterly, 40*(2), 256–267.

Pare-Blagoev, E. (2006). Connecting neuroscience and education: The neural correlates of phonemic awareness in normal reading children. Unpublished Doctoral Dissertation (Ed.D.), Harvard University, Cambridge, MA. AAT 3221615.

Pugh, K., Shaywitz, B. A., Shaywitz, S. E., Shankweiler, D. P., Katz, L., & Fletcher, J. M. (1997). Predicting reading performance from neuroimaging profiles: The cerebral basis of phonological effects in printed word identification. *Journal of Experimental Psychology: Human Perception and Performance, 23,* 299–318.

Shaywitz, B., Shaywitz, S. E., Blachman, B. A., Pugh, K. R., Fulbright, R. K., Skudlarski, P., Mencl, W. E., Constable, R. T., Holahan, J. M., Marchione, K. E., Fletcher, J. M., Lyon, G. R., & Gore, J. C. (2004). Development of left occipito-temporal systems for skilled reading in children after a phonologically-based intervention. *Biological Psychiatry, 55,* 926–933.

Willis, J. (2008). *Teaching the brain to read: Strategies for improving fluency, vocabulary, and comprehension.* Alexandria, VA: ASCD.

Wolf, M. (2007). *Proust and the squid: The story and science of the reading brain.* New York: Harper.

Art and Creativity in MBE Science

Abraham, A., & Windmann, S. (2007). Creative cognition: The diverse operations and the prospect of applying a cognitive neuroscience perspective. *Methods 42*(1), 38–48.

Carlson, N. (2004). *Physiology of behavior* (8th ed.). Boston, MA: Pearson Publisher.

Carlsson, I., Wendt, P. E., & Risberg, J. (2000). On the neurobiology of creativity. Differences in frontal activity between high and low creative subjects. *Neuropsychologia, 38,* 873–885.

Csikszentmihalyi, M. (1996). *Creativity: Flow and the psychology of discovery and invention.* New York: HarperPerennial.

Diamond, M., & Hopson, J. (1998). *Magic trees of the mind: How to nurture your child's intelligence, creativity, and healthy emotions from birth through adolescence.* New York: Plume.

Dietrich, A. (2004, Dec.). The cognitive neuroscience of creativity. *Psychonomic Bulletin & Review, 11*(6), 1011.

Fink, A., Benedek, M., Grabner, R. H., Staudt, B., & Neubauer, A. C. (2007). Creativity meets neuroscience: Experimental tasks for the neuroscientific study of creative thinking. *Methods, 42*(1), 68–76.

Gardner, H. (1994). *Creating minds: An anatomy of creativity seen through the lives of Freud, Einstein, Picasso, Stravinsky, Eliot, Graham, and Gandhi.* New York: Basic Books.

Gardner, H. (1994). *The arts and the human development: A psychological study of the artistic process.* New York: Basic Books.

Gruber, H. E. & Bödeker, K. (2005). *Creativity, psychology, and the history of science.* New York: Springer.

Kaufman, J. C., & Sternberg, R. J. (2006). *The international handbook of creativity.* Cambridge, UK: Cambridge University Press.

Sousa, D. (2008). The brain and the arts. In *The Jossey-Bass reader on the brain and learning* (pp. 331–358). San Francisco: John Wiley & Sons.

Srinivasan, N. (2007). Cognitive neuroscience of creativity: EEG based approaches. *Methods, 42*(1), 109–116.

Sylwester, R. (1998). Art for the brain's sake. *Educational Leadership,* 56(3), 36–40.

Culture and MBE Science

Ehrlich, P., & Feldman, M. (2007). Genes, environments, behaviors. *Daedalus,* 5–12.

Posner, M., Rothbart, M. K., & Harman, C. (1994). Cognitive science contributions to culture and emotion. In S. Ktayma & H. Marcus (Eds.), *Culture and emotion,* (pp. 197–216). Washington, DC: American Psychological Association.

Siok, W., Perfetti, C. A., Jin, Z., & Tan, L. H. (2004). Biological abnormality of impaired reading is constrained by culture. *Nature, 431,* 71–76.

Sylwester, R. (2003). *A biological brain in a cultural classroom: Enhancing cognitive and social development through collaborative classroom management.* Thousand Oaks, CA: Corwin Press, Inc.

Tomasello, M. (1999). *The cultural origins of human cognition.* Cambridge, MA: Harvard University Press.

Music and MBE Science

Brown, S., Martinez, M., & Parson, L. (2006). Music and language side by side in the brain: A PET study of the generation of melodies and sentences. *European Journal of Neuroscience, 23*(10), 2791–2803.

Cassity, H., Henley, T. B., & Markley, R. P. (2007). The Mozart effect: Musical phenomenon or musical preference? A more ecologically valid reconsideration. *Journal of Instructional Psychology, 34*(1), 13–17.

Gaser, C., & Schlaug, G. (2003). Brain structures differ between musicians and nonmusicians. *Journal of Neuroscience, 8*(27), 9240–9045.

Gruhn, W., Galley, N., & Kluth, C. (2003). Do mental speed and musical abilities interact? *Annals of the New York Academy of Sciences, 999,* 485–496.

Immordino-Yang, M., & Fischer, K.W. (2007). Dynamic development of hemispheric biases in three cases: cognitive/hemispheric cycles, music and hemispherectomy. In D. Coch, K. W. Fischer, & G. Dawson (Eds.), *Human behavior, learning, and the developing brain: Typical development* (pp. 74–114). New York: The Guilford Press.

Janata, P., & Grafton, S. T. (2003). Swinging in the brain: Shared neural substrates for behaviors related to sequencing and music. *Nature Neuroscience, 6*(7), 682–687.

Koelsch, S. (2005). Neural substrates of processing syntax and semantics in music. *Current Opinion in Neurobiology, 15*(2), 207–212.

Korenman, L., & Peynircioglu, Z. F. (2007). Individual differences in learning and remembering music: Auditory versus visual presentation. *Journal of Research in Music Education, 55*(1), 48–55.

Levitin, D. (2008). My favorite thing: Why do we like the music we like? In *The Jossey-Bass reader on the brain and learning* (pp. 370–384). San Francisco: John Wiley & Sons.

Meister, I., Krings, T., Foltys, H., Boroojerdi, B., Miller, M., & Topper, R. (2004). Playing piano in the mind: An fMRI study on music imagery and performance in pianists. *Cognitive Brain Research, 19*, 219–228.

Menon, V. & Levitin, D. J. (2005). The rewards of music listening: response and physiological connectivity of the mesolimbic system. *NeuroImage, 28*(1), 175–184.

O'Herron, P., & Siebenaler, D. (2005). The intersection between vocal music and language arts instruction. *A Review of the Literature Applications of Research in Music Education, 25*(2), 16–26.

Pantev, C., Oostenvel, R., Engelien, A., Ross, B., Roberts, L. E., & Hoke, M. (1998). Increased auditory cortical representation in musicians. *Nature, 392*, 811–814.

Peretz, I., & Zatorre, R. J. (2005). Brain organization for music processing. *Annual Review of Psychology 56*, 89–114.

Rauscher, F., Shaw, G., Levine, L., Wright, E., Dennis, W., & Newcomb, R. (1997). Music training causes long-term enhancement of preschool children's spatial-temporal reasoning. *Neurological Research, 19*(1), 2–8.

Sack, O. (2008). *Musicophilia: Tales of music and the brain*. New York: Vintage.

Stewart, L., Henson, R., Kampe, K., Walsh, V., Turner, R., & Frith, U. (2003). Brain changes after learning to read and play music. *NeuroImage, 20*(1), 71–83.

Tervaniemi, M., & Huotilainen, M. (2003). The promises of change-related brain potentials in cognitive neuroscience of music. *Annals of the New York Academy of Sciences, 999*, 29–39.

Zatorre, R., Chen, J. L., & Penhune, V. B. (2007). When the brain plays music: Auditory-motor interactions in music perception and production. *Nature Reviews Neuroscience, 8*(7), 547–558.

Science and MBE Science

Carey, S. (2000). Science education as conceptual change. *Journal of Applied Developmental Psychology, 21*(1), 13–19.

Grotzer, T. (2003). Learning to understand the forms of causality implicit in scientific explanations. *Studies in Science Education, 39*, 1–74.

Grotzer, T. (2004, October). Putting science within reach: Addressing patterns of thinking that limit science learning. *Principal Leadership*.

Holloway, J. (2000). How does the brain learn science? *Educational Leadership*, *58*(3), 85–86.

Schwartz, M., & Fischer, K. W. (2003). Building versus borrowing: The challenge of actively constructing ideas in post-secondary education. *Liberal Education*, *89*(3), 22–29.

Schwartz, M., & Fischer, K. W. (2006). Useful metaphors for tackling problems in teaching and learning. *About Campus*, *11*(1), 2–9.

Nutrition and Learning in MBE Science

Cotman, C., & Berchtold, N. C. (2002). Exercise: A behavioral intervention to enhance brain health and plasticity. *Trends in Neuroscience*, *25*, 295–301.

Dwyer, T., Sallis, J. F., Blizzard, L., Lazzarus, R., & Dean, K. (2001). Relation of academic performance to physical activity and fitness in children. *Pediatric Exercise Science*, *13*(3), 225–237.

Eimer, J., Salazar, W., Landers, D. M., Petruzzello, S. J., Jan, M., & Nowell, P. (1997). The influence of physical fitness and exercise upon cognitive functioning: A meta-analysis. *Journal of Sport & Exercise Psychology*, *19*(3), 249–277.

Liu, J. (2004). Malnutrition at age 3 years and externalizing behavior problems at ages 8, 11, and 17 years. *American Journal of Psychiatry*, *161*(11), 13.

Marcason, W. (2005). Can dietary intervention play a part in the treatment of attention deficit and hyperactivity disorder? *Journal of the American Dietetic Association*, *105*(7), 1161–1161.

Reynolds, D., Nicolson, R. I., & Hambly, H. (2003). Evaluation of an exercise-based treatment for children with reading difficulties. *Dyslexia*, *9*, 48–71.

Stein, D., Collins, M., Daniels, W., Noakes T. D., & Zigmond, M. (2007). Mind and muscle: The cognitive-affective neuroscience of exercise. *CNS Spectrums*, *12*(1), 19–22.

Nature Versus Nurture (Genetics, Environment) in MBE Science

Byrne, B., Olson, R. K., Samuelsson, S., Wadsworth, S., Corley, R., DeFries, J. C., & Willcutt, E. (2006). Genetic and environmental influences on early literacy. *Journal of Research in Reading*, *29*(1), 33–49.

Coltheart, M. (2006). The genetics of learning to read. *Journal of Research in Reading*, *29*(1), 124–132.

Hayiou-Thomas, M., Harlaar, N., Dale, P. S., & Plomin, R. (2006). Genetic and environmental mediation of the prediction from preschool language and nonverbal ability to 7-year reading. *Journal of Research in Reading*, *29*(1), 50–74.

Mascolo, M., & Fischer, K. W. (2003). Beyond the nature-nurture divide in development and evolution. Review of Gilbert Gottlieb's "Individual development and evolution." *Contemporary Psychology*, *48*, 842–847.

Nation, K. (2006). Reading and genetics: An introduction. *Journal of Research in Reading*, *29*(1), 1.

Pace-Schott, E., & Hobson, J. A. (2002). The neurobiology of sleep: Genetics, cellular physiology, and subcortical networks. *Nature Reviews Neuroscience*, *3*, 591–605.

Ridley, M. (2003). *Nature via nurture: Genes, experience, and what makes us human.* New York: HarperCollins.

Atypical Behavior, Anomalies, and Disabilities and MBE Science

Ansari, D., & Karmiloff-Smith, A. (2002). Atypical trajectories of number development: A neuroconstructivist perspective. *Trends in Cognitive Sciences, 6,* 511–516.

Ansari, D., Donlan, C., Thomas, M., Ewing, S., & Karmiloff-Smith. (2003). What makes counting count? Verbal and visuo-spatial contributions to typical and atypical number development. *Journal of Experimental Child Psychology, 85,* 50–62.

Attwood, T. (2002). *Dyscalculia in schools: What it is and what you can do.* Northants, UK: First and Best in Education Ltd.

Butterworth, B. (2004). *Dyscalculia guidance: Helping pupils with specific learning difficulties in maths.* Coventry, UK: David Fulton Publications.

Chinn, S. (2004). *The trouble with maths: A practical guide to helping learners with numeracy difficulties.* London: Routledge Falmer.

Coch, D., Dawson, G., & Fischer, K. W. (2007). *Human behavior, learning, and the developing brain: Atypical development.* New York: Guilford Press.

Desoete, A., & Grégoire, J. (2006). Numerical competence in young children and in children with mathematics learning disabilities. *Learning & Individual Differences, 16*(4), 351–367.

Fiorello, C., Hale, J. B., Holdnack, J. A., Kavanagh, J. A., Terrell, J., & Long, L. (2007). Interpreting intelligence test results for children with disabilities: Is global intelligence relevant? *Applied Neuropsychology, 14*(1), 2–12; discussion 13–51.

Henderson, A., Came, F., & Brough, M. (2003). *Working with dyscalculia.* Wiltshire, UK: Learning Works International, Ltd.

Immordino-Yang, M. (2007). An evolutionary perspective on reading and reading disorders? In K. W. Fischer, J. H. Bernstein, & M. H. Immordino-Yang, (Eds.), *Mind, brain and education in reading disorders.* Cambridge, UK: Cambridge University Press.

McCandliss, B., & Noble, K. G. (2003). The development of reading impairment: A cognitive neuroscience model. *Mental Retardation and Developmental Disabilities Research Reviews 8,* 196–205.

Nigg, J. (2005). Neuropsychologic theory and findings in attention-deficit/hyperactivity disorder: The state of the field and salient challenges for the coming decade. *Biological Psychiatry, 57*(11), 1424–1435.

Nigg, J. & Casey, B. J. (2005, July). An integrative theory of attention-deficit/hyperactivity disorder based on the cognitive and affective neurosciences. *Development and Psychopathology, 17*(3), 785–806.

Pugh, K. R., Mencl, W. E., Jenner, A. R., Katz, L., Frost, S. J., Lee, J. R. (2001). Neurological studies of reading and reading disability. *Communication Disorders, 34,* 479–492.

Rourke, B., & Conway, J. A. (1997). Disabilities of arithmetic and mathematical reasoning: Perspectives from neurology and neuropsychology. *Journal of Learning Disabilities, 30,* 34–46.

Shaywitz, S., Shaywitz, B. A., Fulbright, R. K., Skudlarski, P., Mencl, W. E., Constable, R. T., Pugh, K. R., Loan, J. M., Marchione, K. E., Fletcher, J. M., Lyon, G. R. & Gore J. C. (2003). Neural systems for compensation and persistence: Young adult outcome of childhood reading disability. *Biological Psychiatry, 54*(1), 25–33.

Stewart, L., von Kriegstein, K., Warren, J. D. & Griffiths, T. D. (2006). Music and the brain: Disorders of musical listening. *Brain, 129*(10), 2533–2553.

Evolution, the Brain, and MBE Science

Anderson, M. (2007). Evolution of cognitive function via redeployment of brain areas. *The Neuroscientist: A review journal bridging neurobiology, neurology and psychiatry, 13*(1), 13–21.

Baldwin, M. (1896). A new factor in evolution. *The American Naturalist*, 30(354), 441–451.

Immordino-Yang, M. (2007b). An evolutionary perspective on reading and reading disorders? In K. W. Fischer, J. H. Bernstein, & M. H. Immordino-Yang, (Eds.), *Mind, brain and education in reading disorders*. Cambridge, UK: Cambridge University Press.

Jackendoff, R. (2003). Précis of Foundations of language: Brain, meaning, grammar, evolution. *The Behavioral and Brain Sciences, 26*(6), 651–665; discussion 666–707.

Joseph, R. (1993). *The naked neuron: Evolution and the languages of the body and brain*. New York: Plenum Publishing Corporation.

Linden, D. (2007). *The accidental mind: How brain evolution has given us love, memory, dreams and God*. Cambridge, MA: The Belknap Press of Harvard University.

Posner, M., & Rothbart, M. K. (1990). The evolution and development of the brain's attention system. *Quarterly Journal of Experimental Psychology, 42A*, 189–190.

Wolf, M. (2008). A triptych of the reading brain: Evolution, development, pathology, and its interventions. In A. Battro, K. W. Fischer, & P.J. Léna, *The educated brain* (pp. 183–197). Cambridge, UK: Cambridge University Press.

Important Websites in MBE Science

International Mind, Brain, and Education Society: www.imbes.org
Journal of MBE: www3.interscience.wiley.com/journal/117982931/home

References

Ambady, N., & Rosenthal, R. (1993). Judging social behavior using "thin slices." *Chance, 10,* 12–18.

Ansari, D. (2005a). Paving the way towards meaningful interactions between neuroscience and education. *Developmental Science, 8*(6), 466–467.

Ansari, D. (2005b). Time to use neuroscience finding in teacher training. *Nature, 437*(7055), 26.

Armstrong, T. (1998). *Awakening genius in the classroom.* Alexandria, VA: Association for Curriculum and Development.

Armstrong, T. (2006). *The best schools: How human development research should inform educational practice.* Alexandria, VA: Association for Supervision and Curriculum Development.

Bain, K. (2004). *What the best college teachers do.* Cambridge, MA: Harvard University Press.

Barsalou, L., Breazeal, C., & Smith, L. B. (2007). Cognition as coordinated noncognition. *Cognitive Processing, 8*(2), 79–91.

Battro, A., Fischer, K. W., & Léna, P. J. (Eds). (2008). *The educated brain: Essays in neuroeducation.* Cambridge, UK: Cambridge University Press.

Benar, J., & Miikkulainen, R. (2003). Learning innate face preferences. *Neural Computation, 15,* 1525–1557.

Benfenati, F. (2007). Synaptic plasticity and the neurobiology of learning and memory. *Acta Bio-Medica: Atenei Parmensis, 78*(Suppl 1), 58–66.

Berk, L. (2001). Modulation of neuroimmune parameters during the eustress of humor-associated mirthful laughter. *Alternative Therapies in Health and Medicine, 7*(2), 62–72, 74–76.

Berninger, V., & Abbott, R.D. (1992). The unit of analysis and the constructive processes of the learner: Key concepts for educational neuropsychology. *Educational Psychology, 27,* 223–242.

Berninger, V., & Corina, D. (1998). Making cognitive neuroscience educationally relevant: Creating bidirectional collaborations between educational psychology and cognitive neuroscience. *Educational Psychology Review, 10*(3), 343–354.

Best, J. (2006). From fad to worse. *Chronicle of Higher Education, 52*(32), B6–B7.

Best, J., Diniz Behn, C., Poe, G. R., & Booth, V. (2007). Neuronal models for sleep-wake regulation and synaptic reorganization in the sleeping hippocampus. *Journal of Biological Rhythms, 22*(3), 220–232.

Bettelheim, B. (1959). Feral children and autistic children. *American Journal of Sociology, 64*(5), 455–467.

Billington, D. (1997). *Seven characteristics of highly effective adult learning environments.* Retrieved January 4, 2005, from www.newhorizons.com

Bjorkman, S. (2007). *Relationships among academic stress, social support, and internalizing and externalizing behavior in adolescence.* Unpublished doctoral dissertation, Northern Illinois University, AAT 3279173.

Blakemore, S., & Frith, U. (2007). *The learning brain: Lessons for education.* Malden, MA: Blackwell.

Bloom, B. (1956). *Taxonomy of educational objectives: Handbook I. Cognitive domain.* New York: Longman.

Bonwell, C. (1993). *Active learning: Creating excitement in the classroom.* Retrieved August 20, 2007, from www.Active-Learning-Site.com

Bonwell, C., & Eison, J. (1991). *Active learning: Creating excitement in the classroom.* Washington, DC: Jossey-Bass.

Borich, G. (2006). *Effective teaching methods: Research based practice* (6th ed.). New York: Prentice Hall.

Boud, D., Cohen, R., & Sampson, J. (2001). *Peer learning in higher education: Learning from & with each other.* London: Kogan Page.

Bourgeois, J. (2001). Synaptogenesis in the neocortex of the newborn: The ultimate frontier for individuation? In C.A. Nelson & M. Luciana (Eds.), *Handbook for developmental cognitive neuroscience* (pp. 23–34). Cambridge, MA: MIT Press.

Bransford, J., Brown, A. L., & Cocking, R. R. (Eds.). (2003). *How people learn: Brain, mind, experience and school.* Washington, DC: National Academy Press.

Briggs, D. (2008). Synthesizing casual inferences. *Educational Researcher Journal, 37*(1), 15–22.

Brookfield, S. D. (2005). What it means to think critically. In S.B. Merriam (Ed.), *Critical thinking in adult education* (pp. 3–12). Hoboken, NJ: Wiley.

Brown, R., & Bjorklund, D. F. (1998). The biologizing of cognition, development, and education: Approach with cautious enthusiasm. *Educational Psychology Review, 10*(3), 355–374.

Bruer, J. (1997). Education and the brain: A bridge too far. *Educational Researcher, 26*(8), 4–16.

Caine, G., & Caine, R. N. (2001). *The brain, education and the competitive edge.* Lanham, MD: Scarecrow.

Caine, G., Nummela-Caine, R., & Crowell, S. (1999). *Mindshifts: A brain-based process for restructuring schools and renewing education* (2nd ed.). Tucson, AZ: Zephyr.

Cajal, S. (1911). *Histologie du système nerveux de l'homme et des vertébraux.* Paris: Maloine.

Calvin, W. (1996). *How brains think: Evolving intelligence, then and now.* New York: Basic Books.

Campbell, D. (1997). *The Mozart effect: Tapping the power of music to heal the body, strengthen the mind, and unlock the creative spirit.* New York: William Morrow & Company.

Carroll, R. T. (2009). Placebo effect. *The Skeptics Dictionary.* Retrieved on August 4, 2009, from http://www.skepdic.com/placebo.html

Carskadon, M., Acebo, C., & Jenni, O. G. (2004). Regulation of adolescent sleep: Implications for behavior. *Annals of the New York Academy of Sciences, 1021,* 276–291.

Carskadon, M., Wolfson, A. R., Acebo, C., Tzischinsky, O., & Seifer, R. (1998). Adolescent sleep patterns, circadian timing, and sleepiness at a transition to early school days. *Sleep, 21,* 871–881.

Chance, P. (1986). *Thinking in the classroom: A survey of programs.* New York: Teachers College Press.

Chatterjee, A. (2004). Cosmetic neurology: The controversy over enhancing movement, mentation, and mood. *Neurology, 63*(6), 968–974.

Chickering, A. W., & Gamson, Z. F. (1987). Seven principles for good practice in undergraduate education. *AAHE Bulletin, 39,* 3–7.

Coch, D., Fischer, K. W., & Dawson, G. (Eds.) (2007). *Human behavior, learning, and the developing brain: Typical development.* New York: Guilford Press.

Compton, R., Heller, W., Banich, M. T., Palmieri, P. A., & Miller, G. A. (2000). Responding to threat: Hemispheric asymmetries and interhemispheric division of input. *Neuropsychology, 14*(2), 254-264.

Copinschi, G. (2005). Metabolic and endocrine effects of sleep deprivation. *Essential Psychopharmacology, 6,* 341–347.

Cotman, C., & Berchtold, N. C. (2002). Exercise: A behavioral intervention to enhance brain health and plasticity. *Trends in Neuroscience, 25,* 295–301.

Cromie, W. J. (1999, Sept). Mozart effect hits sour notes. *Harvard Gazette Archives.* Retrieved August 4, 2009 from http://www.news.harvard.edu/gazette/1999/09.16/mozart.html

Dehaene, S. (2004). Evolution of human cortical circuits for reading and arithmetic: The "neuronal recycling" hypothesis. In S. Dehaene, J. R. Duhamel, M. Hauser, & G. Rizzolatti (Eds.), *From monkey brain to human brain.* Cambridge, MA: MIT Press.

deHann, M., Pascalis, O., & Johnson, M. H. (2002). Specializations of neural mechanisms underlying face recognition in human infants. *Journal of Cognitive Neuroscience, 14,* 199–209.

Denckla, M. (2005, April). *Paying attention to the brain and executive function: How learning and memory are impaired by the syndrome called ADHD.* Paper presented at the Learning and the Brain Conference. Cambridge, MA.

Depue, R., & Collins, P. F. (1999). Neurobiology of the structure of personality: Dopamine facilitation of incentive motivation, and extraversion. *Behavioral & Brain Science, 22*(3), 491–517.

De Raedt, R. (2006). Does neuroscience hold promise for the further development of behavior therapy? The case of emotional change after exposure in anxiety and depression. *Scandinavian Journal of Psychology, 47*(3), 225–236.

Dewey, J. (1998). *How we think: A restatement of the relation of reflective thinking to the educative process.* Chicago: Henry Regenery Co. (Original work published 1933) Excerpts retrieved on July 20, 2008, from http://www.infed.org/thinkers/et-dewey.htm

Diamond, M., Krech, D., & Rosenzweig, M. R. (1964). The effects of an enriched environment on the rat cerebral cortex. *Journal of Comparative Neurology, 123,* 111–119.

Doidge, N. (2007). *The brain that changes itself: Stories of personal triumph from the frontiers of brain science.* New York: Penguin.

Durmer, J., & Dinges. D. F. (2005). Neurocognitive consequences of sleep deprivation. *Seminars in Neurology, 25*(1), 117–129.

Dwyer, T., Sallis, J. F., Blizzard, L., Lazzarus, R., & Dean, K. (2001). Relation of academic performance to physical activity and fitness in children. *Pediatric Exercise Science, 13*(3), 225–237.

Edin, F., Macoveanu, J., Olesen, P., Tegnér, J., & Klingberg, T. (2007). Stronger synaptic connectivity as a mechanism behind development of working memory–related brain activity during childhood. *Journal of Cognitive Neuroscience, 19*(5), 750–760.

Education Commission of the United States. (1998). *Bridging the gap between neuroscience and education.* Denver, CO: Education Commission of the States.

Eisenhart, M., & DeHaan, R. L. (2005). Doctoral preparation of scientifically based education researchers. *Educational Researcher, 34*(4), 3–14.

Elder, L., & Paul, R. (1996). *Critical thinking development: A stage theory with implications for instruction.* Retrieved March 1, 2007, from http://www.criticalthinking.org/page.cfm?PageID=483&CategoryID=68.

Endo, T., Roth, C., Landolt, H. P., Werth, E., Aeschbach, D., & Borbély, A. (1998). Selective REM sleep deprivation in humans: Effects on sleep and sleep EEG. *American Journal of Physiology, 274* [electronic version].

Erikson, E. H. (1950). *Childhood and society.* New York: Norton.

Erikson, E. H. (1959). *Identity and the life cycle.* New York: International Universities Press.

Erlauer-Myrah, L. (2006). Applying brain-friendly instructional practices. *School Administrator, 63*(11), 16–18.

Facione, P. A. (2004). *Critical thinking: What it is and why it counts.* Millbrae, CA: Insight Assessment.

Fernandes, M., & Moscovitch, M. (2000). Divided attention and memory: Evidence of substantial interference effects at encoding and retrieval. *Journal of Experimental Psychology: General, 129*, 155–176.

Filipowicz, A. (2003). The influence of humor on performance in task-based interactions. Doctoral dissertation, Harvard University. AAT 3051159.

Fink, L. D. (2003). *Creating significant learning experiences: An integrated approach to designing college courses.* San Francisco: Jossey-Bass.

Fischer, K. (2007, April). *Mind, brain, and education: Analyzing human learning and development.* Podcast of the inaugural launch of the journal *Mind, Brain, and Education.* Cambridge, MA: Harvard University.

Fischer, K. & Fusaro, M. (2006, May). From the president's desk: Building Mind, Brain, and Education. *The.MBE.PONS, 1*(2), 1.

Fisher, J. (2005). *The development of perceptual expertise in the visual categorization of complex patterns.* Doctoral dissertation, Northwestern University. AAT 3200931.

Fitzgerald, D., Angstadt, M., Jelsone, L. M., Nathan, P. J., & Phan, K. L. (2006). Beyond threat: Amygdala reactivity across multiple expressions of facial affect. *NeuroImage, 30*(4), 1441–1448.

Funahashi, S., Takeda, K., & Watanabe, Y. (2004). Neural mechanisms of spatial working memory: Contributions of the dorsolateral prefrontal cortex and the thalamic mediodorsal nucleus. *Cognitive, Affective and Behavioral Neuroscience, 4*(4), 409–421.

Furnham, A., Christopher, A., Garwood, J., & Martin, N. (2008). Ability, demography, learning style, and personality trait correlates of student preference for assessment method. *Educational Psychology, 28*(1), 15.

Gardner, H. (1987). *The mind's new science: A history of the cognitive revolution.* New York: Basic Books.

Gardner, H. (1993). *Frames of mind: The theory of multiple intelligences.* New York: Basic Books. (Original work published 1983)

Gardner, H. (2007). *Five minds for the future*. Cambridge, MA: Harvard Business School Press.

Garner, R. (2006). Humor in pedagogy: How ha-ha can lead to aha! *College Teaching, 54*(1), 177–180.

Gaustad, J. (1992, December). School discipline. *ERIC Digest*, p. 78.

Gauthier, I., Tarr, M. J., Moylan, J., Skudlarski, P., Gore, J. C., & Anderson, A. W. (2000). The fusiform "face area" is part of a network that processes faces at the individual level. *Journal of Cognitive Neuroscience, 12*, 495–504.

Gazzaniga, M. (Ed.). (2005a). Smarter on drugs. *Scientific American Mind, 11*, 32–37.

Gazzaniga, M. (Ed.). (2005b). *The cognitive neurosciences, III*. Cambridge: MIT Press.

Gazzaniga, M., Ivry, R. B., & Mangun, G. R. (Eds.). (2002). *Cognitive neuroscience: The biology of the mind*. New York: W. W. Norton & Company.

Geake, J. (2004a). Cognitive neuroscience and education: Two-way traffic or one-way street? *Westminster Studies in Education, 27*(1), 87–98.

Geake, J. (2004b). How children's brains think: Not left or right but both together. *Education, 32*, 65–72.

Geake, J. (2005a). Educational neuroscience and neuroscientific education: In search of a mutual middle way. *Research Intelligence, 92*, 10–13.

Geake, J. (2005b). The neurological basis of intelligence: Implications for education: An abstract. *Gifted and Talented, 9*(1), 8.

Giordano, P. (2004). *Teaching and learning when we least expect it: The role of critical moments in student development*. Excellence in Teaching, Psych Teacher electronic discussion. Retrieved November 14, 2004, from http://www.chronicle.com

Given, B. (2002). *Teaching to the brain's natural learning systems*. Alexandria, VA: Association for Supervision and Curriculum Development.

Goldberg, E. (2006). *The wisdom paradox: How your mind can grow stronger as your brain grows older*. New York: Gotham Books.

Golombek, D. A., & Cardinali, D. P. (2008). Mind, brain, and education and biological timing. *Mind, Brain, and Education, 2*(1), 1–6.

Goswami, U. (2005a). The brain in the classroom? The state of the art. *Developmental Science, 8*(6), 468–469.

Goswami, U. (2005b). Neuroscience and education: The brain in the classroom. Target article with commentaries. *Psychology of Education Review, 29*(2), 17–18.

Goswami, U. (2006). Neuroscience and education: From research to practice. *Nature Reviews Neuroscience, 7*(5), 406–413.

Goswami, U. (2008a). *Cognitive development: The learning brain*. London: Taylor & Francis.

Goswami, U. (2008b). Neuroscience and education. In *The Jossey-Bass reader on the brain and learning* (pp. 33–50). San Francisco: Wiley.

Guild, P., & Chock-Eng, S. (1998). Multiple intelligence, learning styles, brain-based education: Where do the messages overlap? *Schools in the Middle, 7*(4), 38–40.

Gunn, A., Richburg, R.W., & Smilkstein, R. (2007). *Igniting student potential: Teaching with the brain's natural learning process*. Thousand, Oaks, CA: Corwin.

Gurian M., & Stevens, K. (2007). *The minds of boys: Saving our sons from falling behind in school and life*. San Francisco: Jossey-Bass.

Hake, R.R. (1998). Interactive engagement versus traditional methods: A six-thousand-student survey of mechanics test data for introductory physics courses. *American Journal of Physics, 66*, 64–74.

Halary, K., & Weintrayub, P. (1991). *Right-brain learning in 30 days*. New York: St. Martin's Press.

Hall, J. (2005). Neuroscience and education. *Education Journal, 84*, 27–29.

Halpern, D., & Hakel, M. D. (2002). *Applying the science of learning to university teaching and beyond*. San Francisco: Jossey-Bass.

Hauser, M. D., Chomsky, N., & Fitch, W. T. (2002). The faculty of language: What is it, who has it, and how did it evolve? *Science, 298*(5598), 1569–1580.

Hebb, D. (1949). *The organization of behavior*. New York: Wiley.

Henry, N. B. (Ed.). (1960). *Rethinking science education: The fifty-ninth yearbook of the National Society for the Study of Education*. Chicago: University of Chicago Press.

Hitachi. (2008). *Optical topography and Hideaki Koizumi*. Retrieved April 4, 2008, from http://www.hitachi.com/New/cnews/040311b.html

Hobson, J. (2004). *Dreaming: An introduction to the science of sleep*. New York: Oxford University Press.

Hobson, J., & Pace-Schott, E. F., (2002). The cognitive neuroscience of sleep: Neuronal systems, consciousness and learning. *Nature Reviews Neuroscience, 3*, 679–693.

Hobson, J., Pace-Schott, E. F., & Stickgold, R. (2000). Dreaming and the brain: Toward a cognitive neuroscience of conscious states. *Behavioral and Brain Sciences, 23*, 793.

Holcombe, K., & Johnson, M. H. (2005). Educating executive attention. *Proceedings of the National Academy of Sciences of the United States of America, 102*(41), 14479–14480.

Holtzer, R., Stern, Y., & Rakitin, B. C. (2004). Age-related differences in executive control of working memory. *Memory & Cognition, 32*(8), 1333–1346.

Hong, E. (1999). Test anxiety, perceived test difficulty, and test performance: Temporal patterns of their effects. *Learning & Individual Differences, 11*(4), 431–448.

Howard-Jones, P. (2005). An invaluable foundation for better bridges. *Developmental Science, 8*(6), 470–471.

Howard-Jones, P. (2007). *Neuroscience and education: Issues and opportunities. Commentary by the Teacher and Learning Research Programme*. London: TLRP. Retrieved January 14, 2008, from http://www.tlrp.org/pub/commentaries.html

Hurd, P. (2008). *The state of critical thinking today*. Dillon Beach, CA: Foundation for Critical Thinking. Retrieved December 10, 2008, from http://www.criticalthinking.org/professionalDev/the-state-ct-today.cfm.

Huttenlocher, P., & Dabholkar, A. S. (1997). Regional differences in synaptogenesis in human cerebral cortex. *Journal of Comparative Neurology, 387*, 167–178.

Iidaka, T., Aderson, N., Kapur, S., Cabeza, R., & Craik, F. (2000). The effort of divided attention on encoding and retrieval in episodic memory revealed by positron emission tomography. *Journal of Cognitive Neuroscience, 12*(2), 267–280.

Illes, J. (2005). *Neuroethics in the 21st century*. Oxford: Oxford University Press.

Illes, J. (Ed.). (2006). *Neuroethics*. Oxford: Oxford University Press.

Immordino-Yang, M. (2007a). A tale of two cases: Lessons for education from the study of two boys living with half their brains. *Mind, Brain, and Education, 1*(2), 66–83.

Immordino-Yang, M. (2007b). An evolutionary perspective on reading and reading disorders? In K. W. Fischer, J. H. Bernstein, & M. H. Immordino-Yang (Eds.), *Mind, brain and education in reading disorders* (pp. 16–29). Cambridge, UK: Cambridge University Press.

Immordino-Yang, M., & Damasio, A. (2008). We feel, therefore we learn: The relevance of affective and social neuroscience to education. In *The Jossey-Bass reader on the brain and learning* (pp. 183–198). San Francisco: Wiley.

James S. McDonnell Foundation. (2005). *The neuro-journalism mill: Separating the wheat from the chaff of media reporting on brain sciences.* Retrieved September 13, 2007, from http://www.jsmf.org/about/jpubs.htm

Japikse, K. (2002). *Interference in procedural learning: Effects of exposure to intermittent patterns.* Doctoral dissertation, Georgetown University, Washington, DC. AAT 3046279.

Jehee, J., Rothkopf, C., Beck, J. M., & Ballard, D. H. (2006). Learning receptive fields using predictive feedback. *Journal of Physiology* (Paris), *100*(1–3), 125–132.

Jensen, E. (2006). *Enriching the brain: How to maximize every learner's potential.* San Francisco: Wiley.

Jolles, J., de Groot, R., van Benthem, J., Dekkers, H., de Glopper, C., Uijlings, H., & Wolff-Albers, A. (2005). *Brain lessons. A contribution to the international debate on brain, learning & education.* Maastricht, Netherlands: Neuropsych Publishers.

Jonides, J., & Nee, D. E. (2006). Brain mechanisms of proactive interference in working memory. *Neuroscience, 139*(1), 181–193.

The Jossey-Bass reader on the brain and learning. (2008). San Francisco: Wiley.

Kacinik, N., & Chiarello, C. (2007). Understanding metaphors: Is the right hemisphere uniquely involved? *Brain and Language, 100*(2), 188–207.

Kalueff, A. (2007). Neurobiology of memory and anxiety: From genes to behavior. *Neuralplasticity, 78,* 171.

Kandel, E. (2007). *In search of memory: The emergence of a new science of mind.* New York: Norton.

Kanwisher, N., & Yovel, G. (2006, December). The fusiform face area: A cortical region specialized for the perception of faces. *Philosophical Transactions of the Royal Society of London, Series B, Biological Sciences, 361*(1476), 2109

Keuler, D., & Safer, M. A. (1998). Memory bias in the assessment and recall of pre-exam anxiety: How anxious was I? *Applied Cognitive Psychology, 12,* S127–S137.

Killgore, W., Blakin, T. J., & Wesensten, N. J. (2005). Impaired decision making following 49 h of sleep deprivation. *Journal of Sleep Research 15,* 7–13.

Kilts, C., Kelsey, J. E., Knight, B., & Ely, T. D. (2006). The neural correlates of social anxiety disorder and response to pharmacotherapy. *Neuropsychopharmacology, 31*(10), 2243.

Kimura, D. (2002, August). Sex differences in the brain. *Scientific American,* 32–34.

King, A. (1993). From sage on the stage to guide on the side. *Questia, 41,* 1.

King, D. (1999). *Exercise seen boosting children's brain function.* Retrieved January 23, 2008, from http://www.pelinks4u.org/news/bgbrain.htm

Korenman, L., & Peynircioglu, Z. F. (2007). Individual differences in learning and remembering music: Auditory versus visual presentation. *Journal of Research in Music Education, 55*(1), 48–55.

LeDoux, J. (2003). *Synaptic self: How our brains become who we are.* New York: Penguin.

Leppo, M., & Davis, D. (2005). Movement opens pathways to learning. *Strategies, 19*(2), 11–16.

Lesser, M. (2003). *The brain chemistry plan: The personalized nutritional prescription for balancing mood, relieving stress, conquering depression.* New York: Berkeley Publishing Group.

Levine, M. (2000). *A mind at a time.* New York: Simon & Schuster.

Lieberman, M. (2007). Social cognitive neuroscience: A review of core processes. *Annual Review of Psychology, 58,* 259.

Lindblom-Ylänne, S., & Lonka, K. (1999). Individual ways of interacting with the learning environment—Are they related to study success? *Learning and Instruction, 9*(1), 1–18.

Linden, D. (2007). *The accidental mind: How brain evolution has given us love, memory, dreams and God.* Cambridge, MA: The Belknap Press of Harvard University.

Littleton, J. (1998). Learning to laugh and laughing to learn. *Montessori Life, 10*(4), 42–44.

Liu, J. (2004). Malnutrition at age 3 years and externalizing behavior problems at ages 8, 11, and 17 years. *American Journal of Psychiatry, 161*(11), 13.

Lucas, B. (2006). *Boost your brain power week by week: 52 techniques to make you smarter.* London: Duncan Baird.

Maloney, K. (2004). *The evolutionary development of the scientific mind: A grounded theory of adventuring.* Unpublished Ed.D. dissertation (Ed.D.), Fielding Graduate Institute, AAT 3120901.

Mangels, J., Butterfield, B., & Lamb, J. (2006). Why do beliefs about intelligence influence learning success? A social cognitive neuroscience model. *Social Cognitive and Affective Neuroscience,* (2), 75–86.

Marcason, W. (2005). Can dietary intervention play a part in the treatment of attention deficit and hyperactivity disorder? *Journal of the American Dietetic Association, 105*(7), 1161–1161.

Mareschal, D., Johnson, M. H., Sirios, S., Spratline, M., Thomas, M., & Westermann, G. (2007). *Neuroconstruictivism: How the brain constructs cognition.* Oxford, UK: Blackwell.

Martin, S., & Morris, R. G. M. (2002). New life in an old idea: The synaptic plasticity and memory hypothesis revisited. *Hippocampus, 12,* 609–636.

Marzano, R. (2007). *The art and science of teaching: A comprehensive framework for effective instruction.* Arlington, VA: Association for Supervision & Curriculum Development.

Marzano, R., Pickering, D. J., & Pollock, J. E. (2004). *Classroom instruction that works: Research-based strategies for increasing student achievement.* New York: Prentice Hall.

Mascolo, M., & Fischer, K. W. (2003). Beyond the nature-nurture divide in development and evolution. Review of Gilbert Gottlieb's "Individual development and evolution." *Contemporary Psychology, 48,* 842–847.

Maslow, A. (1943). A theory of human motivation. *Psychosomatic Medicine, 15,* 85–92.

McCann, E., & Garcia, T. (1999). Maintaining motivation and regulating emotion: Measuring individual differences in academic volitional strategies. *Learning & Individual Differences, 11*(3), 259–270.

McCutcheon, L.E. (2000). Another failure to generalize the Mozart effect. *Psychological Reports, 87*, 325–30.

McKeachie, W. J., Pintrich, P. R., Yi-Guang, L., & Smith, D. A. F. (1986). *Teaching and learning in the college classroom: A review of the research literature.* Ann Arbor: Regents of the University of Michigan.

McKinsey & Company. (2007). *How the world's best performing school systems come out on top.* Retrieved December 19, 2007, from http://www.mckinsey.com/clientservice/socialsector/resources/pdf/Worlds_School_Systems_Final.pdf

Mednick, S., Nakayama, K., & Stickgold, R. (2003). Sleep-dependent learning: A nap is as good as a night. *Nature Neuroscience, 6*(7), 697.

Meltzoff, A. (2007). "Like me": A foundation for social cognition. *Developmental Science, 10*(1), 126–134.

Meltzoff, A., & Decety, J. (2003). What imitation tells us about social cognition: A rapprochement between developmental psychology and cognitive neuroscience. *Philosophical Transactions of the Royal Society B: Biological Science, 358*(1431), 491–500.

Mezirow, J. (1991). *Transformative dimensions of adult learning.* San Francisco: Jossey-Bass.

Michigan Department of Education. (2006). *Brain breaks.* Retrieved March 22, 2009, from http://www.emc.cmich.edu/brainbreaks/

Mignot, E. (2008). Why we sleep: The temporal organization of recovery. *PLoS Biol 6*(4) [electronic version].

Miller, G. (2004). Brain cells may pay the price for a bad night's sleep. *Science, 306*(5699), 1126.

Miller, M., Van Horn, J. D., Wolford, G. L., Handy, T. C., Valsangkar-Smyth, M., Inati, S., Grafton, S., & Gazzaniga, M. S. (2002). Extensive individual differences in brain activations associated with episodic retrieval are reliable over time. *Journal of Cognitive Neuroscience, 14*(8), 1200–1214.

Molfese, D. (2000). Predicting dyslexia at 8 years of age using neonatal brain responses. *Brain and Language, 72*, 238–245.

Molteni, R. (2002). A high-fat, refined sugar diet reduces hippocampal brain-derived neurotrophic factor, neuronal plasticity, and learning. *Neuroscience, 112*(14), 803–814.

Morasch, K. (2007). *Explicit memory and brain-electrical activity in 10-month-old infants.* Unpublished doctoral dissertation, Virginia Polytech University. Retrieved September 14, 2007, from http://scholar.lib.vt.edu/theses/available/etd-04202007-152907/

Moss, M., & Scholey, A.B. (1995). Oxygen administration enhances memory formation in healthy young adults. *Psychopharmacology, 124*(3), 255–260.

Muris, P., Merckelbach, H., & Damsma, E. (2000). Threat perception bias in non-referreed, socially anxious children. *Journal of Clinical Child Psychology, 29*, 348–359.

Nigg, J. (2005). Neuropsychologic theory and findings in attention-deficit/hyperactivity disorder: The state of the field and salient challenges for the coming decade. *Biological Psychiatry, 57*(11), 1424–1435.

Nummela-Caine, R., & Caine, G. (1994). *Making connections: Teaching and the human brain* (rev. ed). Bel Air, CA: Dale Seymour Publications.

Nummela-Caine, R., & Caine, G. (1994). *Making connections: Teaching and the human brain* (rev. ed). Bel Air, CA: Dale Seymour Publications.

Nummela-Caine, R., Caine, G., McClintic, C., & Klimek, K. J. (2008). *12 brain/mind learning principles in action.* Thousand Oaks, CA: Corwin.

O'Boyle, M. (2008). Mathematically gifted children: Developmental brain characteristics and their prognosis for well-being. *Roeper Review, 30*(3), 181–186.

Organisation for Economic Co-Operation and Development (OECD). (2002). *Understanding the brain: Towards a new learning science.* Paris: Author. Retrieved from www.oecd.org

Organisation for Economic Co-operation and Development (OECD). (2007). *The brain and learning: The birth of a new learning science.* Retrieved March 10, 2007, from http://www.oecd.org/department/0,2688,en_2649_14935397_1_1_1_1_1,00.html

Ortega-Perez, I., Murray, K., & Lledo, P. M. (2007). The how and why of adult neurogenesis. *Journal of Molecular Histology, 38*(6) [electronic version].

Pace-Schott, E., & Hobson, J. A. (2002). The neurobiology of sleep: Genetics, cellular physiology and subcortical networks. *Nature Reviews Neuroscience, 3*, 591–605.

Paul, R. (1992). Características de un pensador crítico. In A. C. Muñoz Hueso & J. Beltrán Llera (2001), *Fomento del Pensamiento Crítico mediante la intervención en una unidad didáctica sobre la técnica de detección de información sesgada en los alumnos de Enseñanza Secundaria Obligatoria en Ciencias Sociales Universidad Complutense de Madrid.* Departamento de Psicología Evolutiva y de la Educación. Retrieved November 11, 2005, from http://www.psicologia-online.com/ciopa2001/actividades/54/.

Pelegrina, S., Bajo, M. T., & Justicia, F. (1999). Allocation of time in self-paced memory tasks: The role of practice, instructions, and individual differences in optimizing performance. *Learning & Individual Differences, 11*(4), 401–410.

Piaget, J. (1955). *The child's construction of reality.* London: Routledge & Kegan Paul.

Piaget, J. (1972). Intellectual evolution from adolescence to adulthood. *Human Development, 15*(1), 1–12.

Pickering, S., & Phye, G. D. (2006). *Working memory and education.* Burlington, MA: Academic Press.

PISA. (2009). OECD PISA competencies. Retrieved March 20, 2009, from http://www.pisa.oecd.org/

Popham, J. W. (2001). *The truth about testing: An educator's call to action.* Alexandria, VA: Association for Supervision and Curriculum Development.

Poppel, E. (2004). Lost in time: A historical frame, elementary processing units and the 3-second window. *Acta neurobiologiae experimentalis, 64*(3), 295–301.

Posner M. (Ed). (2004). *Cognitive neuroscience of attention.* New York: Guilford.

Presseisen, B. (1999). *Teaching for intelligence: A collection of articles.* Thousand Oaks, CA: Corwin.

Purhonen, M., Kilpelainen-Lees, R., Valkonen-Korhonen, M., Karhu, J., & Lehtonen, J. (2004). Cerebral processing of mother's voice compared of unfamiliar voice in 4-month-old infants. *International Journal of Psychophysiology, 52*(3), 257–266.

Putnam, J., Spiegel, A. N, & Bruininks, R. H. (1995). *Future directions in education and inclusion of students with disabilities: A Delphi investigation.* Retrieved November 19, 2007, from http://www.eric.ed.gov:80/ERICWebPortal/custom/portlets/recordDetails/detailmini.jsp?_nfpb=true&_&ERICExtSearch_SearchValue_0=EJ503064&ERICExtSearch_SearchType_0=no&accno=EJ503064

Ramos-Voigt, L. (2007). Examining the relationship of instructional time to student achievement. Doctoral dissertation, Capella University. AAT 3251337.

Rauch, S., Shin, L. M., & Wright, C. I. (2003). Neuroimaging studies of amygdala function in anxiety disorders. *Annals of the New York Academy of Sciences, 985*, 389–410.

Rauscher, F. H., Shaw, G. L., & Ky, K. N. (1993). Music and spatial task performance. *Nature, 365*, 611.

Rauscher, F., Shaw, G., Levine, L., Wright, E., Dennis, W., & Newcomb, R. (1997). Music training causes long-term enhancement of preschool children's spatial-temporal reasoning. *Neurological Research, 19*(1), 2–8.

Raz, A., & Buhle, J. (2006). Typologies of attentional networks. *Nature Reviews Neuroscience, 7*(5), 367–379.

Reeve, J. (2004). *Understanding motivation and emotion* (4th ed.). New York: Wiley.

Restak, R. (2008). How our brain constructs our mental world. In *The Jossey-Bass reader on the brain and learning* (pp. 3–11). San Francisco: Wiley.

Reynolds, D., Nicolson, R. I., & Hambly, H. (2003). Evaluation of an exercise-based treatment for children with reading difficulties. *Dyslexia, 9*, 48–71.

Ridley, M. (2003). *Nature via nurture: Genes, experience, and what makes us human.* New York: HarperCollins.

Ronis, D. (2007). *Brain-compatible assessments* (2nd ed.). Thousand Oaks, CA: Corwin.

Rose, D. H., & Meyer, A. (Eds.). (2006). *A practical reader in Universal Design for Learning.* Cambridge, MA: Harvard Education Press.

Rosenzweig, M., Krech, D., & Bennett, E. L. (1958). *Neurological basis of behaviour.* (Ciba Foundation Symposium). London: Churchill.

Rueda, M., Fan, J., McCandliss, B. D., Halparin, J. D., Gruber, D. B., Lercari, L. P., & Posner, M. I. (2004). Development of attentional networks in childhood. *Neuropsychologia, 42*(8), 1029–1040.

Sander, D., Grandjean, D., Pourtois, G., Schwartz, S., Seghier, M., Scherer, K. R., & Vuilleumier, P. (2005). Emotion and attention interactions in social cognition: Brain regions involved in processing anger prosody. *NeuroImage, 28*, 848–858.

Sapolsky, R. (2001). Depression, antidepressants, and the shrinking hippocampus. *Proceedings of the National Academy of Science, 98*(22), 12320–12322.

Schacter, D. (2007). *The seven sins of memory: How the mind forgets and remembers.* New York: Houghton Mifflin.

Schacter, D., & Addis, D. R. (2007). The cognitive neuroscience of constructive memory: Remembering the past and imagining the future. *Philosophical Transactions of the Royal Society of London Series B, Biological Sciences, 362*(1481), 773–786.

Scherer, M. (2006). *Celebrate strengths, nurture affinities: A conversation with Mel Levine.* Retrieved August 31, 2007, from http://www.ascd.org/authors/ed_lead/ el200609_scherer2.html

Schrimer, A. (2003). Emotional speech perception: Electrophysiological insights into the processing of emotional prosody and word valence in men and women. Unpublished dissertation, Leipzig Universitat, Max Planck Institute of Cognitive Neuroscience.

Schwartz, C., Wright, C. T., Shin, L. M., Kagan, J., & Rauch, S. L. (2003). Inhibited and uninhibited infants "grown up": Adult amygdalar response to novelty. *Science, 300*, 1952–1953.

Scientific Learning Corporation. (2009). *Scientific learning: FastForWord.* Retrieved August 4, 2009, from http://www.scilearn.com/

Sheridan, K., Zinchenko, E., & Gardner, H. (2005). Neuroethics in education. In J. Illes (Ed.), *Neuroethics* (pp. 281–308). Oxford: Oxford University Press.

Sheridan, K., Zinchenko, E., & Gardner, H. (2006 May). Neuroethics in education. *The.MBE.PONS, 1*(2), 4–5.

Skinner, B. (1974). *About behaviorism*. New York: Knopf.

Slobin, D.I. (Ed.). (1992). *The crosslinguistic study of language acquisition*. Mahwah, NJ: Erlbaum.

Smilkstein, R. (2003). *We're born to learn: Using the brain's natural learning process to create today's curriculum*. Thousand Oaks, CA: Corwin.

Smith, A. (2004). *Accelerated learning in practice: Brain-based methods for accelerating motivation and achievement*. London: Network Education Press.

Smith, M., Gosselin, F., & Schyns, P. G. (2007). From a face to its category via a few information processing states in the brain. *NeuroImage, 37*(3), 974–984.

Society for Neuroscience. (2007a). *Depression and stress hormones*. Retrieved September 11, 2007, from www.sfn.org/index.cfm?pagename=brainbriefings_depressionandstresshormones

Society for Neuroscience. (2007b). *Humor and laughter in the brain*. Retrieved September 11, 2007, from http://www.sfn.org/index.cfm?pagename=brainBriefings_humorLaughterAndTheBrain

Society for Neuroscience. (2007c). *Stress and the brain*. Retrieved September 11, 2007, from http://www.sfn.org/index.cfm?pagename=brain Briefings_stressAndTheBrain

Sohn, Y., Doane, S. M., & Garrison, T. (2006). The impact of individual differences and learning context on strategic skill acquisition and transfer. *Learning & Individual Differences, 16*(1), 13–30.

Sousa, D. (2000). *How the brain learns*. Thousand Oaks, CA: Corwin.

Steen, R. (2007). *The evolving brain: The known and the unknown*. New York: Prometheus.

Stewart, L., von Kriegstein, K., Warren, J. D., & Griffiths, T. D. (2006). Music and the brain: Disorders of musical listening. *Brain, 129*(Pt 10), 2533–2553.

Stickgold, R. (2005). Sleep-dependent memory consolidation. *Nature, 437*(7063), 1272–1279.

Stickgold, R. (2006). Neuroscience: A memory boost while you sleep. *Nature, 444*(7119), 559–560.

Sylwester, R. (1985). Research on memory: Major discoveries, major educational challenges. *Educational Leadership, 42*(7), 69–75.

Sylwester, R. (1997). Unconscious emotions, conscious feelings, and curricular challenges. Originally printed in *MindShift Connection 1(1)*, Zephyr Press. Retrieved August 20, 2007, from www.newhorizons.org/neuro/sywester3.htm

Sylwester, R. (2003). *A biological brain in a cultural classroom: Enhancing cognitive and social development through collaborative classroom management*. Thousand Oaks, CA: Corwin.

Tainturier, M., Schiemenz, S., & Leek, E. (2006). Separate orthographic representations for reading and spelling? Evidence from a case of preserved lexical reading and impaired lexical spelling. *Brain and Language, 99*(1–2), 31–32.

Taylor, D., Jenni, O. G., Acebo, C., & Carskadon, M. A. (2005). Sleep tendency during extended wakefulness: Insights into adolescent sleep regulation and behavior. *Journal of Sleep Research, 14*, 239–244.

Taylor, J. (2008). *My stroke of insight: A brain scientist's personal journey*. New York: Viking.

Thomas, J. (1972). The variation of memory with time for information appearing during a lecture. *Studies in Adult Education, 4*, 57–62.

Thompson, P., Giedd, J. N., Woods, R. P., MacDonald, D., Evans, A. C., & Toga, A. W. (2000). Growth patterns in the developing brain detected by using continuum mechanical tensor maps. *Nature, 404,* 190–193.

Thompson, W. (1999). Individual differences in memory-monitoring accuracy. *Learning & Individual Differences, 11*(4), 365–377.

Tinnesz, C. G., Ahuna, K. H., & Kiener, M. (2006). Toward college success: Internalizing active and dynamic strategies. *College Teaching, 54*(4), 302–306.

Tokuhama-Espinosa, T. (2008a). *Living languages: Multilingualism across the lifespan.* Westport, CT: Greenwood.

Tokuhama-Espinosa, T. (2008b). *The scientifically substantiated art of teaching: A study in the emerging standards in neuroeducation.* Unpublished doctoral dissertation, Capella University. Retrieved on October 3, 2009, from http://www.proquest.com/en-US/products/dissertations/pqdt.shtml.

Tokuhama-Espinosa, T., Sanguinetti, V., & Guerra, S. (in press). *¿Qué hacen los mejores profesores?* Quito, Ecuador: Universidad San Francisco de Quito.

Tomlinson, C. (1999). *The differentiated classroom: Responding to the needs of all learners.* Alexandria, VA: Association for Supervision and Curriculum Development.

Tomlinson, C., & Kalbfleisch, M. L. (1998). Teach me, teach my brain: A call for differentiated classrooms. *Educational Leadership, 56*(3), 52–56.

Tomlinson, C., & McTighe, J. (2006). *Integrating differentiated instruction & understanding by design: Connecting content and kids.* Alexandria, VA: Association for Supervision and Curriculum Development.

Touyarot, K., Venero, C., & Sandi, C. (2004). Spatial learning impairment induced by chronic stress is related to individual differences in novelty reactivity: Search for neurobiological correlates. *Psychoneuroendocrinology, 29*(2), 290–305.

Tucker, P., & Stronge, J.H. (2005). *Linking teacher evaluation and student learning.* Alexandria, VA: Association for Supervision and Curriculum Development.

UNESCO (United Nations Educational, Scientific and Cultural Organization). (2008). *Educational Strategies.* Retrieved January 28, 2008, from http://portal.unesco.org/education/en/ev.php-URL_ID=48792&URL_DO=DO_TOPIC&URL_SECTION=201.html.

U.S. National Institute of Child Health and Human Development. (2009). *Human health and development information.* Retrieved March 20, 2008, from www.nichd.nih.gov

Van Der Jagt, J., Ramasamy, R., Jacobs, R. L., Ghose, C., & Lindsey, J. D. (2003). Hemisphericity modes, learning styles, and environmental preferences of students in an introduction to special education course. *International Journal of Special Education, 18*(1), 24–35.

Varma, S., McCandliss, B., & Schwartz, D. (2008). Scientific and pragmatic challenges for bridging education and neuroscience. *Educational Researcher, 37*(3), 140–152.

Vianna, E., & Stetsenko, A. (2006). Embracing history through transforming it: Contrasting Piagetian versus Vygotskian theories of learning and development to expand constructivism within a dialectical view of history. *Theory & Psychology, 16*(1), 81–108.

Voelkle, M., Wittmann, W. W., & Ackerman, P. L. (2006). Abilities and skill acquisition: A latent growth curve approach. *Learning & Individual Differences, 16*(4), 303–319.

Vuilleumier, P., Harmony, J., & Dolan, R. (2003). Reciprocal links between emotion and attention. In R. S. J. Frackowiak (Ed.), *Human brain function* (pp. 419–444). San Diego: Academic Press.

Wager, K. (2009). Biological psychology: An illustrated survival guide. *Journal of Mental Health, 18*(3), 274.

Walker, D., Toufexis, D. J., & Davis, M. (2003). Role of the bed nucleus of the stria terminalis versus the amygdala in fear, stress, and anxiety. *European Journal of Pharmacology, 463*, 199–216.

Walker Tileston, D. E. (2003). *What every teacher should know about learning, memory, and the brain.* Thousand Oaks, CA: Corwin.

Wallis, C. (2006). Viewpoint: the myth about homework. *Time, 168*(10), 57.

Weiss, R. (2000). Brain-based learning. *Training & Development, 54*(7), 20.

Westwater, A., & Wolfe, P. (2000). The brain-compatible curriculum. *Educational Leadership, 58*(3), 49–52.

Wiggins, G., & McTighe, J. (1998). *Understanding by design.* Alexandria, VA: Association for Supervision and Curriculum Development.

Wiggins, G., & McTighe, J. (2005). *Understanding by design* (2nd ed.). Alexandria, VA: Association for Supervision and Curriculum Development.

Willis, J. (2006). *Research-based strategies to ignite student learning: Insights from a neurologist and classroom teacher.* Alexandria, VA: Association for Supervision and Curriculum Development.

Willis, J. (2007). *Brain-friendly strategies for the inclusion classroom.* Alexandria, VA: Association for Supervision and Curriculum Development.

Willoughby, A. (2005). *Medial frontal brain potentials following feedback during probabilistic learning.* Unpublished doctoral dissertation, University of Michigan. AAT 3163969.

Wolf, M., Barzillai, M., Gottwald, S., Miller, L., Spencer, K., Norton, E., Lovett, M., & Morris, R. (2009). The RAVE-O intervention: Connecting neuroscience to the classroom. *Mind, Brain, and Education, 3*(2), 84–93.

Wolfe, P. (1996). *Mind, memory, and learning: Translating brain research into classroom practice, a staff developer's guide to the brain.* Napa, CA: Author.

Wolfe, P. (2001a). *Brain matters: Translating research into classroom practice.* Alexandria, VA: Association for Supervision and Curriculum Development.

Wolfe, P. (2001b). *Brain research and education: Fad or foundation?* Retrieved July 17, 2007, from http://www.brainconnection.com/content/160_

Wolfe, P. (2006). Brain-compatible learning: Fad or fashion? *School Administrator, 63*(11), 10–15.

World Bank. (2008). *Economics of education.* Retrieved January 28, 2008, from http://web.worldbank.org/WBSITE/EXTERNAL/TOPICS/EXTEDUCATION/0,,contentMDK:20264769~menuPK:613701~pagePK:148956~piPK:216618~theSitePK:282386,00.html.

Wunderlich, K., Bell, A., & Ford, A. (2005). Improving learning through understanding of brain science research. *Learning Abstracts, 8*(1), 41–43.

Yan, Z., & Fischer, K. W. (2007). Pattern emergence and pattern transition in microdevelopmental variation: Evidence of complex dynamics of developmental processes. *Journal of Developmental Processes, 2*(2), 39–62.

Yordanova, J., Falkenstein, M., Hohnsbein, J., & Kolev, V. (2004). Parallel systems of error processing in the brain. *Neuroimage, 22*(2), 590–602.

Zemelman, S., Daniels, H., & Hyde, A. (1998). *Best practice: New standards for teaching and learning in America's schools.* Portsmouth, NH: Heinemann.

Index

About the Author

Tracey Tokuhama-Espinosa is a Professor of Education at the Universidad San Francisco de Quito in Ecuador. She is the director of the University's Institute for Research, Development and Educational Excellence, where she is in charge of teacher training for 600 teachers and students and leads community outreach programs for public schools and teachers.

Tracey received her Ph.D. in education with a dissertation focus on Mind, Brain, and Education Science from Capella University in July 2008 and earned her M.Ed. from Harvard University in International Educational Development. Tracey has a B.A. in International Relations and a B.S. in mass communication from Boston University, magna cum laude and with distinction.

Tracey is an international educational consultant and conducts workshops for parents, teachers, and educational professionals on themes of language acquisition, brain development, critical thinking, and teaching methodologies. While her main work is within schools, her commercial clients include Procter & Gamble, Early Childhood Education in the Netherlands, Shell OUTPOST Schools, Ares Serono, the Diplomatic Women's Guild of the United Nations, and the University of Melbourne (Australia). She has worked with dozens of schools around the world, including conferences in Argentina, Colombia, Peru, Ecuador, Mexico, Costa Rica, Australia, Norway, Germany, Italy, Thailand, Switzerland, the United Kingdom, the Netherlands, Belgium, and France. Tracey works with the European Council of International Schools, the East Asia Regional Council of Overseas Schools, and the Association of American Schools of Central America, Colombia, Caribbean and Mexico. Tracey also serves as the Educational Director for Grupo FARO, a nonprofit organization devoted to social, educational, and economic development in Latin America.